D1612785

The Battle for Syria
1918–1920

The Battle for Syria 1918–1920

JOHN D. GRAINGER

THE BOYDELL PRESS

First published 2013
The Boydell Press, Woodbridge

ISBN 978 1 84383 803 6

The Boydell Press is an imprint of Boydell & Brewer Ltd
PO Box 9, Woodbridge, Suffolk IP12 3DF, UK
and of Boydell & Brewer Inc.
668 Mount Hope Ave, Rochester, NY 14620–2731, USA
website: www.boydellandbrewer.com

A catalogue record for this book is available
from the British Library

The publisher has no responsibility for the continued existence or accuracy
of URLs for external or third-party internet websites referred to in this book,
and does not guarantee that any content on such websites is,
or will remain, accurate or appropriate

Papers used by Boydell & Brewer Ltd are natural, recyclable products
made from wood grown in sustainable forests

Printed and bound in Great Britain by
TJ International Ltd, Padstow, Cornwall

Contents

Illustrations

Maps

Preface

The Middle East has been a disturbed region, to put it no stronger, throughout the twentieth century, and it looks as though that reputation will continue on into the twenty-first. In fact, its disturbance as a major international concern only began during the Great War, when the Ottoman Empire fell into war on the German side, and became subject to attacks by the Allies.

Every section or region of that former empire has been part of the 'disturbances', from Libya to the Caucasus, from Constantinople to the Yemen, from Cairo to Baghdad, but the most violent, confused, and complex region has been Syria. This is a geographical term which includes the modern states of Syria, Lebanon, Israel, the Palestinian West Bank, and Jordan, together with parts of Egypt and Turkey. It is, and has been for fifteen centuries and more, a land whose society is much divided, particularly among religious communities – in their census in 1906/1907 the Ottoman authorities distinguished nineteen separate religious groups, and this in a country half the size of Britain.

The proximate cause of the change from a group of fairly somnolent Ottoman provinces to the most notorious hotbed of warfare and intrigue in the modern world was its conquest by British forces in 1917 and 1918. In the course of the fighting a series of promises were made by the British to other peoples and countries which were all impossible to keep. In the stress of an appallingly difficult war the British government was lavish in agreeing to reward others, without bothering too much that these rewards and promises overlapped. In 1918 and 1919, of course, the contradictions emerged. Hence the constant troubles ever since.

The capstone to this unstable edifice of nods, winks, agreements, and promises was the victory in September 1918 of British forces – though they were mainly non-British as it happens, Indians, Australian, New Zealanders, and others. Had that battle not been the overwhelming victory it was, or had it been never been fought, it is possible, if unlikely, that the British could have found excuses not to honour some of their wartime promises. If the region of modern Syria and Lebanon had not been conquered, France could have been denied it, the Arabs could have been given only Jordan, maybe the Jews would not have so exuberantly 'returned' to Palestine. The new international boundaries which emerged after 1918, most notably the boundary between Turkey and

Syria, resulted from these campaign,. Where the armies stopped, there the lines were drawn.

The battle in Palestine in September 1918, therefore, is a crucial event in modern Middle Eastern history. The intention, in Britain at least originally, was to conquer only Palestine – 'from Dan to Beersheba', in Lloyd George's phrase – to drive Turkish power from Egypt and the Suez Canal. As it happened, the victory in September was so overwhelming that General Allenby decided to take Damascus, which his Arab allies in particular wanted, and then Aleppo and Lebanon, which both the Arabs and the French wanted. So the sheer unexpected scale of the exploitation of the victory was to lead to a Franco-Arab war and to a Franco-Turkish conflict in 1919 and 1920, both of which the British were quite content to observe without becoming involved in. But it also led to an Arab-Jewish conflict in which the British were the victims of both sides.

This battle was fought in the coastal plain of Palestine just north of Jaffa, a region now covered with roads, houses, factories, and all the paraphernalia of modern life, to such an extent that the land is totally different from what it was in 1918. But this is also the narrow waist of the Israeli state, only a dozen miles wide, which is now defined by the sea on one side and the concrete wall separating Israel from the Palestinian West Bank on the other. This wall follows more or less the line established by the British imperial infantry forces at the end of the fighting on 19 September 1918, an indication of the power of geography to determine events.

The British gave the overall name of Megiddo, popularised as 'Armageddon', to the battles that took place in that September. In fact Megiddo itself did not feature in any way in the conflict, but it suited the British to adopt the apocalyptic name for a decisive battle in the 'War to end Wars'. For the Middle East it was the reverse, of course, a war to begin wars, while for far too many of the people it was a battle whose results changed their world radically.

This book follows from another on the conquest of southern Palestine in 1917, but in this case the scale of events is wider, its effects deeper and more complex. An account of the battle itself is a necessary element in the overall story, since it was the way the battle was planned, conducted, and exploited which is a fundamental element in the historical development of the whole region in the following decades. It was, if not 'Armageddon', at the least it was a decisive 'battle for Syria'.

Introduction

THE British army in Egypt came under attack as soon as the war with Turkey began in 1914.[1] A Turkish army invaded Egypt, hoping that the Egyptians would respond to a call for *jihad*, but they did not. The Turks were stopped at the obstacle of the Suez Canal, which, not for the last time, acted as a defensive moat, keeping the invader out of Egypt proper. For a time, attention centred on the Allied attack on Gallipoli, but by late 1915 this was clearly a failure; attention shifted back to Egypt and Palestine. The Gallipoli troops were evacuated to Egypt where they recovered and were reinforced, above all, by regiments from Australia and New Zealand and became part of the Egyptian Expeditionary Force. The Force then attacked the Turks by the Canal. It took two years to clear the Sinai Peninsula of the enemy, and another eight months to break into Palestine through the Turkish defence lines at Gaza and Beersheba.[2]

Once these Turkish defences in southern Palestine had, at the third attempt, been broken through in October 1917, the invasion of Palestine could begin. By December the subsequent pursuit had taken the British forces as far as the conquest of Jerusalem and the crossing of the Auja River north of Jaffa; at that point weariness, logistical problems, and the Palestinian winter halted further progress.[3]

The two opposing armies had undergone the usual shake-up which happens to peacetime forces when they find themselves fighting rather than parading and occupying. On the Turkish side a lack of manpower and equipment had been in part remedied by German assistance, and the lack of command capability by the insertion of skilled German officers. The Turks had even permitted Germans to direct the whole campaign, though there was a good deal of antagonism between them. Djemal Pasha, the overall Turkish commander in the region, was mainly a politician, a member of the Committee of Union and Progress which had seized power in the Ottoman Empire in 1908. He had some sensible ideas and was to become generally competent at military

---

[1] In the notes the practice is to provide author's name and short title; full details are available in the Bibliography.

[2] These events are well detailed in MacMunn and Falls, *Official History* Vol. I.

[3] I have detailed this in my book *The Battle for Palestine 1917*, which contains full references.

command. The German Colonel Kress von Kressenstein had emerged as the effective army commander during 1916. After three years of fighting, the Turks had evolved a competent command structure and their troops were tough and skilled - those who had survived, that is.

On the British side the army command in Egypt had to cope with many problems besides the Ottoman army in Sinai: the aftermath of Gallipoli, the Senussi rebellion in Libya, a rebellion in Darfur in the Sudan, not to mention the repeated misbehaviour of Australian troops in Cairo. The Suez Canal had been useful as a moat to prevent the Turks getting into Egypt proper, and the Turks had eventually been pushed away from it without too much difficulty, but Egypt was always restless under British rule (it had been made a formal British Protectorate in 1914) and a large section of British forces was held in Egypt as an occupying force. Cairo's civilian temptations led to slackness and laziness within the military command and an overmanning in the headquarters. When the army in Sinai was beaten for the second time at Gaza, in April 1917, the commanding general, Sir Archibald Murray, was sacked; General Sir Edmund Allenby, until then commanding an army in France on the Western Front, was sent out to replace him. The troops at the front were very pleased to hear of the swift clear-out of fat colonels from comfortable billets in Cairene offices, but were startled to find that the main headquarters was shifted to the front, and that Allenby himself arrived at the front, inspecting conditions and aiming to exercise direct command.

The result was a reorganization of the Expeditionary Force, and the well-planned and carefully conducted third battle of Gaza. Gaza city by then had been formed into the western anchor of a Turkish defensive line of trenches and strongpoints, which stretched to the edge of the Judaean hills at Beersheba, and the battle Allenby conducted had comprised a series of well disguised blows at this line, each employing forces which decisively outnumbered the Turkish defenders on the spot. He did not reduce the whole line at the first blow, and by the time the Turkish line had broken, Allenby knew that the Turks he was fighting were tough and adaptable, even if they were always hungry and often sick. Several of the blows he struck at the Turkish line were blunted before they could succeed. At last, the capture of Beersheba by a wild Australian charge did succeed in capturing one of the strongpoints, and from then on the line was broken in other places as well. The battle lasted a fortnight; the line was broken, but much of the Turkish army got away to fight on.

This military success was highly pleasing to the British government, whose Prime Minister, David Lloyd George, had been desperate for a victory to set against the continuing lack of success in France, and to justify the *coup* a year before by which he had displaced the previous Prime Minister. In appointing Allenby he had set him a target of capturing 'Jerusalem by Christmas', which, with only a few days to spare, had been achieved. But during this victorious invasion of Palestine, events elsewhere cast a pall of apprehension over the whole Allied war effort. True, the United States had joined the Allies in April 1917 (at the time of the earlier Gaza defeats), but that gain – which was still largely in the future at the end of 1917 – was more than offset by the collapse of Russia and the seizure of power there by the Bolshevik Communists. Their policy of peace at any price was sufficient to gain them enough popularity to keep them in power. By the end of 1917 their delegates were talking peace terms with the German army command. The Eastern Front had been closed down.

The problem for the Allies which followed was, of course, that the end of fighting on the Eastern Front would permit the Germans to concentrate their attention and their manpower on the front in the West, in France and Belgium. As it happened they did have to leave a large proportion of their forces in the East, in part because they became greedy in the peace negotiations and had to police their huge acquisitions.

Then, in November 1917, the Italian army in the Dolomites suffered a catastrophic defeat at the battle of Caporetto. Italy was rescued by the emergency transfer of British and French forces from the Western Front, but in effect she was a passenger from then on. So the whole winter of 1917/18 was one of expectation, even dread, and feverish preparations on all sides. The assumption was that the German offensive in the West would come in the spring.

For the British command in Palestine there was a comparable problem. The closing down of the Russian war, where the Turks had been fighting the Russians in the Ukraine, but above all in the Caucasus and Armenia, would also release Turkish forces, and they could be used in Palestine and Mesopotamia. In fact, the Turkish government was more interested in conquering territory in the north and east and not much concerned to defend its position in the Arab lands. Perhaps Enver Pasha, the driving force in the Committee regime, assumed that the British would be content with having conquered Palestine, and would now concentrate their forces and their attention on the Western Front, for he pushed the Turkish forces forward in the East, first to retake the lands which Russian forces had conquered, but then in pursuance of a dream of his to construct a great new Turkish empire in Central Asia.

In Palestine, therefore, two major consequences followed the Russian and Italian collapses. The threat to the Western Front meant that as much of the

British force as possible would have to be moved to France. They would be replaced from elsewhere, India probably, but also from other, less active or less important areas. But these troops would take some time to arrive and they would be a mixture of experienced and inexperienced personnel, all new to the theatre. The largely homogeneous, overwhelmingly British force Allenby had commanded in 1917 would change drastically. The troops would have to be retrained for the peculiar conditions of Palestinian warfare; nor could Allenby be sure just what forces he would have in the end. It was also to be expected that Turkish forces facing the British would be reinforced. This would not necessarily imply a Turkish attack, but it would certainly mean that an even more determined and effective Turkish defence would be mounted.

It had been difficult enough to get as far as Jerusalem. To much surprise on the Allied side, the Ottoman Empire, long perceived to be weak and inefficient, had proved to be a very difficult nut to crack. After defeats in the Balkan Wars and in Libya in the years before 1914, the Ottoman Empire seemed to be on its last legs. But its army had put up a stubborn and successful defence against the major attack at Gallipoli in 1915; it had defeated a British invasion of Mesopotamia at Kut el-Amara, also in 1915; it had taken the initiative by invading Egyptian territory as far as the Suez Canal, an invasion which it had taken nearly three years to repel. For an ancient and decrepit state which had been casually dubbed the 'sick man of Europe' for decades, this was a performance to be proud of. To be sure, the Russian front in the Caucasus had seen repeated Turkish defeats and a Russian invasion of Anatolia – but then Russia itself had collapsed under the strain of war, while the Ottoman Empire did not.

In 1917, however, the Allied armies had at last made some progress in the Turkish war. The Russians may have faltered, so that the Turks recovered lost territory and moved into the Caucasus region, but the British revived in Mesopotamia, capturing Baghdad in March, and at the third attempt finally took Gaza, and then Jerusalem. In north-east Africa, the rebellions in Darfur and in Libya had been suppressed and the threat of trouble in Egypt had faded, at least for the moment. And although an Allied army which had landed at Salonica (in neutral Greek territory) made no progress against Bulgarian and Turkish defences, neither had it been thrown into the sea, as had happened at Gallipoli.

The fighting in Palestine had been overwhelmingly a British affair. It had been a British army which had defended the Canal, and it was under British command that the army advanced across the Sinai Peninsula and into Palestine. But its original Britishness had been diluted by the mounted regiments from Australia and New Zealand, which had arrived partly by way of Gallipoli. Small forces had also been sent by France and Italy as tokens of their political hopes for slices of Turkish territory to add to their empires in the event of victory. Even so, the great majority of the Egyptian Expeditionary Force was composed of British regiments, cavalry and infantry, and almost all the artillery was British; a few Indian cavalry regiments had been added, as had small groups from South Africa, Polynesia and the West Indies. And great numbers of Egyptians had been recruited, or conscripted, as labourers to bring up supplies.

The difficulties of the fighting in this Turkish war had persuaded the British to extend a conspiratorial hand into Arabia. The Sultan of Turkey was also Caliph of Islam, the successor to the Prophet Muhammad. He had proclaimed a *jihad* at the beginning, which had helped along the rebellions in Libya and Sudan, and which was an obvious threat to the British in Egypt. The rebellions had been put down, and Egypt was under control, with regular military demonstrations to intimidate likely disturbers of the peace, and acceptance by Egyptian politicians that they would support the British. But in Arabia, where a response to the call to *jihad* might have been expected, it was not answered. At Mecca political power was in the hands of the Sharif, Husain, who was inveigled into an alliance by British promises, after tortuous negotiations. As a descendant of the Prophet Muhammad, he could usefully negate the religious influence of the Turkish Caliph, who was known to be manipulated by the Young Turks. At the same time, the agreements between Husain and the British were woolly, even ambiguous, in their wording, and predictive of future difficulties. Nevertheless, during 1916 and 1917 a new Turkish front opened up in Arabia. The Arabs succeeded in isolating a Turkish army which had unsuccessfully attacked the British in Aden, while another which had concentrated into Medina came under pressure and was effectively immobilized. Husain's Arab Army could not capture Medina, but it could cut the Turks' communications and prevent them advancing against Mecca. This campaign involved ambushing supply trains using the railway which ran south from Damascus, and destroying selective parts of the line itself, though Turkish and German engineers proved adept at repairing breaks fairly quickly. Built originally to carry Hajj pilgrims to Mecca, and funded in part by popular subscription, it was now being destroyed by Muslims under British direction to help defeat a Muslim Turkish army.[4]

---

[4] The negotiations have been subjected to much study. A couple of the more useful and extensive works include Tibawi, *Anglo-Arab Relations*, and Kedourie, *Anglo-*

To get the Arabs to rebel in the first place had taken much hard work, intricate negotiation, strong promises and supplies of munitions. The Arabs had required assurances which several of those involved in the negotiations in Egypt had been unwilling to provide. They had also required arms – since their Turkish enemies were better equipped and trained - and when the arms were provided they had to be trained in their use. Once the Arab rebellion began, in June 1916, the British could help with providing weaponry. Recruiting among their Arab prisoners provided the Arab Army with a nucleus of trained soldiers, above all, officers. The bureaucrats in Cairo were not too pleased when the Sharif proclaimed Arab independence, and tended to avoid addressing him as a king. His son Feisal, however, proved to be an intelligent, even an inspiring, leader, who understood how to get the best out of his people and his European partners.

In the negotiations over the future of Syria the French had insisted that they were to be awarded a good slice of the spoils. This conflicted with Arab wishes, of course, but the French, who clearly knew of Arab aspirations to unite the Arabs in Mesopotamia, Syria, and Palestine with those in Arabia, nevertheless sent a mission to represent their interests with the Sharif. Curiously, as good republicans, they had no hesitation in referring to him as *Sa Majesté*, which some of the monarchist British would not do. Both Britain and France were sparing with direct military assistance – early on, the British sent an Egyptian mountain gun battery to assist in the siege of Medina, only to find that their guns were outranged by those of the Turks inside the city. Nevertheless artillery of various sorts was particularly useful, as were machine guns.

The new Arab Army was quickly built up to a strength of perhaps 10,000 fighters, though only about half had rifles. This force was mainly occupied in the blockade of Medina, while small groups of better trained fighters were taken north to operate as a guerrilla force, against the railway. It was here in the second half of 1917 that T.E. Lawrence emerged as a leader of the guerrillas, along with a group of British and French officers. By the end of the year the Arab Army had finally isolated the Turkish Ninth Army in Medina, and had carried out raids as far north as et-Tafilat, south-east of the Dead Sea, where a Turkish detachment was defeated. Et-Tafilat was reoccupied by the Turks not long after, for the Arabs could not hold any position. Allenby was well aware of the usefulness of these actions, but it was still his own army which had to do

Arab Labyrinth. Also useful is Fisher, *Curzon and British Imperialism*. There is a host of other studies, usually partisan.

most of the work. In October and November it had been the British Imperial army that had beaten the Turkish main army.

The Turks fought hard and well at Third Gaza. However, they were outnumbered and outgunned, and were increasingly coming under German control, which many of them resented. The Arab soldiers in the Turkish army were never fully trusted once Sharif Husain proclaimed Arab independence, and any who were captured were solicited by the British to join the Arab Army – several of that army's most effective officers were former Turkish soldiers. The Turkish rank-and-file and the junior officers were tough and very capable fighters. They were ill-fed, badly clothed, under-equipped, ravaged by diseases, and short of guns, rifles, ammunition and supplies of all sorts. But they had defeated the British twice in front of Gaza, and had only been prised out of that ruined city by an army which had tanks, aircraft, twice their numbers, and a commander in Allenby who was to prove to be one of the most capable on any side in the whole war.

The involvement of the Arab rebels had immensely complicated the political aspects of affairs in the Near East. As soon as the Turkish war began, the Allies began to eye Ottoman territories for choice plums to extract for themselves. Assuming, reasonably enough at the beginning, that the Ottoman Empire would be defeated in fairly short order, Britain, France, and Russia in March 1915 set out in a series of memoranda and agreements the sections each wanted. In the same year, Italy joined in and she was accommodated. The Italians wanted the south-western corner of Anatolia, the ancient Lycia, and Pamphylia, which was close to the Dodecanese Islands they had taken from the Empire in 1911; the French wanted the northern part of the Levant, the area now called Lebanon and Syria, plus a large slice of southern Anatolia; the British wanted Mesopotamia and Palestine. There was disagreement between Britain and France over boundaries, but there seemed quite enough for everyone. The Russians were promised Constantinople, European Turkey (Thrace), and Armenia, and control of the Straits of the Bosporus and the Dardanelles.[5] This last division of the spoils caused much perturbation in France, but not in Britain, whose policy for much of the previous century had been to prevent this very thing from happening. Once the Bolsheviks seized power and ceased fighting these promises to Russia could be disregarded. (The Bolsheviks pub-

---

5   An intelligible summary of all this is in Anderson, *Eastern Question*, pp. 316–26; later accounts downplay the Russian involvement, but it was crucial at the time; see also Holt, *Egypt and the Fertile Crescent*, pp. 262–3.

lished the texts of the various treaties, which had been kept secret until then; this caused further diplomatic ructions, but since everyone had assumed that such agreements already existed, the general damage was slight.)

The involvement of the Arabs changed this picture, for Sharif Husain and his family were keen to expand their control over all the lands of the Arabs, first all the Arabian peninsula, but also the lands to the north, in particular, Palestine, Syria, and Mesopotamia. In effect this was what they believed had been promised to them by the British, though Husain knew that coastal areas and parts of Mesopotamia were going to be occupied by Britain and France. In March the British in Baghdad had studiously avoided any assumptions that Mesopotamia was to become part of the Arab state when they captured the city. And there was the further problem for Husain that many of those in the Arabian peninsula were not interested in being ruled by him. His most persistent enemy, even more so than the Turks, was Ibn Saud, ruler of a large part of the centre of Arabia – and Ibn Saud was another of Britain's allies.

The difficulty with attempts such as these to organize the future is that when the time comes to implement the plan the problem has changed. The basic outline of British and French plans had been laid out in the 'Sykes-Picot Agreement' of January 1916; within six months the Arab Revolt had upset this plan, not to mention the fact that neither Sykes nor Picot had any real authority to conclude international agreements.[6] And so it went on, any agreement scarcely surviving long enough for the ink to dry on the signatures. They could never take account of events which were still to happen. The Arabs may well have thought that they had been promised a large kingdom, but that did not take account of the fact that the British did most of the fighting, nor that the one country which the British had to keep on side at all costs was France. Russia had counted itself out by late 1917; Italy could be ignored after the disaster at Caporetto (and anyway its demands did not conflict with anyone else's); but it was absolutely essential that France be accommodated. Even if France did not take much of a part in the fighting in Palestine, it was France which had borne the heat and burden on the Western Front for three hard years. And France wanted some reward; in particular she required a substantial slice of the Levant.

This had been clear from the beginning, and the Sykes-Picot Agreement had

---

[6] Sykes was an MP, Picot a diplomat; both knew something of the Arab lands. Their agreement only came about in order to avoid an Anglo-French quarrel. The British in particular never intended it to be definitive. See Barr, *A Line in the Sand*, pp. 7–36.

formalized French intentions and wishes. The French had sent a small force to take part in the Palestinian fighting, an active mobile artillery battery, under Captain Pisani's mission, to assist the Arab Army. (The Italians sent a small force to Palestine as well, but it was regarded as a joke by the British forces. By 1918 the contingent had been relegated to guard duties in Jerusalem.)

Then in the midst of the British army's advance against Jerusalem, the British government stirred the pot even more. In November 1917 the Foreign Secretary A.J. Balfour published a letter he had written to Lord Rothschild in which he promised that Palestine would in future be understood as a 'national home' for the Jews. Again, this was hardly a crystal clear commitment, nor was its meaning easily understood, but it did bring in another interested party with interests and influence in many Allied states. It also antagonized Britain's Arab allies.

This initiative that emerged had two origins: first, in the Sykes-Picot Agreement, Palestine had been designated as an 'International Zone', since it was seen as indelicate to claim to rule in the Holy Land. It also functioned as a neutral zone which would separate the British in Egypt from the putative French possessions in northern Syria. Second, Jewish support for the Allies was hoped for, notably in the United States (whose government had been consulted by Balfour before the letter was issued) and in continental Europe, notably Russia.

By the time the British army, at a cost of over 5000 casualties, had won the battle for Jerusalem in December 1917 the number of fingers in the Near Eastern pie had increased once more: British, French, Arabs, Jews, Italians, though the Russians were counted out. Yet most of the territory which was being divided up was still under the rule of the Ottoman Empire, while the United States, never actually at war with Turkey, had been calculatedly involved in the diplomacy by the British. Little account had been taken as yet of the interests or preferences of the inhabitants of the land that was being fought over and potentially divided. The Arabs of Arabia regarded the population of the whole Fertile Crescent as Arabs who should be pleased to come under Arab rule. The French saw them as people being rescued from Ottoman oppression, and the Lebanese in particular, many of whom were Christian, seemed almost to be surrogate Frenchman. The British had entered Mesopotamia in 1914 for the purpose of protecting their great oil refinery at Abadan against attack, and the potential oil reserves in the future Iraq were of interest, since the Royal Navy was now dependent on such supplies. Palestine as an International Zone might or might not be an effective forward defence for Egypt (in particular against any French moves once they had been established in Syria), and as the Holy Land it was a place to be held 'in trust' for Jews and Christians alike for access, though once the British had conquered Palestine and organized its administration the idea of an International Zone was discarded. But the Palestinians and Syrians and Lebanese and Iraqis were never consulted.

In Syria in particular, before the war several societies had developed whose interest was in being Arab, not Ottoman, but Syrian above all else. At first they looked to raise their profile within the Turkish Empire, in some cases envisaging a sort of partnership with the Turks in the empire, though others looked to separation. The movement was mostly small in both numbers and influence, confined to the middle classes and concentrated in the cities, particularly Damascus. But the groups existed and when the war came their ideas spread among the general population thanks to the heavy tread of Ottoman rule, brutal taxation, conscription, famine and Turkish (and German) arrogance.[7] In 1915 Sharif Husain's son Faisal contacted these groups in Damascus, and the desert Arabs and the city Arabs found themselves more or less in agreement,[8] so that when the Sharif negotiated with the British he felt fully able to speak for the 'Arab nation' – a term originally employed by Lord Kitchener in his first approach to the Sharif – by which he meant all those in Arabia, in Iraq, in Palestine, and in Syria, as far north as the Taurus Mountains. This was not necessarily accepted by the British, but to ensure Arab participation in the war, they contrived to fudge the issue.

In early 1918 there were therefore manifold problems for every government and army and community in Syria, Palestine, and Arabia. There was confusion between the British and the Arabs over the precise meaning of their agreements; there was deep suspicion among the Arabs about the meaning of the Balfour Declaration, whose precise consequences few of the British considered or guessed at; there was much suspicion in French political and diplomatic circles about British ambitions and intentions in Syria. None of the territories the French were interested in had yet been reached by the British in Palestine, and there was no guarantee that the British would ever attempt to conquer them, or if they did, that they would ever allow the French to take them over.

Much investigative attention has been directed at discovering the precise chronology, meaning, and development of the continuing negotiations between all the parties involved in these affairs. Much of this research is designed not to

---

[7] Petran, *Syria*, pp. 51–3; Dawn, *Ottomanism to Arabism*, ch 6; Gelvin, *Divided Loyalties*, pp. 51–86.

[8] See Gelvin, pp. 57–8, and references there.

understand what took place, but as justification for later claims and attitudes, intentions and positions, as though such temporary agreements could confer legitimacy, an especially futile notion since they were contradictory and over-lapping. Thus Sykes and Picot made an 'Agreement', Balfour's letter became a 'Declaration', each with capital initials, though the first was informal, and the second only a letter giving a view.

The reality is that all the agreements and treaties were only provisional. At base, no one knew who would win the war - until mid-1918 it looked very much as though it would be Germany. These various positions and maps and treaties must therefore be regarded only as aspirations of the particular moment at which they were agreed. The extreme positions proclaimed by the various par-ties were the most anyone hoped for, and the agreements merely reflected the state of the parties, or the hopes they represented. The actual achievement of any of these extreme hopes was never likely to happen, and it is probable that everyone involved realized this. Most of those involved were quite prepared to adjust their intentions to the momentary facts on the ground. This meant that the British government, through its army in Palestine, inevitably had the greatest say, just as it had in Mesopotamia.

That army was more or less immobile for well over a month after the capture of Jerusalem in early December. It beat off an attempt by the Ottoman army to recover the city late in that month, and in February Allenby sent a force down into the Rift Valley to seize Jericho and the northern end of the Dead Sea.[9] This move effectively blocked any Turkish attempt to move southwards along the western side of the Sea, and opened up the possibility of linking, or at least communicating with, the Arab Army, if it could make any headway on the eastern plateaux across the Sea. But the winter weather pinned the Arabs down even more firmly than it did the Turks or the British. And the news was bad from Europe. Allenby knew by now he would soon face the wholesale destruction of his army, not at enemy hands but by his superiors.

---

[9]   MacMunn and Falls, *Official History* Vol. I, p. 302.

CHAPTER 1

Defeats

THE British move into the Jordan Valley to secure Jericho was also aimed at gaining control of crossing places over the river, blocking the Turkish supply route across the Dead Sea, and hoping to join up with the Arab forces. The equivalent of two divisions were used, the 60th London Division, commanded by Major-General John Shea, to which 231 Brigade was attached from the 74th Yeomanry Division. Along with these infantry units were the New Zealand Mounted Brigade (three regiments) and the 1st Australian Light Horse Brigade, both from the Australian and New Zealand (Anzac) Mounted Division.

Their task was to climb down the steep western slope of the Rift Valley into the plain of the Jordan north of the Dead Sea. They faced an old enemy, the Turkish 53rd Division, but above all, they had to cross extremely difficult territory as well – rocky slopes and narrow tracks – where there were plenty of good positions available for the defence. The Turks defended with well-sited machine guns, and held a series of positions, all of which had to be taken. The infantry of the London Division did the main work. The New Zealand riflemen had to dismount to capture at least one place. The Australian brigade climbed down by a separate track to the south of the main fighting and in a neat flanking move captured Jericho behind the Turkish defenders. This operation moved the northern flank of the British position north to the Wadi el-Auja, a tributary of the Jordan, and it became anchored on hills at Musallabeh just north of the wadi.

The operation took three days, but at the end was only partly completed. The Turks quietly withdrew to the east side of the river on the night of 20/21 February, but held on to a bridgehead on the west bank at el-Ghoraniyeh. It was evident that the attack had not been seriously contested, except by the machine gunners on the scarp descent. The Turks had obviously expected it, yet it had cost 500 casualties, mainly among the Londoners. Allenby, who had left the operation to General Sir Philip Chetwode, remarked that the country was 'awful', and noted that the valley was very unhealthy. The troops were kept out of Jericho itself, where typhus was rife.[1]

---

[1]   Wavell, *Palestine Campaign*, pp. 177–8; Anglesey, *British Cavalry*, pp. 215–17;

During this operation Allenby was visited by General Smuts, the South African politician who had acquired a large, if somewhat undeserved, reputation in Britain. He had conducted the main campaign in East Africa for a time, and was popularly regarded as successful, though that had been a very costly and badly managed campaign, which was still unfinished at the end of the war. He was, however, seen as an independent voice by the British government, which had become very suspicious of the Army High Command. He came out to investigate what should now be done in the Near East, and had a remit to consider the naval, Palestinian and Mesopotamian campaigns. He was, in fact, a stooge for Lloyd George, being employed to provide separate advice from that which was coming from the army in the voice of the Chief of the Imperial General Staff, General Sir William Robertson. Smuts was a politician and his military experience and understanding were thoroughly deficient. When he discussed possibilities with Allenby, Chetwode, and others in Jerusalem he was listened to, but his ideas were then ignored, at least those he had not picked up from Allenby while out east. When he reported to Lloyd George he said just what the Prime Minister wanted: that the way to defeat Turkey was to reinforce Allenby's army and attack in order to conquer Syria as far as Aleppo. He did not apparently appreciate that a stubborn Turkish army, several mountain ranges and deserts, and 400 miles of poor roads lay between Allenby's army and the objective. Nor did he appreciate what Robertson and others had pointed out, that Aleppo was hardly a worthwhile objective if the purpose was to force Turkey out of the war, since it was not a vital Turkish position.[2]

By then Allenby's conquest of Jericho had taken place (while Smuts was in Palestine, but it had clearly been planned beforehand), and Allenby was certainly considering a further exploitation eastwards to cut the Turkish Hajj railway decisively. He proposed the move as soon as he had secured Jerusalem.[3] He had also been considering options beyond that. Within a week of the capture of Jerusalem, Robertson had asked him to comment on two suggestions, which clearly came from the War Cabinet in London, that he should exploit his victory in two alternative, or possibly successive, ways: conquer the rest of Palestine as far as 'Dan', or advance as far as Aleppo.[4] He replied

---

Advance, plate 33; Hughes (ed.), *Correspondence*, pp. 126 and 133, Allenby to Robertson, 3 January 1918 and 25 February 1918.

[2]   Smuts' final report is at TNA CAB/4/4/G199; it is noted in most accounts of the campaign, most thoroughly by Hughes, *Allenby and British Strategy*, pp. 67–9.

[3]   Hughes (ed.), *Correspondence*, p. 83, Allenby to Robertson, 14 December 1917.

[4]   Ibid., p. 85, Robertson to Allenby, 18 December 1917.

on 20 December that he could probably do the first by July, 'assuming that Dan means Paneas', but would need to double his present forces to attempt the second. (The invocation of 'Dan' marks the origin of the suggested objectives as from Lloyd George, who more than once defined Palestine in the biblical phrase as 'from Dan to Beersheba'; Allenby's redefinition indicated that he fully understood that Robertson was quoting the Prime Minister.)[5]

There followed discussions on moving troops to increase his forces. The expedition in Mesopotamia was to revert to the defensive, and two of its divisions were to be transferred to Allenby; one would come from France. One of the Mesopotamian divisions, the 7th Indian, was beginning to move right away. Then only one division and some artillery was to come from Mesopotamia. The division from France was to be an Indian cavalry division. Allenby's yeomanry battalions were to be broken up to fill up his depleted units, and the remainder – calculated at a 'surplus' of 5000 men – would go to France to be retrained as machine gunners for the Western Front. But all this depended on shipping – it was estimated that it would take two months to move one division from Basra to Suez.[6] So the idea of reinforcing Allenby's command was whittled down to a net increase of one division at the most, and Robertson acquired reinforcement for the Western Front as well.

Allenby meanwhile put in some minor local attacks to push the Turks further from Jerusalem, to straighten his line, and to seize some positions which might be used as the bases for Turkish attacks. General Chetwode, the XX Corps commander, used the 10th Irish Division and part of the 74th Division to push north from Tell Asur on the Nablus road. Captain J.J. Kennedy of the Royal Inniskillings describes the objective as 'a series of strongly held ridges, intersected by great wadis and ravines'. An early advance captured several of these places, but then came up against a strong defensive based on hills overlooking a deep wadi, and the attack failed, as did a second attack next day (10 March). Two platoons of the 5th Royal Irish Fusiliers became separated from the rest in the first attack, but survived. They were now located, and rescuing and reinforcing them became the basis for a new attack. The men

> had to descend the wadi in broad daylight under severe artillery fire and
> a barrage of seven or eight machine guns, these latter firing from the
> front and obliquely. Men rushed down the hillside, doing acrobatic feats,

---

5   Ibid., p. 87, Allenby to Robertson, 20 December 1917.
6   Ibid., p. 100, Robertson to Allenby, 7 March 1918, states the essential division.

jumping from terrace to boulder carrying full equipment, performing feats that would not be thought of in cold blood. The ascent of Hill K4, the enemy side of the wadi, was made under frontal and oblique fire. Hill K4 was captured by a charge, the garrison holding out to the last.[7]

This broke the Turkish position, and neighbouring positions were abandoned. A further attack, by three companies, captured Jiljilya, the main objective.

This type of operation straightened out the Turks' line as well as that of the British. The Turks pulled out some units from the line they occupied in order to rest them. Also, on the Turkish side General Falkenhayn was replaced in command by General Liman von Sanders, to Turkish relief. Liman replaced Falkenhayn's all-German staff with Turks, since the Germans had long rasped Turkish nerves. He also replaced Falkenhayn's policy of a flexible defence with a more determined policy of refusing to give up any position without a stiff fight.[8] The Inniskillings and the Irish Fusiliers were the first to encounter this new policy, and their Turkish enemies the first to suffer from it. Liman claimed to have foiled an attempt to advance on Nablus, fifteen or more miles north of the line at which the fighting stopped. The British had no immediate plans for such an advance, but it was sensible of Liman to boost his authority by such a claim. (He cites orders found on a dead British officer as his source, but seems to have misunderstood the implications.)[9]

However, those two operations – Jericho and Tell Asur and others – also indicated that a policy of 'active defence', which Falkenhayn had implemented and had operated at Jericho, usually meant losing territory. There had been only a relatively small force defending the place. The capture of Hill K4 had led to the evacuation of two neighbouring hills and the retreat of the Turkish line in that section, and the stubborn fight put up by the defenders of K4 had been unsuccessful. That is, neither active nor stubborn defence was likely to succeed. The only way to stop the British was to put an army equal or superior to Allenby's in the field, and attack. On the other hand, a stubborn defence also meant inflicting greater casualties on the British, which was clearly Liman's aim. An advance in small bites such as Tell Asur would soon wear the British down.

[7]   Kennedy, *The Sprig of Shillelagh*, [1920], p. 44.
[8]   Liman von Sanders, *Five Years*, p. 204.
[9]   Ibid., p. 205.

Allenby developed a new strategy – to initiate a major attack across the Jordan River to cut the Turkish railway and destroy a substantial section of the track. The Arabs had done this often enough already further south, but never with any permanent effect; Allenby aimed to destroy fifteen miles of track. The attacking forces would seize and hold the small town of es-Salt, which would provide an advanced base on the summit of the plateau. From there raids against the railway could be made, or it could be a base for a major attack later.[10] The northern moves about Tell Asur had the effect, as Liman's reaction showed, of implying that Allenby's attention was directed towards that area. Some of the Turkish units east of the river were brought across the river to thicken up the defences before Nablus.

This sequence of attacks bears all the hallmarks of Allenby's methods: first to the east and the capture of Jericho, then to the north and the apparent threat to Nablus, now to the east again, in each case concentrating a force much greater than that of the Turkish defenders. Similarly the details of the attack on Jericho show the use of the pinning frontal attack (by the Londoner infantry) followed by the enveloping cavalry ride by the Australians to seize the main object in rear of the enemy defenders. This was hardly a measure possible on the Western Front where there were no enemy flanks to be turned, but it shows that the basic command and tactical skills still existed in the British army when it was possible to use them. At the same time the ease with which the Turks escaped the trap indicated comparable skills (that is, flexible defence) on their side.

The attack to the east across the Jordan was conducted by a mixed force commanded by Major-General Shea. He had his own division, the 60th London, the full Anzac Mounted Division, the Imperial Camel Brigade (mainly Australians and New Zealanders), two batteries of artillery, and a Royal Engineers' bridging party. He was given the general instruction that the infantry should take and hold the town of es-Salt, twenty miles along the road, and the cavalry should seize Amman, another twenty miles further on, and destroy the Turkish railways there over a distance of fifteen miles of track. This section was chosen because it included a sequence of vulnerable constructions, a viaduct, a tunnel, two or more bridges, and the equipment at two stations, at Amman itself and at Libban to the south. Shea was to leave a substantial force east of the river, holding es-Salt, when the main force was withdrawn; this garrison was intended to prevent the Turks repairing the railway by making continual raids on the working parties.

---

[10] The operation order is printed in Falls, *Official History* Vol. II, Appendix 20.

The attack began on 21 March. The first task was to seize the Turkish bridgehead at el-Ghoraniyeh, then lay bridges to get the main force across. Shea had a 'Pontoon Park' of the Royal Engineers and the Divisional Bridging Train from the Desert Mounted Corps at his disposal. But it rained, the river became swollen, and the engineers faced unexpected difficulties. They did get three bridges laid, but it took two days instead of one night to establish them and then to get the main force across to the east bank. Then it took until noon on the 24th to capture a nearby hill, Shunet Nimrin, which the Turks defended stubbornly. The tracks which had to be used were not strong enough or wide enough to cope with the motor transport it had been intended to use. Camels took the place of the lorries, but more time was lost in transferring the ammunition and explosives, and the movement forward of these supplies was clearly much slower than intended.

The territory was much more difficult to traverse than on the west bank. The steep Rift Valley side this time had to be climbed, not descended. It rained. Horses and camels could move only slowly and with great labour; they even had to be lifted over some of the obstacles. Only two tracks could be used, in single file. Even when the heads of the columns reached the plateau, no further progress could be made until the rest of the column had arrived. It was late on the 25th when es-Salt was taken, and midnight before the first infantry brigade moved in. The attackers were already three or four days late.

The opposition to all this, apart from the rain and the country, was the Turkish 48th Division, which consisted of a cavalry regiment and a locally recruited cavalry unit called the Circassian Irregulars, two battalions of the Fourth Army at es-Salt (the 2/150 and the 2/159), and another battalion of the 150th at Amman, which had spread its men along the railway line as guards. This was clearly an inadequate force to prevent the advance of two whole Allied divisions, but reinforcements were on the way and the 48th concentrated into Amman. From the south, from et-Tafilat, the 703rd German battalion was already moving north along the railway, though its progress was delayed for a time when a raiding party from the New Zealand Mounted Brigade blew up part of the line several miles south of Amman. Also from the south came several units from as far away as Ma'an, who were also able to use the railway for most of the journey, moving more quickly than the British and the Australians could on horseback and on foot. From the north and west Liman sent the four cavalry regiments of the 3rd Cavalry Division and two infantry battalions from the main force, crossing the river at the bridge at Jisr ed-Damieh; a second small German and Turkish force came south along the railway. In other words, the delays imposed on the attackers by difficulties with the weather and the country, and the Turkish resistance enabled the Turkish reinforcements to concentrate from three directions. By the time the Londoners had reached es-Salt the raid had already begun to look more like a trap.

The mounted men had to rest themselves and their horses for a day at es-Sir, several miles short of Amman. By the time they, the Camel Brigade, and the infantry of 181 Brigade launched an attack, the Turks had assembled a strong defence force. The German units in particular were heavily equipped with machine guns, and the defence had fifteen pieces of artillery, whereas the attackers had only three batteries of light mountain guns. It proved to be impossible to take either Amman village or station, and the defences of the tunnel and the viaduct were also too strong. Behind these forward units, the garrison at es-Salt had also come under attack by the Turkish 3rd Cavalry and the two infantry regiments from the north, and further back the Jordan River had risen nine feet and had already destroyed two of the bridges at el-Ghoraniyeh; it now threatened to sweep the last one away.

Blaming the weather was a convenient excuse for failure, but the fact was that the attack had tried to reach too far. The difficulties of climbing the steep slope of the Rift Valley had been badly underestimated – though the experience of climbing down the west scarp should have been a clear warning – and the rapidity of the Turkish response had also been unexpected. At Amman the mounted troops had been unable to prevail against well-placed, well-armed infantry, and this should have been expected, while the defence of es-Salt was as isolated as the Amman operation. The Turkish use of the railway to move reinforcements had been swift and intelligent. The slow British advance had allowed a good Turkish response, and the lengthy communications between the bridge and the forward forces at es-Salt and Amman were dangerously vulnerable. It may have been a typical British reaction to defeat to blame the rain – and no doubt such an excuse resonated well at home – but the result was a clear defeat; not one of the aims of the attack was achieved, and the railway was not badly damaged – five miles of track was claimed to have been destroyed, but only one bridge was damaged, and the other bridges, the viaduct and the tunnel were untouched. Allenby in a report to the War Office estimated that the damage could be repaired in three days once equipment and materials were assembled. The only concrete results were the elimination of the Turkish bridgehead at el-Ghoraniyeh, and the acquisition of a British bridgehead on the east bank at the same place; the intended hold on es-Salt was abandoned. Holding a bridgehead implied that there would be another attack, and Allenby set the engineers to constructing a permanent bridge, but some of the Turks' forces were moved to the east bank, so any new attacks would clearly face an earlier and tougher defence.

The significance of the defeat was devalued by calling it a 'raid' with the implication – if one did not look too closely at the original aims – that much had gone well. The Turks on the other hand called it 'The First Battle of the Jordan', and this is a better term than 'Amman Raid'. The Allies had intended to hold more than a small bridgehead, and had envisaged a more extensive destruction of the railway than what was achieved, with the further aim of keeping the railway under attack and permanently broken. None of this happened; it was a clear defeat.[11]

This attack coincided with the expected massive German attack in France, which turned out to be even more destructive and dangerous than anticipated. Almost at once calls went out to Allenby to send many of his European soldiers to France. By 27 March he had arranged to send the 52nd Lowland Division together with the artillery of the 7th Indian Division (which was closer to the embarkation point). Another division was to follow when the 7th Indian arrived from Mesopotamia. Allenby was also asked for more artillery and four hospitals, and was told he would not be receiving promised railway equipment and four squadrons of aircraft. But Allenby understood the problem - he had fought for two years and more on the Western Front - and he was more than generous in his response. When asked, he agreed to send the 74th Yeomanry Division, without waiting for the 3rd Indian to reach him. The yeomanry battalions would, however, be sent only when their Indian replacements arrived, which happened during May.[12]

The role of the Palestinian force was thus now to be one of 'active defence',[13] and this became all the more necessary once the 74th Division, as well as the 52nd, was withdrawn. It was all very upsetting to Allenby's organization, and a substantial set of changes was also forced on him. The net reduction in manpower was not very great, but Allenby had to accept that the increase he had been expecting would not now arrive, and that the Indian troops he would

---

[11] MacMunn and Falls, *Official History* Vol. I, p. 335; *Advance* pp. 17–20, and plates 34–36; Liman von Sanders, *Five Years*, pp. 210–14; Hughes, *Allenby and British Strategy*, pp. 78–81; Hughes (ed.), *Correspondence*, pp. 104, 196, 107, 110, Allenby to War Office, 26 March–5 April 1918.

[12] Falls, *Official History* Vol. II, pp. 411–14.

[13] Hughes (ed.), *Correspondence*, p. 108, War Office to Allenby, 27 March 1918; since both sides were now committed to an 'active defence', the front lines scarcely changed for the next six months.

receive would need to be retrained – even trained, for those who came direct from India – and acclimatized before they could be used.

Another of Allenby's alternate east-west attacks was intended for the 10th Irish Division's section of the line for early April, and another was planned for close to the coast, but both were cancelled because of the withdrawal of the divisions for France. The 52nd began moving south from Lydd, the railhead, on 4 April, and the 74th on the 15th April, both to embark in Egypt. When the railway was clear, battalions from other divisions would need to go as well.

The two armies facing each other were now both supposed to be in a state of 'active defence'. Something of what this actually meant came in mid-April. On the 11th the Turks launched serious attacks against the trans-Jordan bridge-head, in combination with an attack from the north against the 160 Brigade, which was holding the northern flank on the west bank at el-Musaballeh, north of the Wadi el-Auja. Both attacks were beaten off with, supposedly, heavy Turkish casualties. Then at the bridgehead an attempted counter-attack failed; the continued vigour of the Turkish forces was obvious.[14]

It must be pointed out here, and kept in mind all along, that claimed casualty figures are unreliable. Numbers of prisoners are probably acceptable, since such men would have to be counted and fed and accommodated, but enemy dead and wounded are always overestimated, sometimes wildly. Similarly there is a tendency to assume all casualties were killed, where the proportion of dead to wounded was perhaps one to four – and many of the wounded would return to the fighting, sooner or later. Consequently very few figures will ever be quoted in this account.

A second attempt was made to establish a British presence on the plateau across the Jordan. This time es-Salt was to be the principal target, in a cut-down version of the Amman attack. The assault began on 29 April, brought forward several days in an attempt to cooperate with an Arab tribe, the Beni Sakhr, which claimed to be willing to help by blocking one of the Turkish tracks from Amman. But the Turks had made preparations and the tracks across the plateau from Amman westwards had been improved. The position at Shunet Nimrin close to the el-Ghoraniyeh crossing had been developed and fortified and was well manned by six infantry battalions flanked to north and south by cavalry. The crossings of the river north of el-Ghoraniyeh were well guarded.

[14] Anglesey, *British Cavalry*, pp. 224–48; *Advance*, p. 21 and plates 37 and 38; Hill, *Chauvel of the Light Horse*, pp. 151–2; Liman, *Five Years*, pp. 221–37; Hughes (ed.), *Correspondence*, p. 116, Allenby to War Office, 2 May 1918; Hughes, *Allenby and British Strategy* pp. 82–7.

The Londoners of 179 and 181 Brigades of 60 Division attacked the line of fortifications on either side of Shunet Nimrin on 30 April. Their southern flank was guarded by the cavalry of one regiment of the New Zealand Mounted Rifles, and the Imperial Service Regiment of the Hyderabad Lancers. The infantry took the first Turkish line by storm, but failed entirely to get any further, despite continuing their attacks for several more days. This was, if unpleasant, not necessarily unwelcome. It could be regarded as a pinning attack which would prevent the Turkish infantry at Shunet Nimrin from acting elsewhere.

Behind the Londoners, the Australian Mounted Division – two Australian Light Horse Brigades and the (British) 5th Mounted Brigade – together with the 1st and 2nd Light Horse Brigades from the Anzac Division, crossed the bridges and turned north. They had two tasks: first, to block the approach of any possible Turkish reinforcements which were likely to come from the west by seizing control of the crossings, and second, to seize es-Salt, the main object of the expedition.

The 4th Light Horse Brigade headed north along the river aiming to take control of the bridge at Jisr ed-Damieh, which the Turks had used in the previous raid, eighteen miles north of el-Ghoraniyeh. But the bridge was strongly defended, so the horsemen of the 11th Regiment stayed clear, though they did control the track from that bridge to es-Salt, and a detachment occupied the prominent Red Hill, half way between the bridges at el-Ghoraniyeh and ed-Damieh. The 4th Regiment moved east along the track towards es-Salt. Meanwhile the rest of the horsemen moved along other tracks, and the 3rd Brigade reached es-Salt first, only just missing capturing the headquarters of the Turkish Fourth Army. Soon it was joined by the 2nd Brigade. The several regiments adopted defensive positions all round the town. The 5th Mounted Brigade should also have gone on to es-Salt, but was diverted south to threaten the flank of the Turkish main position at Shunet Nimrin. So the force at es-Salt was only two-thirds what had been intended, and was entirely made up of mounted infantry.

This might have been satisfactory, but the Turkish infantry was very obdurate at Shunet Nimrin, and it soon became clear why. First, the failure of the Beni Sakhr tribe to rise left the track from Amman to Shunet Nimrin available for the Turks to being up supplies and reinforcements; second, the Australians at the river had missed a new crossing point, a pontoon put across the river by the Turks at Mafid Jozele, five miles south of Jisr ed-Damieh. This should have been in plain sight of the 11th Regiment's post at Red Hill, but they did not see it. The sudden arrival on the east bank of the Turkish 3rd Cavalry Division, which crossed at Jisr ed-Damieh, and the 24th Infantry Division, which crossed at Mafid Jozele, therefore startled the 4th Light Horse Brigade and drove the men back towards the steep Rift Valley side. Their accompanying artillery, a battery of the Honourable Artillery Company, had to abandon nine of its twelve guns, though the men and the horses escaped. The horsemen were almost trapped against the hillside, but escaped southwards along the last track open to them, through the tangled and difficult country. With the help of the 6th Mounted Brigade and two regiments of the New Zealand Mounted Rifles Brigade, the line was stabilized by noon on 1 May. But this new line ran close to the only track left by which troops in es-Salt could be supplied – or could escape.

The troops at es-Salt were also under attack from the north by the 3rd Cavalry, and from the east by three regiments of the Fourth Army and the Circassians. Attack and counter-attack took place throughout 2 and 3 May, with neither side prevailing, but the threat to the Australians' communications was obvious, and only one supply of ammunition had got through to them since their arrival. They were reduced to iron rations by the 2nd, which would only last for two days. Allenby cut his losses and ordered a withdrawal to the bridgehead, which was covered by 181 Brigade. The Turks, no doubt as exhausted as their enemies, in effect let them go.

Allenby and his admiring historians claimed a modicum of success in all this. Blame was cast on the Arab tribe, the Beni Sakhr, which had proposed to rebel and which had been expected to cut the repaired track from Amman through es-Sir. But they did not make the offer until after the operation began, and it was not planned on the assumption of their participation; further, no Arab tribe, armed at most with swords and a few old guns, and not subject to the stiffening effect of military discipline, could have been expected to face a Turkish force even as small as a battalion armed with rifles and machine guns, and there were many more Turks than that. Further, the Arabs had been expected to cut a track at es-Sir, but the Turks scarcely used it, so the fact that the Arabs did not rise had no effect. Allenby had not understood the 'unreliability' of the Arabs – for which one must actually read their unwillingness to commit suicide.

Blaming the Arabs' failure to rebel will not do, any more than blaming the rain is a sufficient excuse for the failure of the first attack (and this time the weather was good, which is said to have favoured the Turks – the weather, good or bad, was apparently always on the side of the Turks). The real failure was the underestimation of Turkish resistance, though, after three years of fighting them, there is no excuse for this, and the continuing failure to appreciate the difficulties of the country east of the Jordan. By pushing a force into the east, and maintaining a bridgehead on the east bank, it is claimed that Allenby was persuading the Turks that he was still interested in further adventures there, and so the Turks kept a larger force there than before. But the Turks had shown, in both operations, that they were quite capable of moving back and forth across the river between the east and west banks rapidly, so their troops in the east were fully available for use in the west, if Allenby chose to attack there. It is also claimed that the withdrawal of Turkish forces from southern posts such as et-Tafilat and Ma'an to combat the seizure of es-Salt made life easier for the Arabs who were harassing those posts, but this hypothesis does not work either, for, since the Turks had shifted more troops to the east, they were able to cope with the Arab pinpricks the more easily.

The aim of the Amman operation had been to achieve a worthwhile strategic objective – the decisive cutting of the Turks' railway – but the aim of the es-Salt operation had no such clear and important aim. It should have been obvious that the steep climb up the Rift Valley side would be a choke-point which the Turks would exploit, so any force which was established at es-Salt would be continually threatened by the severing of its communications. That this threat materialized within a day only emphasizes the futility of the exercise. And the precise purpose of a garrison at es-Salt, when the main force west of the river was being so decisively weakened, is not clear. The original objective in the Amman Raid had been to maintain pressure on the railway, but this was no longer possible. No evident aim or purpose can be discerned.

Any claims to partial success, or deceiving the enemy as to Allenby's intentions, falls down before the plain fact that for the second time Allenby had been defeated in an eastern thrust. Also, his attempts to push northwards had met with unwelcome stiff resistance, and this was likely to increase in the face of Liman's policy of stubborn defence, seen to be most successful at Shunet Nimrin. On top of these setbacks and difficulties his force was being drastically reduced in numbers and expertise to feed the great holocaust in France. Allenby had been defeated both by the Turks and by his own superiors. For the present he was reduced, as the War Office had told him, to an 'active defence'.

CHAPTER 2

The Turks

THE Ottoman Empire had entered the Great War quite willingly, even if it did so at a push from Germany. For the empire the main enemy was always Russia, a country which had been a constant and repeated enemy for centuries. Russia had gradually chopped off parts of the empire, either by annexations or by encouraging provinces to grasp at independence. The other Ottoman enemies in this war, Britain and France, became so because they were allied with Russia. At the same time, both of these countries had also sliced off choice Ottoman morsels in the past, notably in Britain's case by taking Egypt. For the Ottoman Empire there were plenty of reasons to be fighting all three states.

By 1914, after recent losses in the Balkans and in Africa, the empire comprised two main national groups, Turks and Arabs, along with several smaller groups, such as Armenians and Kurds. The Committee of Union and Progress, popularly referred to as the 'Young Turks', who had seized power in a series of *coups* between 1908 and 1913, had instigated a fairly chaotic policy of Turkification.[1] This had alienated most of the rest of the empire, in particular the Arabs, and the Armenians had been driven into alliance with the invading Russians as a result. The Turkish government had replied with massacre and expulsion so that when the Russian armies finally invaded the region in 1916 there were few Armenians left.[2] As Muslims – the Armenians were Christians – the Arabs were not treated as harshly as that, but as Arabs they were subjected to discrimination. This was one of the elements in the Sharif Husain's willingness to rebel against the Caliph, and it turned the Arabs of Syria and Iraq against their Turkish rulers. The Young Turks' Turkish nationalism acted on the Arabs to produce a rival Arab nationalism.

---

[1]   Ramsaur, *The Young Turks*; Anderson, *The Eastern Question*, pp. 273–8; Kedourie, *Politics in the Middle East*, ch. 3.

[2]   This is a controversial subject between Turks and Armenians. Both sides exaggerate. There was a massacre, for that was the way Ottoman army dealt with rebels. It was not genocide since plenty of Armenians survived, and some served in the Ottoman army.

The Young Turks' general aim was to modernize the empire whose government they had usurped. This meant, in contemporary European terms, legal and economic reforms, greater bureaucratic efficiency, a well-armed professional army recruited by conscription, and nationalism (defined in terms of the Turkish nation). Local exceptions and privileges should be removed, everyone should speak Turkish.[3] The various wars the empire fought under the Young Turks' rule – the Balkan Wars in 1911 and 1912, the Italian War of 1911, the Great War beginning in 1914 – simultaneously enabled their work and hindered it. For example, the outbreak of the war with the European Great Powers allowed the Committee to proclaim the abolition of the Capitulations, the old concessions which exempted the members of various European states from regulations and legal processes.[4]

The energies of the government were harnessed to the war effort from 1914 onwards, and this obviously hindered their work of modernization. The central direction remained in the nervous hands of Enver Pasha, and in Syria Djemal Pasha, the Minister of Marine, took control. The army was probably no larger than about 150,000 men in 1914[5] (about the same size as the British army), but conscription swelled it. Conditions for the soldiers were bad, and disease and desertion continually thinned their numbers, so any estimate of actual Turkish fighting strength is therefore no more than an approximation – record keeping was not efficient. It is said that during the war 2,700,000 men were conscripted (out of an eligible male population of less than four and a half million), but that at any one time the actual number in arms and uniform was perhaps half a million. By 1918 the number was less than that.[6]

The geography of the empire meant that there were several well-separated fronts on which to fight, but all of them were fairly narrow. Gallipoli, of course, was the main test, which the Turkish army passed but at great cost. Elsewhere there were three main fronts. Mesopotamia and Sinai (later Palestine) were narrow in geography and therefore favoured the Turkish defence; thus, relatively small numbers of troops could be deployed in each region. After Gallipoli, however, the main Turkish front was in the Caucasus against the

---

3   For the effect in Syria, see Petran, *Syria*, pp. 51–3.

4   In fact the Turks had denounced the Capitulations even before the war began. They became an issue later in the peace conference at Lausanne, but Turkey won her point in the end. See Anderson, *The Eastern Question*, pp. 312–14, 373–4.

5   Murphy, 'The Turkish Army in the Great War', in *Soldiers of the Prophet*, 175–96, at 175.

6   Ibid., 176–7.

Russians (other Turkish divisions fought on the main Russian front in the Ukraine). It was in the Caucasus that defeat by 1916 looked probable, with a Russian invasion having penetrated as far as Erzerum and Erzincan. But Russia collapsed, and Enver saw his chance to recover both lost Turkish territory and to go on to build a new, specifically Turkish, empire in the Caucasus and in Central Asia at Russian expense. He pursued this hope even after being ousted from the Ottoman Empire, dying in Central Asia, still fighting for his dream, in 1922.[7]

This concentration on fighting Russia and recovering lost lands in Anatolia was of great benefit to the British campaigns in Mesopotamia and Sinai, since instead of turning the forces released by the Russian collapse in 1917 southwards, Enver raised new forces and used them in the Caucasus. (Given that in both Mesopotamia and Sinai, the British had already suffered humiliating defeats, this, from their point of view, was just as well; from the Turkish point of view it may have seemed that the British would not – or might not want to – recover.) This direction of advance is an indication of Enver's priorities, one which did not change, and perhaps that of many of his colleagues. The Arab lands were now of less importance than Anatolia, the centre of Turkish strength. They would fight for them, of course, but their main purpose was to keep the British at a safe distance from the Turkish homeland.

This approach explains the background to the policy of 'active defence' which both Falkenhayn and von Sanders had to pursue in the face of Allenby's attacks after the fall of Jerusalem. The Arab lands were not regarded as particularly valuable in Constantinople as compared with lands inhabited by Turks, in Anatolia. That is, they were regarded as expendable. This was not, of course, an announced preference, for it would conflict with the Islamist hue which also bathed Turkish policy as a whole. The Committee was composed of men who were largely indifferent to religion, but their head of state was still the Sultan-Caliph. He had proclaimed *jihad* when the war began, and the Committee's secular nationalists were perfectly willing to ride along with that, particularly as Islam was the ideology which drove the ordinary soldiers. But it put a conflict at the heart of Turkish war policy, and compelled the government to retain a considerable force to defend the Ottoman position in Arabia.

---

7 Hopkirk, *Setting the East Ablaze*, pp. 154–71. It is worth noting that Enver's ambition revived in Turkish policy in the wake of the collapse of the Soviet Union in 1991. Relations were very quickly established with the newly independent Central Asian republics, and with Azerbaijan regarded as Turkish, the idea of union with Turkey was aired, and must remain a geopolitical possibility.

This became, with the Arab revolt in mid-1916, yet another front for the Turkish army, and a particularly vicious one in that it was in effect a civil war.

The Turkish defenders of the Ottoman provinces in Palestine and Syria therefore faced considerable difficulties, political as well as military. They were defending a region which was becoming less and less amenable to Turkish rule and well down the list when available forces were being allocated. The Ottoman position in Arabia had already been reduced to the blockaded Ninth Army in Medina, and a detachment supposedly attacking Aden, the latter completely isolated, the former almost so. Apart from these the southernmost town still under Ottoman rule was Ma'an east of the Dead Sea, which was under intermittent attack by the Arab Sharifian Army.

The Arab rebellion had stirred responses throughout the Arab lands. Arab officers in the Ottoman army were very liable to be recruited into the Sharifian army when captured. Two of the most effective commanders in the Arab Army were Ja'afar al-Askeri and Nuri es-Said, both originally from Iraq. Ja'afar had been captured when the Senussi rebellion in Libya was defeated. He had been recruited into the Sharifian Arab Army and had organized and trained the most effective force in that army. He was operating from his headquarters at Aqaba towards Ma'an, and defeated a Turkish attack near Petra in October. Nuri operated as Chief of Staff to Faisal, the Commander-in-Chief of the Arab Army, under his father, King Husain.[8]

Faisal had contacted the disaffected Arab groups in Damascus in 1915 (and in Constantinople in 1914), but it was scarcely possible for these men to rebel in a city which was the Turkish military headquarters, and when their influence and support was still very limited. Several prominent Syrians were arrested and executed by Djemal in that year, and this quelled any overt display of opposition.[9] Yet the Turkish policies of conscription, grinding taxation, requisition of foodstuffs (producing famine) and Turkification, drove the mass of the population to detest the Turkish regime by 1917.[10]

The British raids into the Trans-Jordan lands had also encountered another aspect of Arab affairs, which would complicate everyone's lives. The Bani Sakhr, who had proposed to rebel but then did not do so, were only one of many relatively small groups whose loyalty was principally to themselves, and

---

8   Wavell, *Palestine Campaign*, pp. 35, 37. Nuri es-Said was Enver's half-brother.

9   Petran, *Syria*, p. 55, says thirty-four were executed; Dawn, *From Ottomanism to Arabism*, pp. 155–6, has a slightly different figure.

10   Petran, *Syria* p. 55.

who had no affection for Turks, nor Sharifians, nor Europeans. They did not like the Turks, though they were able to deal with them in time-honoured ways, and the Turks made efforts to keep them friendly, or at least neutral.[11] They were by no means happy at the prospect of someone else – Arab, British, Sharifian, French – ruling them. Most of these groups were also in a feud with someone else, normally a neighbour. So, during the Amman operation in March 1918 the advance of 179 Brigade from es-Salt towards Amman was interrupted when the brigade found itself in the midst of a fight between the Christian Arabs of el-Fuheis and the Circassians of Suweileh.[12] The Circassians were refugees from the Russian conquest of their homeland in the Caucasus several decades before, resettled in various parts of the Trans-Jordan lands, and were inevitably staunch Ottoman loyalists. Their arrival and settlement on land already regarded as someone else's inevitably upset the locals.[13] Hence the feud, which neither the Ottoman government nor that of the Committee much bothered with, since such conditions meant that at least one side would be loyal. General Allenby reported to the War Office on a comparable situation to the south of Amman, which indicated the variety of local problems he had to take into account:

> Belga Arabs were found ready to co-operate with our forces, but not so ready to assist Sherif. Made[b]a townsfolk (Christian) also entirely with us but nervous of Belga Arabs with whom they have an old feud. A section of the Beni Sakha came out further south and raided Ziza Station during Amman operations but appeared to have retired again probably owing to old feud with Belga tribes. There is no sign of Sherifian co-ordination of tribes north of Kerak at present.[14]

The Turkish army in Palestine had been reinforced by a German contingent. The original intention had been to use this force, codenamed *Yilderim*, in Mesopotamia, but it had been switched to Palestine when it seemed that the front there would collapse. Two successive German forces, *Pasha I* and *Pasha II* had been organized, but in the result one of the infantry brigades did not arrive. *Yilderim* (Turkish for 'lightning' and the nickname of a particularly

---

[11] Only one Trans-Jordanian tribe, the Howeitat, took part in the Arab revolt before the final months.

[12] Falls, *Official History* Vol. II, p. 335.

[13] Lewis, *Nomads and Settlers*, ch. 6.

[14] Hughes (ed.), *Correspondence*, p. 110, Allenby to War Office, 5 April, 1918.

successful Ottoman medieval sultan) became the name for the whole Palestine army, as the Yilderim Army Group, and the German contingent with it became the Asien Korps.[15]

The Turkish Palestine forces were now organized as three armies under the Yilderim Army Group. Djemal Pasha – not the Minister of Marine, but a competent soldier known to the British as Djemal the Lesser – commanded the IV Army, which comprised the units east of the Jordan. It had the responsibility of combating the Arab Army approaching from the south, and had been the object of the attack in the Amman and es-Salt operations. West of the Rift Valley, in Palestine proper, there were two armies: VII Army, commanded by General Fevzi Pasha at Nablus, was in the eastern half of Judaea, including the western part of the Jordan Valley; VIII Army, with its headquarters at Tulkarm under General Jevad Pasha, defended the land from the coast to the boundary of VII Army's territory in the hills.

VIII Army had also Asien Korps under its command. This consisted of artillery and machine-gun detachments and three infantry battalions (701st, 702nd, and 703rd), one of which (703rd) had been posted east of the Jordan and had fought against the Amman Raid. Each of these three battalions had an artillery company, a machine-gun company, and a cavalry component, so they were particularly versatile. The quantity of machine guns in the Korps as a whole made it notably formidable.

A further German contingent – 'Pasha II Reinforcement' – was sent to Palestine in the spring of 1918. It included the 146th Infantry Regiment, part of which also took part in the repulse of the Amman Raid, a Jager battalion (but this was reduced in size before it set out) and more artillery and machine-gun detachments. This was thus another more or less integrated force. Its commander was Colonel von Oppen, who soon became commander of the whole Asien Korps. These German units were tough, experienced, well commanded, well armed and well organized, as would be expected, but their presence should not lead us to ignore the fact that by far the greatest number of troops on the Palestine front were Turks, and it was these Turks who did most of the fighting.[16]

In December 1917 the General Staff in London and Allenby's staff were both concerned about actual and potential Turkish strength. The assumption both operated on was that the end of the Russian war, which was expected

---

[15] Liman von Sanders, *Five Years*, pp. 177–81; Falls, *Official History* Vol. II, pp. 444–5.
[16] Ibid.

soon, would release Turkish forces for other fronts. In London the General Staff calculated that 180,000 Turkish soldiers could be released and might be used to reinforce the Palestine front. Allenby's staff members were a little less pessimistic, but only comparatively so. It was these figures which lay behind Allenby's request for reinforcement, and London's agreement to transfer forces from Mesopotamia and India for his use.

The large figures produced in both London and Cairo were based on several assumptions, the unreliability of which were gradually taken into account as time passed. The major error was in assuming that since the Turks had suffered defeat in Palestine they would wish either to recover their lost territory, or at least strongly fortify the defence of their remaining territory. To do either of these they would send in more troops. This might be termed a self-referential viewpoint, since it was assumed that the war against the British army was necessarily seen to be the most important for the Turks. But Turkish policy, as noted earlier, was in fact devoted principally by 1918 to the reconquest of lost land in Anatolia, and then to extending Ottoman power farther eastwards, into the Caucasus and beyond.

Then there were the combined problems of transport and logistics. The Turkish transport system in Syria/Palestine depended on a single railway, which was subject to breakdown and interruption. Being single track and comprising a succession of railways, it operated slowly. It was interrupted in the north, where the tunnel through the Amanus Mountain range was not finished until October 1918. It was standard gauge as far as Riyaq in the Bekaa Valley, but narrow gauge from thereon southwards, including the lines in Palestine and the Hajj line on the east of Jordan. (There was also a rack-and-pinion section between Riyaq and Beirut, but this had ceased to work.) Branch lines and the French-built railway from Damascus southwards had been dismantled to use the rails and sleepers to repair breaks elsewhere, and much of the forests east of the Jordan had been cut down to feed the locomotives. This complicated and inadequate system meant that moving troops and supplies was a slow and laborious task; it was also difficult to supply the troops already in the front line. And if a much larger army was actually brought into Palestine the already intractable problems of supply would simply multiply. The British, of course, faced a similar problem. The only reason they had been able to win at the Third Battle of Gaza was because their army was well supplied with water brought by pipeline from the Nile, and with food, fodder and other supplies transported by a new railway from Kantara on the Suez Canal. The line was extended north, partly by cannibalising the Turkish narrow gauge line, as a standard gauge north as far as Ludd, just behind the front line, and a branch went up to Jerusalem. Capturing and/or cutting the Turkish railway north of the front was a priority in later operations.

General Robertson in London appreciated these constraints on Turkish capabilities in part, and on 3 January he wrote to Allenby with a reduced estimate of Turkish capabilities, but one which still assumed the centrality of Palestine in Turkish military minds:

> we are inclined to believe that you may possibly be opposed before long by 60,000 combatants, including about 11,000 Germans, and that this force might be increased to 70,000 or 80,000 by middle of February.
>
> We are inclined to believe that further increases would be prevented by transport difficulties and that in any case the maximum force enemy could subsequently maintain in Damascus area would be 100,000 combatants.[17]

In the event, the Turks sent only a few battalions south to reinforce two of their divisions in Palestine. Given that there was a great deal of desertion from and sickness in all Turkish units, this additional strength did no more than stay the gradual fall in Turkish overall numbers for a time. By June 1918 all Turkish formations were under strength except those on the east bank area (IV Army), and by September these were also below strength.[18]

Desertion was rife because of the bad conditions the troops endured – and perhaps because it must have been clear that a new attack, when it came, would lead to another defeat. Estimates of total desertions from the army range from 300,000 to 400,000;[19] on top of this there had been grievous casualties in other fighting, particularly at Gallipoli and in Armenia. Altogether these reduced the full strength of the army to about 400,000 in total by 1918.[20]

The bad conditions were not entirely the fault of the army organization, the officers, or the difficult supply and transport system – though these inefficiencies and difficulties certainly aggravated the situation. The great majority of the troops were peasants in origin, either from Anatolia or from the Arab lands; their practices and standards of hygiene were rudimentary. The dirt in

---

[17] Hughes (ed.), *Correspondence*, p. 91, Robertson to Allenby, 2 January 1918.

[18] Erickson, *Ottoman Army*, pp. 132–5.

[19] Murphy, 'The Turkish Army in the Great War', in *Soldiers of the Prophet*, 176.

[20] Erickson, *Ottoman Army*, p. 164, discussing the demobilisation numbers.

the trenches bred diseases, such as typhus, and all sickness was aggravated by the poor diet supplied to the troops.[21] But the main disease was malaria, which was endemic in Syria, and particularly so in the Jordan Valley and low-lying areas such as the Vale of Esdraelon. Allenby had also noted the presence of typhus in Jericho – and kept his troops out of the town as a result – and that cannot have been the only case. Combined with shortage of food and consequent malnourishment, the Turkish soldiers were very liable to fall sick.

There was also less concern for the wounded than in western armies, both in recovering the wounded men from the battlefields, and in caring for them later. In April Allenby reported that several instances had occurred of German and British observing local truces to bring dead men and recover wounded after fights. These were dangerous exploits, liable to be misunderstood – indeed Allenby was explaining these events because it had been reported that he had asked for an armistice.

> On 11th April Germans with Red Cross flags … collected dead and wounded and were not fired on. Later 4th Welsh Regiment sent out stretcher-bearers to same locality, they were, however, fired on and returned as did the Germans.
>
> On 17th April a medical officer and burying party were sent out and an enemy medical officer and burying party also appeared…. There was no contact between parties, and except where parties were at work no cessation of artillery or rifle fire.[22]

The significance of these notices – Allenby did not have to explain himself again – is that it was the British and the Germans who were involved. There are no instances, so far as I can see, of Turks acting in such a way. Indeed, it was widely feared on the Allied side that to be taken prisoner by the Turks was likely to lead to one's death, either immediately or by starvation – the Turks put prisoners to work, and many were worked to death. To fall into the hands of Arabs was almost certain death, especially if one was isolated – airmen were often instantly murdered.

In these circumstances – being short of food, heavily outnumbered, and with constant sickness and a lack of supplies – it is not surprising that the commanders of the Turkish forces adopted a policy of staying on the defen-

---

[21] Ibid., pp. 132–3.

[22] Hughes (ed.), *Correspondence*, p. 114, Allenby to War Office, 26 April 1918.

sive. An attack was generally more costly than defence, and the Palestine army could not afford even more losses, on top of desertions and disease. But it must also have been clear that the British, at least after being defeated twice in their Trans-Jordan adventures, were much weakened by the withdrawal of two very competent divisions, and of many experienced battalions. Of course, the Turks missed a trick here. Had they used a good proportion of the troops they had employed in the north to build up their strength in Palestine, it would be quite possible to have caught the British forces off balance and secure a victory. Yet another British defeat in the Near East at a time when the Western Front was so active might well have led to the closing down of British operations in Palestine – Allenby was already in a state of 'active defence'. This would certainly have badly affected morale at home, and quite possibly would have led to disputes with the French and the Arabs, who were both counting on a British victory to enable them to realize their own political ends. But Enver and his government were blinded to military possibilities in the south by their nationalism and it does not seem that the idea occurred to them.

CHAPTER 3

The New Army

THE 52nd and 74th Divisions entrained at Ludd in April and embarked at
Kantara on the Suez Canal on their way to France. Their replacements
had already begun to arrive – though these had originally been intended not
as replacements but as reinforcements. The 7th Indian Division was sent by
sea from Mesopotamia and had arrived in the Suez area in early January. It
surrendered its artillery component to the departing 52nd Division, receiving
that division's guns in their place. Much of this change had been arranged by
early April, but the actual movement of units meant that the disruption of the
Egyptian Expeditionary Force continued for much longer.

The infantry divisions were more deeply affected than the cavalry, but
almost all were changed. Only two of Allenby's divisions, the Anzac Mounted
and the 54th East Anglian, remained as they had been; and the two new Indian
divisions, the 7th Meerut and the 3rd Lahore, sometimes simply called the 7th
and 3rd Indian, were imported whole, except for their artillery. Others suffered
more or less changes. Further, this was not a matter of one change, but several
taking place over a number of months, largely as a result of the changing state
of the fighting in France, where the successive German attacks between March
and July led to repeated demands for more troops from Palestine, not to mention changes of mind at the War Office. But the whole period from March 21
to the end of July was a powerful demonstration that it was in France that the
war was being fought, and that, as Allenby understood all along, Palestine was
as much a sideshow to the British as it was to the Committee of Union and
Progress in Constantinople. The difference was that the British had good reasons to persist with operations in Palestine, while the Young Turks had equally
good reasons to ignore it.

The Mesopotamian divisions were fully manned and organized as normal
Indian Army divisions, each with three British battalions and nine Indian,
organized into three brigades. The 7th had a battalion of the Seaforth Highlanders, one of the Royal Highlanders – that is, the Black Watch – and one
of the Leicestershire Regiment. Most of the Indian battalions were from the
Punjab or other parts of north-west India, with the 28th, 92nd, and 20th Pun-

jabis, and the 56th Punjabi Rifles (Frontier Force). This last was linked with two Sikh battalions, 51st and 53rd, also of the Frontier Force, and their designation implied specialized mountain warfare capability. Similarly the 1st Guides battalion was probably recruited in the north-west. The last two battalions were 125th Napier's Rifles and the 8th Gurkha Rifles. Much as with British regiments, the geographical name did not necessarily mean that all the men came from a restricted area. Some, Gurkhas for example, were composed of one 'race', others tended to have each company of one group, but the battalion might have several; the Bombay Pioneers, for example, had companies of Jats, Mahrattas, Pathans, and Rajasthan Muslims. This simplified feeding since the different groups had different dietary requirements. At the same time being in a single unit would, it was hoped, replace group or religious loyalty with regimental loyalty and pride – and almost always it did so.

Much the same can be said of the 3rd Lahore Division. The three British battalions were the 1st Connaught Rangers, the 1st Manchester, and the 2nd Dorsetshire, and the Indian battalions were once again mainly from the north-west: the 27th and 91st Punjabis, the 59th Scinde Rifles (Frontier force) the 47th Sikhs and the 124th Baluchistan Infantry were all originally raised in the Indus basin region; there were also two Gurkha battalions (7th and 1st), the 93rd Infantry and the 105th Mahratta Light Infantry.[1]

These two Indian divisions each took several months to move from Mesopotamia to Palestine. The 20th Infantry (Brownlow's Punjabis) of 7th Division left their station at Akab north of Baghdad on 9 December, but did not disembark at Suez until 15 January, then stayed in camp at Moascar on the Canal for two months.[2] Other battalions of the division embarked at Basra on 21 December and 8 January, reaching Suez late in January, and again remained in camp at Moascar or Ismailia.[3] These two months were filled by training, and by leave to visit Cairo and Alexandria – some officers even managed leave in Britain.[4] The 3rd Division followed on, leaving Mesopotamia in April, and arriving at Suez at various times between late April and early June. There was, however, no long period of waiting in camp this time.[5] The 7th Division battalions were moved to Ludd by rail at the end of March; most of the 3rd arrived at much

---

[1] These are detailed in Falls, *Official History* Vol. II, Appendix 3.

[2] Anon., *Brownlow's Punjabis*, pp. 39–41.

[3] Wylly, *Leicestershire Regiment*, pp. 186–7; Anon., *53rd Sikhs*, pp. 238–9.

[4] Wylly, *Leicestershire Regiment*, p. 187.

[5] Wylly, *History of the Manchester Regiment*, Vol. 2, p. 192; Chaldecott, *The 1st Battalion*, p. 68; Mackay, *7th Own Gurkhas*, p. 73; Petre, *1st Gurkha Rifles*, p. 175.

the same time, having been in camp near the Canal for only a couple of weeks. From Ludd both divisions moved into the line.

The Indian units had considerably larger number of personnel than the British, and many had to lose some men in drafts to form new battalions. Several sent cadres off to India around which new recruits could be gathered. Brownlow's Punjabis sent eight men to India and were then judged to have a surplus of 137 men, who were sent in March to the Base depot at Kantara.[6] The 7th Gurkhas had similarly sent 200 men to India on leaving Mesopotamia and now sent a full company, including officers, to form a new battalion of the 11th Gurkhas;[7] another company from 1st Gurkhas was similarly transferred.[8] The 124th Baluchis sent a company to help form a new battalion, the 3/153rd Infantry, together with companies from each of the 105th Mahratta Light Infantry, the 23rd Rifles (Outram's Rifles) and the 125th Rifles.[9]

The experience of those divisions already in Palestine was very different, but perhaps even more difficult. Only the 54th East Anglian Division was not changed in any significant degree, and the Anzac and Australian Mounted Divisions suffered only relatively small changes. But all the other divisions gave up nine of their British battalions, which were replaced by nine Indians. That is, the all-British divisions which Allenby had trained in 1917 and with which he had conquered southern Palestine were converted into Indian-type divisions, though they kept their British numbering.

The 10th Irish Division, for example, retained the 1st Leinsters, the 1st Royal Irish Regiment and the 1st Irish Fusiliers; it received two Punjabi battalions, one of Sikhs, one of Dogras, two battalions of Grenadiers, a Kashmir Imperial Service battalion, a Deoli battalion, and a battalion of the 152nd Indian Infantry. Of these, the 46th Punjabis do not seem to have joined before late 1918, but the 74th Punjabis were training at Tel el-Kebir near the Canal by late February, having come from India in January.[10] In the 53rd Welsh Division the retained battalions were two of the Royal Welch Fusiliers and one of the Welch Regiment; these had been reinforced by men from battalions which had been reduced in numbers by casualties. The Indian replacements included the new battalion of the 11th Gurkhas (which had been formed from four sepa-

[6] Anon., *Brownlow's Punjabis*, p. 40.
[7] Mackay, *7th Gurkhas*, pp. 73, 74.
[8] Petre, *1st Gurkha Rifles*, p. 175.
[9] Rawlinson, *Outram's Rifles*, pp. 164–5, 173.
[10] Lawford and Catto, *Solah Punjab*, p. 103; Bethan and Geary, *The Golden Galley*, p. 76.

rate companies from different battalions) – five units are simply described as 'Infantry' or 'Indian Infantry' – and the 1st Cape Corps, a unit of black troops from South Africa.[11]

Hidden under the name of the 1/17th Infantry in the Welsh Division, however, was a battalion of the Mahratta Light Infantry, whose original personnel were largely prisoners of war, having been part of the defeat at Kut el-Amara in Mesopotamia in 1915. The regiment's depot had recruited replacement personnel, but these had been repeatedly removed once they had been gathered in order to supply drafts to other battalions. None of the surviving officers or NCOs who had been exchanged after Kut could serve against the Turks, so when the battalion arrived in Egypt it was composed of new recruits and 'convalescents ... taken from hospital in the hope that they would become effective soon after reaching Egypt'; a huge percentage of troops in the battalion had never even fired a rifle. Little could be done on the voyage from Karachi to Suez – which took place in three separate ships – and when they arrived it was not clear for a few days where they would go. Only on 1 June was the whole battalion reunited, and it was moved to the Surafend camp in Palestine a fortnight later. When the battalion came close to the front line most of its men were still barely trained.[12] By contrast the first battalion of the Kumaon Rifles arrived at Surafend a month later (16 July). Ten days after its arrival it was inspected by the 60th Division commander, Major-General Shea, who was very impressed.[13] Clearly an experienced and well-organized unit, the Kumaonis were soon in action.

The variety of units brought to Palestine was therefore very wide, from the untrained recruits to experienced and tough soldiers, from well-organized and confident battalions to new units composed of disparate companies with different traditions. The changes had been going on since the arrival of the 7th Division in January, and only in July could Allenby be certain that his force was not likely to be suddenly disrupted again. Even in June orders had come to send the 54th Division to France. Allenby was very concerned – this was his only all-British division. He made the point that to rely wholly on Indian Divisions alone would invite trouble in Egypt, where anti-British propaganda was actively courting the Indian Muslims. Wilson, the Chief of the Imperial Gen-

---

[11] Ward, *Royal Welch Fusiliers*, Vol. IV, pp. 181–2; Marden, *The History of the Welch Regiment*, p. 545; Ward, *53rd (Welsh) Division*, pp. 216–17.

[12] Anon., *110 Mahrattas*, pp. 73–5.

[13] Overton, *Kumoan Rifles*, p. 5.

eral Staff (CIGS), quickly relented, but some parts of the division had got as far as the Canal in preparation for embarkation before word of the cancellation of the move arrived. Just as alarming was Wilson's proposal to withdraw the Australian Mounted Division and break it down into drafts to fill up Australian infantry divisions in France. He gave the idea up quickly enough – entangling with the Australian government would not be something he would relish – but the episode is a good indication of the continuing threat of disruption Allenby had to cope with.[14]

The 60th London Division went through the same upheaval as most of the others. Nine of its London battalions went to France, and it received, besides the Kumaonis, three Punjabi and two Baluchi battalions from Mesopotamia, and three others, the 2nd Guides, the 97th Deccan Infantry, and 15th Infantry, direct from India. The 75th Division had been largely a West Country unit, and retained a Wiltshire battalion, one of the Somerset Light Infantry, and one of the Duke of Cornwall's Light Infantry. Its lost battalions were replaced by two Gurkha battalions, two of Punjabis and 'Indian Infantry', and one Kashmir Imperial Service battalion.[15] The disruption was perhaps less felt here than elsewhere because the division already had two Indian battalions, Outram's Rifles and Vaughan's Rifles, as part of its establishment – but the impact of the upheaval can only have been minimally less felt.

Indian cavalry battalions were sent from France in exchange for the British units given up by Allenby. This had led to much greater reorganization than in the infantry divisions where the basic structure remained and the new battalions merely took the places of the departed. In the cavalry the two antipodean divisions remained more or less intact, but the other cavalry division, the Yeomanry Mounted, was dismantled entirely - it had been originally formed in Palestine from a variety of units. Of the regiments from which it had been composed, only three remained with the army in Palestine. These became the British components of a new division, which was eventually called the 4th Cavalry. Two more British Yeomanry units were culled from the Australian Mounted Division and from the 7th Mounted Brigade, and these became the British component of another new division, the 5th Cavalry. These two new divisions then received no less than thirteen Indian cavalry regiments.

[14] Hughes (ed.), *Correspondence, p.* 113, Wilson to Allenby 21 January 1918; p. 131, Allenby to Wilson, 22 June 1918; p. 132, Wilson to Allenby 4 July 1918; Falls, *Official History* Vol. II, p. 418.

[15] *Advance*, pp. 66–72.

Allenby was able to increase his cavalry divisions from three to four by a judicious juggling of his various units. The 5th Mounted Brigade was taken from the Australian Mounted Division and its battalions were spread between the new 5th Cavalry Division (the Gloucester Yeomanry), and corps troops of XX Corps (the Worcester Yeomanry); one was despatched to France.

The 4th Cavalry Division began with the usual three British battalions, the 1st Dorset Yeomanry, the 1st County of London Yeomanry (also called the Middlesex Yeomanry) and the 1st Staffordshire Yeomanry, all retained from the old Yeomanry Mounted Division. To these were added three regiments of Lancers (2nd, 29th and 19th), the 38th Central India Horse, 26th Jacob's Horse, and the 6th Cavalry, all from France.[16]

The 5th Division was rather more diverse in its composition. There were only two British battalions included: the Gloucester Yeomanry, from the Australian Mounted Division, and the 1st Sherwood Rangers from the 7th Mounted Brigade, which had long been attached to the Desert Mounted Corps; also from that brigade came the new division's artillery, the Essex Battery of the Royal Horse Artillery. To these were added the 9th Hodson's Horse and the 19th Lancers with the Gloucesters, and 20th Deccan Horse and 24th Poona Horse with the Sherwood Rangers. The third brigade was composed of three Imperial Service battalions: the Mysore Lancers and the Hyderabad Lancers which were already in Palestine and had proved themselves very effective in the Third Gaza battle and the subsequent pursuit, and the Jodhpore Lancers which came from France.[17]

The Imperial Camel Corps Brigade, which was originally recruited from British, New Zealander, and Australian troops already in Egypt for service primarily in Sinai and southern Palestine, was broken up. The Australian and New Zealand battalions were given back their horses and became the 14th and 15th Australian Light Horse Regiments, assigned to the Australian Mounted Division, which now for the first time became an all-Australian force. The New Zealanders from the Camel Corps became a machine gun squadron. The British battalion stayed on its camels for use in the desert lands beyond the Jordan and to coordinate with the Arab Army. So the Australian Mounted Division became all-Australian though somewhat smaller. The Imperial Camel Corps concentrated on desert work and was reduced to battalion strength. The Anzac Division was unchanged. Allenby also had a number of 'spare' units which

[16]   Barrow, *Fire of Life*, p. 189; Anglesey, *British Cavalry*, pp. 221–2.
[17]   Anglesey, *British Cavalry*, pp. 221–2.

were formed into a mixed brigade, the 20th Indian, a misleading title since it included only four Indian battalions - the Imperial Service units from Alwar, Gwalior, and Patiala, and the 110th Mahratta Light Infantry – along with the 38th and 39th Fusiliers, which were recruited from Jews of several nationalities, and two battalions of the British West Indian Regiment.

Once again, all these changes and developments took time. The Indian regiments in France were given advance warning of a move at the beginning of February, but it was not until April that they arrived in Egypt. There had been rumours since mid-January – officers of Jacob's Horse heard it first in their London clubs[18] – and definitive orders arrived early in February. So they were on their way when the German attack began on 21 March. Indeed two of these regiments entrained for Marseilles the day before, some men going directly from the trenches to the trains. More than one of the contemporary memoirs written at the time is scathing about the staff's work.[19]

The men sometimes travelled by train to Taranto in Italy, though the horses went via Marseilles. The frictions experienced in any war were also evident here. For example, the threat of submarines was ever present in the Mediterranean (one ship carrying some of the Yeomanry to France was torpedoed, and was run aground on Sardinia to save the crew and passengers).[20] The transports had to wait for mines to be cleared and for the destroyers to arrive as escorts – Japanese ships in some cases. In one case, the transport arrived at Alexandria too late in the day to enter the harbour and had to steam about for the night outside – hardly a sensible procedure when the real dangers came from submarines. One horse transport had to stop at Malta after its propeller was damaged when it fouled something – rumour had it that this was a dead horse which had been thrown overboard – and many of the horses fell sick of septic pneumonia, holding up the whole shipment for a fortnight.[21]

Once in Egypt, the men and horses had to be reunited. They were accommodated, as were the infantry from Mesopotamia and India, in the great camps in the Canal area, principally at Kantara, and they then moved gradually into Palestine. This absorbed more time. The 2nd Lancers, for example, arrived at Alexandria on 21 April. Initially travelling by train and then marching, they

---

[18] Maunsell, *Scinde Horse*, p. 174.

[19] Tennant, *Royal Deccan Horse*, p. 63; Hudson, *19th Lancers*, pp. 192–3.

[20] Newbolt, *Naval Operations*, Vol. V, p. 284.

[21] Hudson, *19th Lancers*, pp. 193–4; Whitworth, *2nd Lancers*, pp. 114–15; Watson, *Central India Horse*, p. 383; Maunsell, *Scinde Horse*, pp. 177–82; Tennant, *Royal Deccan Horse*, p. 63.

reached Kantara a week later, moved on to Deir el-Belah near Gaza, and spent five days there 'getting off the dirt which the horses had accumulated on the journey from France'. (One of the regiment's officers had been present at the battle of Tel el-Kebir in 1882 and took a party overground when the regiment stopped there for a night.) Marching throughout the following week, the regiment arrived in the heights above the Jordan valley by 9 May.[22] This was one of the quicker transits, with no obvious delays; yet it had taken three months from the issuing of orders in France to bring the regiment close to the front in Palestine. Most of the other troops took even longer – the Deccan Horse spent two further months in training once it reached the camp at Surafend.[23]

This reorganization and redeployment may have taken time but the sheer range of the activity is worth remarking. Between March and May Allenby sent 60,000 soldiers to France. In exchange he received two divisions from Mesopotamia, the equivalent of one from India, and a cavalry division from France. In the process only one ship had been torpedoed – and no lives were lost. The complex movements took several months, but the condition of the front in Palestine had not suffered in that time. Indeed, both the Turks and the Germans were so preoccupied with their own affairs, in France and Russia and the Caucasus, that, in effect, the British and Allenby were allowed to do all this without any interference. It may have helped that the Amman and es-Salt operations had suggested that he still had considerable aggressive capability, but the disruption of all the changes surely left him vulnerable, particularly once the 52nd and 74th Divisions had left.

The Germans and the Turks were neglecting one of their major advantages in the Palestine war, one which they had already exploited with the old *Yilderim* plan. It was possible for the British to bring soldiers in large numbers from India and Mesopotamia and France, but this took three or four months; it was also possible for the Germans to transport a division, say, by rail from Germany to Palestine in a couple of weeks, or for the Turks to move a division from Anatolia to Palestine in a week. To be sure, the railway system east of Constantinople was skeletal, difficult, and slow, but it did exist. A determined effort could have brought 20,000 men from Germany and Anatolia to the Palestine front while Allenby's men were still at sea. But the attempt was never made.

---

[22]   Whitworth, *2nd Lancers*, pp. 115–17.
[23]   Tennant, *Deccan Horse*, pp. 64–5.

The newly constituted and organized British divisions were spread along the front line from the coast to the Jordan River. The 7th Division held a front of seven miles from the coast at Arsuf inland to the Nahr el-Auja (the westward-flowing of the two rivers of that name). This was an area just north of Jaffa which had been deliberately taken late in 1917 to push the Turks away from the town so that it could safely be used as a base and the harbour for unloading supplies. The line consisted of a series of mutually supporting strong points, with a wide No Man's Land in front of up to 2000 yards. The strong points consisted of a trench system on the forward slopes of small hills strongly wired, with a bivouac area behind the rearward slopes. The trenches were manned by the men only at night; by day the garrison lived in the bivouac area, leaving only an observation post and a Lewis gun team in the trenches. The country was open but undulating, so long communication trenches from the strong points to the rear were not needed.[24]

The 54th Division held the next section, another seven miles or so from the Nahr el-Auja to Medjel Yaba. This was the division which was briefly ordered to France in June. In the biography of a Royal Field Artillery unit, the Hertfordshire Battery, the disruption is described as 'a complex administrative nightmare'. Signallers left the unit to remuster with the Royal Engineers on 26 June. Guns, wagons and other heavy equipment were transferred to other units or sent for storage. Then on 27 June orders came to suspend the operation. On 3 July the news came that the division was not to being dispatched to France. It took ten more days for the signallers to return, together with their equipment. A new set of guns and wagons had to be acquired and filled with first line ammunition.[25] This was in various ways the experience of every unit ordered to France, or sent from elsewhere to Palestine.

The next ten-mile section of the line was held by 75th Division, then the 10th Irish Division held another seven miles. The 10th Irish was for a time a weak division, since it took time for its Indian replacements to arrive, and they were particularly short of experience when they did. The 38th Dogras, a well-experienced unit, however, was present by early May. Then came the 53rd Welsh Division, holding the long section of the line from Jiljilya, captured in the April attack at Tell Asur, to the Rift Valley escarpment. The Indian battalions to fill up this division arrived in June and August. Two battalions of the Welch Regiment were amalgamated, each having been so reduced in numbers

---

[24] Anon., *53rd Sikhs*, p. 240.
[25] Sainsbury, *Hertfordshire Battery RFA*, p. 81.

of soldiers as to have become unviable. Similarly, the 5th and 6th battalions of the Royal Welch Fusiliers were amalgamated, and their brigade, the 158th, also received two of the newly created Indian battalions: the 4/11th Gurkha Rifles and the 3/153rd Indian Infantry, which had been formed from 'surplus' men from several other units. It was clearly going to take some time for the division to recover from the upheaval. Life for the Welch Regiment had been improved 'by the extension and improvement of the railways which brought food and fresh supplies to the troops. There were also concert parties and theatrical parties for units at rest, and short leave to Cairo'. On the other hand, the new Indian battalions 'were so constantly exercised in patrol work and minor attacks, that by the beginning of September they could be relied on to give a good account of themselves'.[26] The Welshmen were clearly using the inexperience of the Indians as an excuse to be lazy.

The Jordan Valley was the station of the Desert Mounted Corps, commanded by Lt-General Sir Harry Chauvel, to which the two new cavalry divisions, 4th and 5th, were allotted. The troops were concentrated in the valley in the summer of 1918, for Allenby decided it was necessary for his domination of the enemy and for the development of his plan of attack to maintain a vigorous and visible presence in the valley even during the summer. The Amman and es-Salt attacks had to a degree fixed Turkish attention on the possibility of the British launching another, even larger, offensive across the Jordan, perhaps in order to outflank the main Turkish forces, and to link up with the Arab Army as the latter advanced northwards. There were few troops on the British side who attracted more attention and made more noise than the Australians, so their presence in the valley all through the summer made it quite certain that the enemy's attention and strength would be directed there. The attachment to the Desert Mounted Corps of the two new divisions made that threat all the more potent.

The Australians and New Zealanders who occupied the valley in the summer of 1918 universally recalled its evil condition – 'Sodom and Gomorrah' and 'Gehenna' were the more polite comparisons. The dry climate, combined with an unusual number of animals and men, cut up the ground so that every campsite was thick with dust – 'whitish-grey, salty and bitter to the tongue', 'yellow and choking'.[27] Insects and vermin swarmed: 'scorpions, tarantulas, centipedes, and snakes, pilgrims of the night mainly among the men's bed-

---

[26] Marden, *Welch Regiment*, p. 545.
[27] Jabotinsky, *Jewish Legion*, p. 131; Kemp, *Queen's Own*, p. 64.

ding. Swarms of flies plagued all during the day.'[28] And it was hot, hotter than any of the men had ever experienced, over 100 degrees Fahrenheit during the day, and still 80 degrees at night.

The troops were usually stationed in the valley for a month at a time; they then spent a month on the cooler highlands, enjoying leave and engaging in sports and training. On their return they halted first at the watering place of Talaat ed-Dum (also called the Samaritan Inn) at the edge of the Rift Valley, and then went down the scarp into the valley once more. Of course, they took a perverse pride in enduring all this, though one account quotes what the author describes as an Arab proverb, to the effect that God made the Jordan Valley, then laughed sarcastically at his work.

The Turks well understood the privations the men were enduring. One account remembers that Turkish 'aircraft dropped messages to say the British were welcome to the valley, and 'in the autumn they would return to bury their bodies.'[29] Not even generals escaped. General Glanville Ryrie, commanding the 2nd Light Horse Brigade, was awakened in the night by a Turkish bombardment and 'sprang hastily out of bed and planted his naked foot right on the tail of a huge black scorpion. For a full half hour Australia was heard at its best.'[30]

Then there was disease. Malaria was endemic, and was ceaselessly fought by the medical staff. Drainage works dried out swamps, and the pools which remained were sprayed with oil to kill the mosquitoes. Some camps were free of the infection, but other areas were not. The two Judaean battalions had contrasted fortunes: 'the American companies ... in the valley of the Auja stream, whose water was sweet and whose banks were first of all lined with rocks to prevent the formation of swampy pools', were relatively free of the disease, 'but with us in the Mellaha, malaria reigned supreme'. The latter battalion began with 550 men and thirty officers; after their sojourn in the valley the battalion had only 150 men and 15 officers fit for duty.[31] This was atypical in that these battalions remained in the valley for two months, instead of the usual one, but it was quite normal for the Australians and New Zealanders to have to evacuate a hundred sick men. In the 3rd Light Horse Regiment, 'in July a total of two

[28] Andrews, *Kiwi Trooper*, p. 175.
[29] Ibid., pp. 174–5.
[30] Patterson, *Judaeans in Palestine*, pp. 120–1.
[31] Jabotinsky, *Jewish Legion*, p. 131.

officers and 100 Other Ranks were evacuated to hospital', and 'casualties for August were two officers, 84 Other Ranks evacuated sick'.[32]

The threat to attack out of the valley was, however, maintained, potentially either northwards along the valley itself, or across the river and into the same territory as the earlier attacks on es-Salt and Amman – the Hejaz railway was obviously a prime target. Engineers were kept busy. The Talaat ed-Dum watering system was much improved,[33] and in the valley the bridges had to be maintained. The Turks shelled them repeatedly, and even though they never actually scored a hit, engineering arrangements for the emergency crossing of the river were organized in case the bridges were destroyed and a quick retreat had to be made. An endless rope crossing was prepared, and the approaches cleared where the horses could be pulled across, with the men swimming beside them; this was an exercise everyone had to practice. 'Much fun was caused when the regiments came down to practice their horses in swimming the river; the horses relishing it as much has the men.' In the event the shelling did not damage the bridges.[34]

After the withdrawal of the Amman attack in early April, the bridge at el-Ghoraniyeh was both held and improved, with a bridgehead across the river always manned, from which occasional patrols went out. The main hostile activity here, however, lay with the artillery. The Turks had two big guns of sufficient range to reach most of the British-held part of the valley. The bridges were always assumed to be the prime target, but the Turks varied their targets. One of the guns, referred to as 'Nimrin Nelly', persecuted General Barrow. He first stayed in 'a large Russian hospice close to Jericho until the enemy shelled us out of it', then he moved to the Gilgal Hotel in Jericho, but the hotel was hit while he was in the bath - 'I hopped out of the bath and went through the drying process quicker than I had ever done before' - and so he moved to 'a charming spot in a garden close to the Mount of Temptation', but 'even here the cursed gun tried to get us and failed'. He became convinced that a spy was reporting his movements, which is quite possible, since the front lines were always porous.[35]

Just having forces present in the valley was, however, scarcely enough. Patrols were constantly on guard, always at night – which meant that those

[32] Blackwell and Douglas, *3rd Australian Light Horse*, pp. 120–1.
[33] Smith, *Third Australian Light Horse*, p. 82.
[34] Annabel, New Zealand Engineers, p. 288.
[35] Barrow, *Fire of Life*, p. 190.

who went out had to sleep during the day, which was almost impossible, due to the heat. On the whole of the line, from coast to river, occasional attacks were made, usually in order to seize control of a hill or a position from which to observe the enemy, or to deprive the enemy of an observation post. On 8 June 21 Brigade of 7 Division attacked to capture two low hills near the coast, which had been used as observation posts by the Turks; the Turks counter-attacked but were eventually driven back. The episode cost perhaps 500 casualties, plus prisoners.[36] The Turks occasionally attempted the same, as on 13 July when the German 701st Battalion of Asien Korps and a company of the Turkish 48th Regiment attempted to take a section of the front of the 75th Division. The attack was beaten off by the 3rd Gurkhas.[37] Another aim of the British side was to blood the Indian troops, particularly the recent recruits, and to give them a taste of what was to come.

The largest of these minor battles during the summer was a German and Turkish attack in the Jordan Valley. The northernmost position held by the British forces was at Musallabeh, captured at the beginning of the Amman Raid as a forward defence against any attack aimed at the bridges across the river. The position was coveted by the Turkish command since it would be a particularly useful observation post. One attempt had been made in April to capture it, and another had been planned for the beginning of May, but abandoned when the raid to es-Salt took place.[38] In Turkish hands it would provide good observation all the way to the el-Ghoraniyeh bridgehead, and so provide information as to British intentions. In British hands it would deny the Turks that opportunity, and so contribute to Turkish doubts about those intentions.

The position was a rocky ridge seamed with ravines and crevasses north of the Wadi el-Auja. To the east was the Wadi Melleha and then the marshy valley of the Jordan. There was a series of hillocks stretching more or less in a line from Musallabeh hill south-westwards to the Auja. The British forces occupied the summits of the hills, with a series of posts, wired and manned, which they had constructed with much labour over the previous months. The valleys and ravines and crevasses separating the hillocks were not held, though they were patrolled irregularly. In July the position, over a mile in length, was held by the 1st Australian Light Horse Brigade of the Anzac Mounted Division. The 1st Light Horse Regiment held the western posts, codenamed 'Zerum' and 'Zeiss',

---

[36] Falls, *Official History* Vol. II, pp. 425–6.

[37] Ibid., p. 426.

[38] Ibid., p. 430; Liman, *Five Years*, p. 220.

and the 3rd Regiment held the next posts, 'Vaux', 'View' and 'Vale'. Located behind these was Abu Tulul hill, a broad-topped plateau dotted with several posts. The 2nd Regiment held 'Vyse' and 'Musallabeh', and, again behind these forward posts, 'Maskera' and 'The Bluff'. Brigade headquarters was across the Auja to the south.

To the east the 2nd Light Horse Brigade held the Melleha valley, a little south of the ford across the Jordan which led to the Umm es-Shert track leading to es-Salt. The ford itself was available to the Turks, and there were several Turkish posts a little to the north, and the east bank of the Jordan was under Turkish control. The bridges at el-Ghoraniyeh were about five miles to the south, held by the newly constituted 5th Cavalry Division (which at the time was still called the 2nd Mounted). The bridgehead east of the river was held by the 14th Mounted Brigade (still at the time the 7th), which consisted of the Poona Horse and the Alwar and Patiala Imperial Service infantry battalions. There were also two smaller bridges, built by the engineers, further south at Hijla and el-Hinu – these were also fords – about three miles south of the main crossing at el-Ghoraniyeh. The Imperial Service Cavalry Brigade and the Sherwood Rangers were posted on the west bank to guard these crossings.

The Turkish/German plan was complicated and concentric. One attack aimed to capture the Musallabeh-Abu Tulul position by an infantry assault from the north; a second was to attack the Wadi Mellaha position by crossing the river from the east; a third was to mount a cavalry attack on the southern bridges. These attacks were intended to be made simultaneously. During 12 and 13 July Turkish shelling of the Abu Tulul and Musallabeh positions increased. This may not normally have been significant, since such erratic changes in bombardments were not unusual, but between bursts of shelling the men of the forward posts heard enemy movements as well, and even commands in German. Some preparations, including the erection of new tents at the Turkish hospitals, had been noted during that day, so surprise was not total. Further, simultaneity was not achieved. The attacks began at 1 a.m. on 14 July at the Abu Tulul posts, but not till near dawn on the Wadi Mellaha, though shelling had taken place there during the night. To the south, the Turkish forces' attacks were anticipated; the Sherwood Rangers and part of the Imperial Service Cavalry Brigade crossed the river to confront them before they could make any attacking moves.

In many ways it was the southern part of the attack against the bridges which was the greatest threat. The Turkish Caucasus Cavalry Brigade approached to within two miles of the crossings at Hijla and el-Hinu. Had these troops pushed across the river they might have been able to cause enough havoc in the rear areas of the British positions to distract the British command long enough to allow the other attacks to succeed. However, the 4th Light Horse Brigade was in reserve south of the Auja, and could have been moved to intercept the Caucasus Cavalry had they crossed. It is clear that the advance of the Turkish cavalry had been noted on the British side well in advance.

The attack on the Wadi Mellaha was not pushed forward with any resolution; even Liman von Sanders called it 'half-hearted'. The plan was to break through the 2nd Light Horse Brigade at two posts, using the 146th (German) Battalion and two Turkish battalions, and then for the 3rd Cavalry Division to sweep through to take other British forces in the rear. But the Turks moved only slowly and reluctantly to the attack, perhaps because they were unused to night fighting, more likely because they had already heard of the failure of the Abu Tulul attack. Liman claims that the 3rd Cavalry was held back by its commander, but he could scarcely attack before the Australian line had been penetrated, and that never happened. The German troops did attack, but no more than 150 men reached the Australian positions. They in turn were counterattacked by a small party of Australians led by Lieutenant J.D. Macansh. His first effort was no more than a reconnaissance, and he tried again two hours later. This time the Germans lost over twenty prisoners to the small attacking party (only twenty-strong) and then lost their nerve as well. The survivors fled in panic.

The Germans who attacked at Abu Tulul complained afterwards that they were not supported properly by their Turkish comrades – this also is the burden of Liman's complaints. The attack here was made by the 702nd and 703rd Battalions and a Jager company, and they were supposed to be supported on either flank by two Turkish regiments. The Germans were able to penetrate between the advanced posts of View and Vale, and then swing round to the left to attack the posts at The Bluff and Maskera. Thus they surrounded the northern part of the Australian line. But they were able to capture only one of the posts, all of which had been deliberately set up to provide for all-round defence. One post was taken when every man had been killed or wounded, but another post held by only twenty men held out against many times their number, though all but three men were casualties.

The failure to capture any more of the Australian posts meant that instead of surrounding the northern end of the line and breaking open a large hole in the defences, the Germans were themselves surrounded by uncaptured posts. The Turks attacked Musallabeh, but were held off by the garrison. At View post they had to climb a cliff, and the first man to reach the top was shot by a sentry. He was carrying incendiary bombs which burst into flames as he fell back. This lit up the rest of the attackers who were picked off by the Australians from the top. Understandably unnerved by the sight of their falling, burning comrade, and by the detection of their surprise attack, the rest could not even try to climb the cliff. (But these are attacks by *Turks*, and so strictures against their 'failure' to support the Germans are clearly wrong.)

By 3.30 a.m. reinforcements arrived for the Australians, and caught the attackers trapped among the posts which were still fighting. One group from the 1st Light Horse cleared Abu Tulul itself in a bayonet attack; a second group recovered The Bluff where the Turks had gained a small lodgement; the Wellington Regiment drove off the attackers from Vaux post. As a result the whole attack had been defeated before any of the other German/Turkish manoeuvres at the Wadi Mellaha and at the southern crossings had really begun. The Mellaha attack only began near dawn, and it was probably by then known that the Abu Tulul attack had failed. An air raid by seven German aircraft had little effect. In the southern attack, the British forces were the aggressors.

Two of the regiments of the Imperial Service Cavalry crossed to the east bank during the night, and in the dawn light they could see the Caucasus troopers. The Jodhpore Lancers moved from the el-Hinu crossing – the southernmost crossing – facing a position at the southern end of the Turkish line. The Mysore Lancers were placed in front of the two crossings at el-Hinu and Hijla. From the el-Ghoraniyeh crossing – the northernmost – the Poona Horse came south to link up with the Sherwood Rangers to attack the northern end of the Turkish line.

The Turks did not apparently react to these moves, perhaps surprised to be attacked when they expected to be the aggressors, perhaps intending to attack the crossings between the British forces when they moved to either flank. But then the Indian soldiers revealed their secret weapon. By their own request the lancers of the Imperial Service Brigade had been re-armed with their nominal weapon, the lance. From the southern end of the Turkish line the Jodhpore Lancers, hidden from Turkish view by approaching along a wadi, suddenly emerged and charged. Their unexpected appearance, their charge, their clear desire to kill, and the sight of their long, sharply pointed and levelled lances, totally unnerved the first two or three troops of the Turks who broke and fled in disorder. A large group on a ridge were attacked by an uphill charge and scattered, several men being speared. A machine gun post finally stopped the charge, after the lancers had destroyed a good half of the Turkish force.

As the Jodhpore Lancers charged, the Mysore Lancers and the Sherwood Rangers advanced at a more sedate pace. The Turks pulled back to the shelter of the Wadi er-Rame, though the Mysores did manage to use their lances on thirty or so of the withdrawing enemy. Both the Jodhpore and Mysore Lancers, however, were exhausted by the exertions of horses and men - it was now daylight and the temperature was well over 100 degrees Farenheit. They had suffered casualties themselves and now had prisoners and captured horses to care for. The surviving Turks, no doubt thoroughly shaken, concentrated into a fairly well defended position in the wadi. The Turkish plan had clearly failed, and they were menaced by the still uncommitted Sherwood Rangers, who were facing their position in a wide semi-circle as the two lancer regiments pulled back. Then came the Poona Horse from the north, which joined up with the Sherwood men. However, one troop of the Poonas did not receive the order to halt and charged into the Turkish position. This cost the lives of six men and their officer, and that of a considerable number of Turks. Late in the day the Rangers and the rest of the Poona Horse advanced, and found that the Turks had retreated.[39]

The whole German/Turkish plan had been totally foiled. But there was more to this episode than merely the defeat of an attack. At Abu Tulul about 450 prisoners were taken, 377 of them German. They complained bitterly that they had not been supported by the Turkish units fighting with them, though the fact that eighty Turks were taken prisoner, and as many were killed, and that their attacks on Musallabeh and the View post are recorded, strongly suggests that this complaint was unjust, and that the Turks were being blamed for German failure. The Germans had captured some beer at one point, and, of course, had actually drunk it, with predictable effects on their military efficiency. The heat of the day was also intense. When the Germans were captured 'a number of them were suffering from sun-stroke and were semi-comatose, while a few were showing the effects of the beer they had drunk'.[40] Clearly the Germans were not in a fully fit state to conduct a war. One group of Turks were

[39] Falls, *Official History* II, pp. 429–37; Anglesey, *British Cavalry*, pp. 233–47; Liman von Sanders, *Five Years*, pp. 249–54 (not a convincing account, merely circumstantial); Blackwell and Douglas, *3rd Australian Light Horse*, pp. 118–19; Browne, *2nd Light Horse Brigade*, pp. 72–7; Richardson, *7th Light Horse*, p. 96; Wylly, *Poona Horse*, pp. 145–7; NZAM, 1986/2731, Trooper Maclean, Wellington Mounted Rifles, 14 July 1918.

[40] Richardson, *7th Light Horse*, p. 96.

attacked by the Wellington Mounted Regiment and sixty of them captured; they were suffering agonies of thirst, so much so that one author even suggested that the 'object of the enemy attack was to gain possession of the fine stream behind the British lines'[41] – the Auja, that is.

The basis for the Germans' complaints against the Turks is more likely to be their own comprehensive defeat, which led them to cast blame on their allies, and perhaps the fact that the regiment they attacked was no more than 259-strong, so they were beaten by a force perhaps a third of their number.[42] Quite probably the Turks' role had been to exploit the gap in the British line which the Germans were supposed to have made, so that their attacks failed because of the prior failure of the Germans to make that hole.

Even more significant than the failure of the attack, (and the evidence of tensions between the enemy allies), was the method of its defeat. The performance of the Indian troopers had been little short of spectacular. The use of lances had been a stroke of military genius (emanating from the soldiers themselves), and led the Turks, even some of the Germans, to look with increased wariness at the Indian cavalry. Further, the German infantry attacks had been defeated with considerable panache by the Australians and the New Zealanders. The Germans were regarded as the best of soldiers, on either side, but at Abu Tulul it is clear that they had more than met their match, being defeated by forces less than half their number.

It is also worth noting that the German tactics at Abu Tulul were a version of those their fellows used in March and April on the Western Front, by infiltrating through the line and leaving the well-defended strongpoints, in this case on the hill tops, to be taken later. It did not work in the end in either place, but the reason at Abu Tulul was mainly because there were not enough soldiers to make it work. And it very much looks as though the Turks did not understand these new tactics, for their attacks were all frontal, and expensive; note also the ability of the German soldiers to be easily distracted into looting and gulping captured beer before the main event was concluded.

The overall result of this fight was to reassure Allenby, who had left the fighting and the tactics to his subordinates, that he commanded an army which was now fully capable of taking on the Turks and Germans in Palestine with a good chance of a decisive victory. In particular he noted and remarked on

---

[41] Nicol, *Two Campaigns*, p. 230.
[42] Browne, *2nd Light Horse Brigade*, p. 72.

the vigorous actions of his new Indian soldiers. It was therefore now up to him and his staff to produce a plan which would permit his soldiers to achieve a comprehensive victory. And he had also to take into consideration the actions, wishes, and purposes of his allies.

CHAPTER 4

The Arabs

T HE Arab Revolt which began in June 1916 moved forward and spread only
slowly. The Arabs who became fighters were generally untrained, unless
they were former Ottoman soldiers. The family of the Sharif Husain was more
interested in establishing itself in power – certainly a necessary first step –
than in liberating fellow Arabs, and it did not altogether trust the British. In
this they had good reason, as the Balfour Declaration had shown, and as the
revelation of the Sykes-Picot Agreement by the Bolsheviks in 1917 confirmed.
The prospect of this particular family rising to prominence and power in Arabia and in Syria disquieted other Arabs, notably their neighbours in Arabia
who were their enemies. But the central element in all this was the need for
anyone who aspired to power in Syria and Iraq and Palestine – the Fertile
Crescent – to be victorious in war. This applied as much to the British and
French as it did to the Sharifian Arabs. Unless and until the Allies could demonstrate that they were winning and were likely to be victorious, most Arabs
would not support them.

The capture of Aqaba in July 1917 provided the Arab forces in the north
with a seaport through which to communicate with, and receive military supplies from, Egypt. This was much more convenient than the ports which had
been used earlier along the middle Arabian coast. The town was defended
successfully soon after its capture, and so it became a base from which the
Hejaz railway could be raided. The Arab Southern Army kept the Ottoman
58th Division and others bottled up in Medina on short commons. The Arabs
had no hope of capturing Medina, but simply preventing the Turkish troops
there from joining their colleagues in the north was a useful accomplishment.

The size of the Turkish force in Medina is too often assumed to be large,
and that it was being kept in place by the Arab besiegers. In fact any Turkish
division was rarely more than 2000 strong by this period in the war, though
the 58th, in Medina, was probably larger, and had been joined by other minor
units - artillery, signals, machine gunners and others. Captain Falls in the *Official History*, Vol. II claims that 'the ration strength' of the Medina garrison was
'12,000', but this is clearly an overestimation. Nevertheless the leadership of its

commander and the spirit of the troops made it a formidable force. At the surrender the British received about 8000 officers and men into captivity, though some of these had been fighting further south. The commander of the Medina garrison, General Fahr ed-Din, controlled a much larger part of Arabia than just that city and oasis. Until well into 1918 he controlled much of the Hejaz railway, almost a far as Ma'an, and he could send expeditions into much of western Arabia. There was never any prospect that the Arab Army, which was never larger than Fahr ed-Din's own force and often smaller, and never as well trained or commanded, could capture Medina, any more than it could take any other urban centre without British help.[1]

The Turks had coped well enough with these Arabian harassments, and were able to repair the broken railway most of the time fairly quickly in the southern part, by using the stockpile of rails which had been assembled before the war in preparation for the extension of the line to Mecca; in the north branch lines had been taken up, and the equipment reused. It took a major and continuous effort to destroy a railway, and, as Allenby noted after the Amman Raid, it needed repeated raids to keep it destroyed. The Medina force was also able to acquire supplies from various parts of Arabia to supplement those which got through by rail. General Fahr ed-Din sent out, by rail, those who wished to leave, thus reducing his requirements of food. By 1918 the civilian population had been reduced from about 70,000 to no more than 3000 or 4000.

Any Arab chief or tribe suspicious of, or hostile to, Sharif Husain was amenable to selling supplies to Husain's enemies. He in turn was assisted by small but specialised British and French forces, so the Arab Army consisted of a small disciplined Arab force, officered by renegade Ottoman officers in the main, a fluctuating collection of Bedouin, an Egyptian Camel Corps, British officers in Rolls Royce armoured cars, a flight of British aircraft, a French mountain gun and machine-gun detachment, and others. Many of the British and French troops were in fact Muslims from India and Algeria respectively. This was not a large force – it could scarcely be so in the desert – but it was very strong in those elements in which the Arabs were deficient, that is, modern weapons. The European allies could also supply money as needed, and military leadership.

In all this T.E. Lawrence was, of course, very active. He much enjoyed the destruction he could cause, and he was always busy in negotiating and cajoling

---

[1]   Wasti, 'Defence of Medina,' in *Middle Eastern Studies* 642–53 at 27; Falls, *Official History* Vol. II, p. 408.

and persuading the various Arab leaders into operating together, or at least not interfering with operations. He had a good eye for military possibilities, but he also needed an organizer to provide support. This was given by Lt-Col. P.C. Joyce, who officially commanded the British contingent, Col. Jaafar al-Askeri, who commanded the Arab Northern Army, and Capt. Pisani who led the French force. All were professional officers with the military expertise Lawrence lacked. These less flamboyant and more professional soldiers were the essential bases on which the erratic success of the Arab rebellion was founded.[2]

From Aqaba the next target north had to be Ma'an, a major Turkish post and railway station. It was the base from which the Turks had attempted to recover Aqaba and was the centre from which they patrolled and repaired the railway southwards towards the next major station at Mudawwarah, and north towards Amman. The Turkish force in the town was substantial, perhaps 6000 men, including some cavalry. This was many more than the Arabs in the north could field, but part of it formed the town's garrison, and only if the town was attacked would such a force be in action. The patrols sent out were much smaller. The trains were 'garrisoned' by only a couple of hundred soldiers, or less. These patrols, trains, and the subordinate stations, were the Arabs' targets. Any attempt to hold on to a captured station or position was dangerous. First of all, any Bedouin who had taken part would probably ride off home as soon as possible with his loot, so the troops attempting to hold the place would be reduced to only a few within a day or two. Using the railway, the Turks could usually bring up a larger force to retake the position. So the methods employed by the Arab Army had to concentrate on destruction, not conquest, at least until the Turkish forces were so worn down that they could be compelled to surrender. But the wearing down process would be very slow if it was left to the Arabs; it had, therefore, to be done by the British in Palestine.

The Arab Northern Army was too far to the south to co-operate effectively with the first of the British attacks across the Jordan, against Amman, at the end of March, but it did lead to the Turks withdrawing some forces from several of the small towns along the southern routes, so rendering them more vulnerable to the Arabs' methods. This was an excellent example of the dependence of the Arabs on British victories in Palestine. These towns were spaced at more or less regular intervals along the old road, the King's Highway, which ran parallel to the railway about twenty miles to the west. Tafilat, where there

---

[2]   Falls, *Official History* Vol. II, Chapter 18.

had been a battle in January, was now retaken by the Arabs after the Turks pulled out.[3]

The intended junction of the Arabs with the British forces, the latter of whom had been supposed to hold onto es-Salt for this purpose, failed. Instead the Arab Army now mounted a series of attacks on the railway north and south of Ma'an. The failure of the British to cut the railway seriously at Amman made this fairly urgent. Some intelligence was received that the Turks were intending to withdraw the Medina force. They had dithered over this for a year or more, caught between the secular nationalism of the Young Turks, which did not find holding Medina a strategic priority and would have withdrawn earlier, and the Islamist substratum of popular belief. This belief saw the defence of Medina as a holy cause. Add to this General Fahr ed-Din's combination of national pride and Islamist determination that fuelled his refusal to abandon the town. But the British had no wish to see the Medina troops, well-trained, well-motivated and successful, joined with the rest of the Turkish army in Palestine. So they made a determined effort to isolate the Medina Army and so keep it in place.

The diplomatic difficulties in linking the Arab aims and methods with those of the British were fully exposed in the failure in April to coordinate the actions of the two. Lt-Col. Alan Dawnay was sent by Allenby to attempt this. He was just the sort of well-trained, logically minded soldier which Lawrence was not, and exactly the sort of careful, professional soldier who was needed for larger operations than raids. They had a conference at Abu Lissan, Faisal's headquarters, on 7 April. The Amman attack had failed; the assault on es-Salt had not yet been arranged. The Arabs were divided over what to do next. They concentrated on the problem of Ma'an, whose capture would decisively isolate the Medina Army. Dawnay warned that an attack would be very costly, and would probably be defeated, an assessment Faisal and Jaafar both agreed upon. But other Arab officers wanted to initiate an action which had greater significance than merely blowing up railway lines. Dawnay's suggestion that they should further attack the railway was not enough for them; they insisted on an attack on Ma'an.[4]

Two sets of attacks were organized. Around Ma'an the town was to be isolated by cutting the railway to the north and the south; the Jebel Semna, the hill overlooking the town, which naturally had a Turkish post on its summit, was to be stormed. The second attack was against the line much further south,

---

3   Ibid., pp. 402–5.
4   Hughes, *Allenby and British Strategy*, pp. 83–4.

towards Mudawwarah, and was led by Dawnay himself, perhaps to distance himself from the disaster he anticipated at Ma'an. He took with him the Egyptian Cameleers, the armoured cars, and some of the Bedouin.

Around Ma'an two attacks went in. Jaafar commanded part of the Arab Army's regular forces to the north of the town. To the south, another section of the army was commanded by Mawlud Pasha, like Jaafar, a former Ottoman officer, who had defected. He was accompanied by a band of undisciplined horsemen led by Auda ibn Tayi, a fierce ruffian and Ottoman outlaw, but a considerable fighter. Jaafar had opposed the idea of a direct attack on Ma'an itself, but Mawlud had advocated it. Evidently there had been a delicate apportionment of responsibility in the two attacks.

Mawlud's force acted first, capturing the next station south of Ma'an, at Ghaidar el-Hajj, in a night attack on 11 April; Jaafar followed two days later by capturing Abu ed-Jurdun, the station north of Ma'an. At that point the troops in the town knew they were in real trouble. Between them these two attacks resulted in the destruction of several miles of the railway. Mawlud meanwhile moved north and stormed the Jebel Semna. It was a hard fight, though regarded as a much easier victory than had been expected. Jaafar moved south towards Ma'an destroying the track and capturing Turkish outposts.

The relative ease of these operations persuaded the Arab officers, already wishing to attack Ma'an itself, that the task was feasible. Jaafar, though he was opposed to it, took command, perhaps to ensure that it was done properly. In the event, as the senior officers had expected, the Turkish defences were staunch. The Arabs, led by Nuri es-Said, reached the station, but most attacks did not seriously penetrate the town itself. After a day's fighting they were driven out. And while the Arabs concentrated on Ma'an, the Turks from the north recaptured Abu ed-Jurdun, and pushed a convoy of supplies on mules into the town. It seems that the town was near starvation point; merely cutting the line to the north and south might well have caused it to capitulate fairly quickly, had the line been kept cut and the mule convoy ambushed. Now it was not likely to give in any time soon.[5]

Dawnay's raid south along the line was moderately successful. It seems that his main aim was to capture Mudawwarah. He did capture the station at Tell esh-Shahin, north of Mudawwarah, and a series of posts along the line to the north. Shahin station was looted and destroyed. Dawnay went on to the south where he found the next station, Ramla, deserted; it too was destroyed. So, the

---

5 Falls, *Official History* Vol. II, pp. 406–7; Barr, *Setting the Desert on Fire*, pp. 231–2.

whole length of the track which he had taken was destroyed. In effect all of it from Mudawwarah to north of Ma'an – a distance of almost a hundred miles – was out of action. But the station at Mudawwarah was now strongly held, having been reinforced by the Ramla garrison and others.[6]

The lesson for the Arabs was driven home by the casualties they had suffered at Ma'an, where ninety of them had been killed, and by their defeat in that attack. The destruction of the railway had been extensive. But it was not repaired, since it seems that the Turkish army engineers had now exhausted their supplies of rails, and the possibility of scrounging them from elsewhere no longer existed. The Medina army was now finally fully isolated. For the British this had been one of the prime objects of the war in Arabia; for the Arabs it was much less important.

Another consequence of the attack on Ma'an was that the Arab Army was incapable of assisting in the second trans-Jordan operation against es-Salt. The Beni Sakhr had offered to assist (they had received a large subsidy) but could not do so without the artillery of the Arab Army, which was detained south of Ma'an. One of the reasons for the defeat at Ma'an was that the French artillery there had run out of ammunition in the middle of the fighting. As pointed out above, the Beni Sakhr could not be expected to fight Turkish regular forces, and so did not actually cut the Ain es-Sir road as the British expected. This was one reason for the failure of the es-Salt operation, most conveniently for the British and Australians who ever since have looked for someone to blame rather than accepting any responsibility themselves.

But there are other reasons. In the discussions at Abu Lissan, Mawlud Pasha and Faisal's Chief of Staff, Nuri es-Said, had argued that the British – in the person of Dawnay – really wanted to prevent the Arabs' revolt from succeeding, and that they were trying to avoid making such conquests as Ma'an (and perhaps Medina).[7] They might have added that the railway which was being destroyed so assiduously by the British would eventually become the property of the Arab kingdom.

This was part of the backlash from the revelation of the British and French double dealing over post-war annexations. The British had always known that Arab ambitions were to expand Husain's kingdom to include all Arabia and the Fertile Crescent as far north as the Taurus Mountains. One of the best ways to

[6] Falls, *Official History* Vol. II, pp. 407–8; Barr, *Setting the Desert of Fire*, pp. 232–5; Lawrence, *Seven Pillars*, pp. 521–2; Rolls, *Steel Chariots*, p. 176.

[7] Hughes, *Allenby and British Strategy*, pp. 83–4.

deny them such a future state was to prevent them from achieving conquests in those regions in the first place. And one of the best arguments the Arabs would have for acquiring territory at the time of peace would be if they had taken a major part in the conquests, and were in physical occupation of the lands they claimed, with the support of their populations.

Of course, the attack on Ma'an made it clear that the Arab Northern Army was actually not capable of capturing such places, and that it had to continue for the moment to depend on the British. At the same time King Husain's attempts to expand his control over other parts of Arabia were also unsuccessful. The presence of Auda ibn Tayi with Jaafar and Mawlud and leading men from his part of the Howeitat tribe (who travelled the desert east of Sinai) was a good insurance against attack by Husain's men. Husain's sons Ali and Abdullah were busy preventing supplies from reaching the Turks in Medina by intercepting convoys from various directions, including Kuwait.[8] The Arab Southern Army was making no progress at Medina, so Husain still only governed Mecca and its surroundings.

Further off he collided with Abdul Aziz ibn Saud, the Emir of Nejd, who had built up his region, centred on Riyadh, into a major Arabian power, and was a direct competitor with Husain; both men harboured ambitions much wider than their present kingdoms. Ibn Saud was in fact at the time much more concerned with a war he was waging against the Shammar tribe of Hail in the north. The Shammar were Turkish allies, and so Ibn Saud passed for a British ally, and had been recognized as such in a treaty in 1915.[9] He was visited by H. St John Philby, who was sent by the Indian government to try to reconcile him with Husain, also a British ally. The two Arabs were far too much at odds, religiously, politically, and personally, for this to be successful, but they also both appreciated that the British were at odds amongst themselves, if in a less violent way. The policies emanating from London, from Cairo, and from Delhi were at variance, each political centre having different priorities – and by 1918 Lawrence was developing another policy, his own. In Arabia, the fact that Ibn Saud was a British ally had no real effect on Husain, other than to fuel his constant suspicions. Indeed about this time the inhabitants of the Kharma oasis, to the south of Mecca, left Husain's alliance and joined Ibn Saud. This followed a quarrel between their chief and Husain's son, Abdullah, but, since the men of Kharma were already Wahhabis, like Ibn Saud, this shift had always

---

8   Lawrence, *Seven Pillars*, p. 83.
9   Hurewitz, *Middle East and North Africa*, Vol. 2, pp. 57–8.

been possible, even likely; the quarrel merely provided the occasion. Husain sent a force to retake the place, but it was defeated.[10]

So neither Ibn Saud nor Husain was interested in peace or reconciliation, only in defeating the other. But to Husain it looked very much as if the British were attempting to block his imperialist ambitions by counting Ibn Saud as their ally. Then again, already in March 1917, after the conquest of Baghdad, the British had issued a proclamation inviting the local inhabitants of Mesopotamia to join in the administration of their own land, which did not sound to Husain as though the British expected him to be their ruler.[11]

The Mesopotamian campaign had been largely closed down after the capture of Baghdad. Even if no announcement was made, the removal of two British Indian divisions could scarcely be hidden. The Turkish response was to withdraw some of their own men for service in the Caucasus and in northern Persia. The arrival in Egypt of the Mesopotamian divisions and the turmoil of exchanging divisions in Palestine was, however, a good sign that the British still intended that the war in the Levant should continue. For Husain it was thus clearly necessary to link up and operate with the British as closely as possible, despite the evidence of contacts with others and the possibility of the British reneging on Husain's assumptions. It is highly unlikely that few of those on the Arab side seriously expected that their full ambitions would be realized. The idea of an Arab empire reaching from Aden to Aleppo and beyond, and from Aqaba to Basra, was clearly a maximum demand. On the other hand, by allying with the victor in the war in Palestine, Syria and Mesopotamia, Husain was likely to make at least some gains.

It was therefore encouraging that the visit of Philby to Ibn Saud and then to Husain (he was sent from Mesopotamia on Delhi's instructions) had provoked complaints from the British in Egypt and London – an envoy from Egypt had met Philby at Jeddah after his meeting with Husain to investigate what he was doing and what effect he had had – and Husain could interpret this intra-British dispute as support for him.[12] It was also helpful that the British army assisted in further reducing the availability of the railway. This also may have been a result of Dawnay's failure in April to take Mudawwarah station. In May, with the assistance of three British aircraft, Abu ed-Jurdun station, north of

[10] Lacey, *The Kingdom*, pp. 147–8.
[11] Monroe, *Britain's Moment in the Middle East*, pp. 41–2.
[12] Barr, *Setting the Desert on Fire*, pp. 216–17; Porte, *Du Caire à Damas*, pp. 298–9.

Ma'an, was again captured, but once more abandoned after more destruction.[13] In August another attack on Mudawwarah was made.

The Turkish force in Medina was threatened with starvation, particularly after the railway line was cut so decisively, but General Fahr ed-Din Pasha was active, popular and vigorous, and any Arab attacks were quickly blocked and driven away. He was also in control the of railway as far as Mudawwarah, a watering place and workshop for locomotives, and therefore well defended. In the circumstances after the cutting of the line between there and Ma'an, it was no longer possible for supplies to get through by rail from the north, though the Bedouin were willing to sell food to the commander, for gold, and his forces were as active at ambushing enemy convoys as the Arab Army was. The possibility did exist however that General Fahr ed-Din might evacuate Medina and move by train to Mudawwarah, load up with supplies and water there, and then march his force to Ma'an. This would be something the Arabs could not stop, and which the British would be able to harass from the air, for example, but not prevent.

The key, therefore, was the control of supplies at Mudawwarah. By the end of July Allenby had decided what aggressive action he would take in Palestine, encouraged by the vigorous performance of the Indian cavalrymen in defence of the Jordan bridges, and the unlikelihood of further disruption to his forces. He did not wish to be surprised by the sudden appearance of a well led and relatively powerful force on his inland flank, so Mudawwarah had to be taken and destroyed. The task was given to the Imperial Camel Corps, of which just one battalion now remained, commanded by Major R.V. Buxton.

But the destruction of Mudawwarah was to be only one of the tasks for the expedition. Having destroyed that station, the force was to make a wide circuit east of the railway towards Amman, where it was to attack the viaduct south of that town which the Amman operation had failed to destroy. On the other hand, it was appreciated that this might not be possible, and the alternative target was the station at Jurf ed-Darwish, north of Ma'an. So the second target of this raid was to isolate Ma'an, presumably to make it possible for the Arabs to starve it out.

Lawrence met the Camel Corps at Aqaba, and warned the men that they would not like the Arabs who would greet and accompany them, but they must put up with it. And certainly the Arabs seemed more likely to kill their British allies than any of the enemy, and spent much ammunition in celebratory firing

---

[13]   Falls, *Official History* Vol. II, p. 408.

– some of it in the air, but also some very close to the heads of the British. This lasted into the night until Lawrence, in a typically theatrical gesture, stood up amid the British targets and at a signal stopped the firing. (No doubt this was all prearranged to reinforce his authority among the British.) Two days were spent in watering at Rumm, halfway between Aqaba and Mudawwarah, and the latter was attacked on 8 August. The station was captured, along with the Turkish garrison. There were three redoubts around it, but only two of them were captured in the night attack which took the station. Attacking the remaining one, Northern Redoubt, in daylight was out of the question. The RAF was called in, and they sent two bombers to attack. Two bombs into the redoubt was enough. The Turks came out and surrendered.

The prisoners were entrusted to the Arabs, who were promised pay for every Turk who was delivered alive to Aqaba, but the money would only be paid on arrival – they all arrived; the wounded were sent back as well. The rifles went to the Arabs, who looted everything. The larger equipment was thrown into the well, and the well, the pumps, the water storage system, and the railway gear, were all blown up, 'making a complete wreck of the place'.[14]

The second objective, the destruction of the viaduct, was thwarted because the viaduct was being held by a Turkish cavalry force and was therefore inaccessible. The Camel Corps and the armoured cars made a great mess out in the desert, hoping to lure the Turks – who soon realized they were there – into thinking that their force was larger than it really was. Their alternative target, the station at Jurf ed-Darwish, was, however, captured and destroyed. Then, by way of a review by Faisal at Abu Lissan and a visit to Petra led by Lawrence (momentarily returning to his archaeological persona) the Cameleers returned to Beersheba.[15]

The main object of the attack, at least from Allenby's point of view, had been achieved in that the northernmost post of the Medina army was now at Madain Salih, well south of Mudawwarah. The line north from Madain Salih to Mudawwarah was not destroyed, except here and there, but without the watering facilities at Mudawwarah the line was militarily useless. This was the definitive isolation of the Medina army. Allenby could be confident that it would not be able to intervene; further, the Arabs of the Northern Army could now concentrate on the Turks to their north.

---

[14] Ibid., p. 408; Inchbald, *Camel Corps*, pp. 129–34; Jones, *War in the Air*, Vol. 6, p. 205; Lawrence, *Seven Pillars*, pp. 432–4, 442.

[15] Inchbald, *Camel Corps*, pp. 134–8; Lawrence, *Seven Pillars*, pp. 432–4, 456–8.

From the Arab point of view, however, all had not gone as well as they had hoped. The attempt to destroy the viaduct near Amman had been Lawrence's responsibility in the expedition. He had persuaded Allenby to add it to the original scheme which had been merely aimed at Mudawwarah. He hoped that if the Arabs could succeed where the British had failed, the Arab cause – to which he was now devoted – would receive a political boost. It would be possible then to take Ma'an, or ignore it, since it would be as cut off from succour from the north as Medina. The destruction at Jurf ed-Darwish was clearly second-best, and the review by Faisal was a way of emphasising the Arab cause, again a second-best ploy. But the Arab Army had still not achieved a real success sufficiently to make the Arabs' political point.

CHAPTER 5

The French

FRANCE claimed to have long had a special interest and place in the Levant, above that of any other European power. Under the influence of national pride in the nineteenth century this interest was said to have dated back to the Crusades, seen in France as a largely French national enterprise, not altogether unjustly. What is more certain is that there was an intermittent alliance with the Ottoman Empire, most notoriously in the sixteenth century, and in extensive trade relations, particularly in the eighteenth century. Napoleon came into this, of course, even though he was defeated and driven out – but even his failed enterprise gave France, at least in French eyes, a claim to interest and influence. A more stable interest developed in the later nineteenth century, based on the recognition of the existence of a substantial Christian community spread throughout Syria, but concentrated especially in the area of Mount Lebanon. Napoleon III had claimed a special status as protector of Catholic Christians and of the holy places in Palestine, a claim which contributed to the outbreak of the Crimean War.[1]

France claimed not only the position of protector of Catholics in the Ottoman Empire, but particularly of the Maronite Christians of Lebanon, who were in communion with the Papacy. It was in fact largely the administrative weakness of the empire which permitted the French to exercise influence in Syria. Ottoman authority had faded in the eighteenth century with the rise of local strongmen, such as the lords of Lebanon and the Governor of Acre.[2] In the later nineteenth century, however, the empire began to recover control. The local strongmen were either suppressed or co-opted. This in turn opened the way for French influence, since the communities who were now re-subjected to Ottoman governmental authority naturally complained about it. The Christians were able to play the religious card, appealing to fellow Christians outside the empire for 'protection'. The population of the Lebanese area was divided

---

[1]   Anderson, *Eastern Question*, Chapter 5.
[2]   Holt, *Egypt and the Fertile Crescent*, pp. 102–33.

into several mutually hostile religious groups, Maronite Christians, Shi'ites, Druzes, and others, so providing many openings for interference.[3]

In 1861, after a further period of violence and an international conference, the region was organized as a separate providence: the Mutasarrifiyya (governorate) of Mount Lebanon. It was to have a Christian governor appointed by the Sultan and to have a wide measure of autonomy. Geographically it included the Lebanese mountains and a part of the Bekaa Valley, but it excluded the three main ports of the coast: Tripoli, Beirut, and Sidon. This was not altogether pleasing to the Ottoman government, which, in a reforming mood, was more concerned with centralizing and enforcing its authority over the provinces. Nor was it wholly pleasing to the Maronites, who had gained some autonomy but who were ambitious to expand their geographical range. Most dissatisfied of all were the non-Christians enclosed within the Mutasarrifiyya. The preliminary violence had resulted in a defeat for these groups, so leaving the Maronites as rescued victims, but it was international pressure from European powers which had been decisive in setting up the autonomous district. This was the foundation of French influence and interest. The whole situation was, of course, a constant source of instability.[4]

In all this the French were in competition with the British. To consider events in the nineteenth century: the British were opposed during Napoleon Bonaparte's expedition to Egypt and Syria; they backed opposing sides during the 1830s when Mohammed Ali of Egypt had briefly conquered Syria; and they backed rival religious factions in Lebanon in 1860. Britain bought up a controlling share of the French-built Suez Canal in 1874, and soon after occupied Egypt itself, an expedition at first encouraged, and then opposed, by the French. The two states competed over financial control of Egypt for the next twenty years, a problem which only faded when the several agreements collectively known as the Entente Cordiale of 1904 were concluded in the face of perceived threats to both countries from Germany. So when the two western powers went to war with the Ottoman Empire in 1914 they had only been on apparently friendly terms for a decade, and the underlying rivalry remained the automatic reaction to both to any event in the region. In the Near East this brittle friendship was especially superficial, and both imperial states were avid to carve off choice joints from the empire which they expected to fall easily into their hands.

---

3   Ibid., pp. 167–75, 231–46.
4   Akarli, *Long Peace*, pp. 28–36.

This Ottoman collapse, of course, did not happen, but the Allies set about arranging the dismemberment in advance in an attempt to reduce their future mutual difficulties. This arrangement in turn gave France a colourable claim which could be produced at the future peace conference, even if the British did most of the fighting. (Most of the fighting on the Western Front was, of course, being done by the French.) The Sykes-Picot Agreement, finally reached in 1916 after long-winded and desultory negotiations, laid out the foundations for the partition of the Near East between the two powers; the details were then adjustable as circumstances changed. The basic division, however, remained constant: Mesopotamia with its oil, was to go to Britain, and Syria was to go to France. There was a vagueness about the desert interior, and a continuing problem over Palestine, which was supposed to become an 'International Zone', a loose term which gradually disappeared when the British occupation from November 1917 continued. This was not helped by the implications of the Balfour Declaration, which, apart from its generosity to the Jews at the expense of the Arabs, was clearly a pre-emptive bid for British imperial control of the area. With Sykes-Picot in the background, however, Britain and France could get on with fighting the war on the Western Front, secure in the knowledge that any political dispute over the Ottoman spoils had been defused in advance.[5]

Of course, neither power assumed that this was really the final decision. Just as with the agreement, or understanding, with the Sharif Husain, the British assumed that the progress of events would necessarily alter the conditions, and that a new agreement, or series of agreements, would be necessary later. The Sykes-Picot Agreement had been made as a result of French urging, but had been negotiated by two fairly low-level diplomats, whom the Foreign Office and the Quai d'Orsay could easily disown or overrule if necessary, and it was subject to adjustment right up to the time of the peace conference. As it happened, the precise terms were not implemented, but the geographical division it sent out, was. Almost as soon as the agreement had been concluded, the Arab Revolt, on Britain's instigation, drastically changed the conditions.

In the end the partition of the Ottoman Empire would obviously depend on the military situation when the fighting stopped, and on the political and diplomatic requirements, above all, of Britain and France. The matter did not

---

5   For the negotiation of the Sykes-Picot Agreement, see, among many other accounts, Barr, *A Line in the Sand*, pp. 31–47; Fromkin, *The Peace to End All Peace*, pp. 188–95; Karsh and Karsh, *Empires of the Sand*, pp. 224–41.

become active between the two powers until General Allenby's successful breaching of the Turkish defence line at Gaza in November 1917, and the capture of Jerusalem a month later. Allenby's predecessor, General Murray, had already rattled French nerves by saying that he expected that the British offensive would reach as far north as Alexandretta.[6] This would leave the British forces in control of all the territory theoretically partitioned between the two states by Picot and Sykes. But that, of course, was before Murray was defeated at Gaza, twice.

Alexandretta, also Iskenderun, on the gulf of that name, and at the geographical junction of Syria and Anatolia, had been mooted as a possible naval-military target from the beginning of the war. It appeared to provide a sheltered naval base and a limited and more or less enclosed geographical area which could be easily conquered and then defended by establishing control of the mountain passes through the Taurus Mountains to the north and the Amanus range to the east. Possession of the region – Cilicia – would sever Ottoman connections to Syria-Palestine and Mesopotamia, above all, by seizing control of a section of the railway. This argument tended to fail, for the required tunnels had not yet been completed. But such an expedition would inevitably be conducted under British auspices and by British enterprise, and would therefore establish British influence in a place the French had all along seen as being potentially their territory. So each time a landing at Alexandretta was suggested, the French blocked the idea. That the British did not insist on the implementation of such a scheme reveals much about the delicacy of the relationship of the two allies.

At the same time the idea of a specifically French attack on the Ottoman position in Syria was repeatedly discussed in French military and diplomatic circles. The island of Arwad, just off the North Syrian coast south of Lattakia, had been seized, and was a useful naval and espionage base close to the complex society of Mount Lebanon. The naval governor there, Capt. Trabaud, was well informed of the internal Syrian situation and sent regular reports to Paris, where there was a lobby called the *Comite d'Action Francais en Syrie*, which included Picot among its members, and had the ears of various French ministers. The suggestion of a French expedition was quickly seen to be impracti-

---

[6] Noted by Tanenbaum, 'France and the Arab Middle East', in *Transactions of the American Philosophical Society* 68, 1–50, at p. 20, quoting a French consular letter of 1 December 1916.

cable, but it was nevertheless a means to keep the issue before the eyes of the ministers.[7]

Allenby was just as unaccommodating to the French as Murray had been, but he was rather more polite. Jerusalem's capture was the key moment which marked the definitive Turkish defeat in southern Palestine, and which raised the future possibility that some areas in the region would be annexed by Britain. The conquest had almost entirely been a British achievement, so whatever happened in the rest of the war it was probable that they would be able to annex that part of Palestine if they wished. A carefully choreographed ceremony of occupation took place on 11 December, with representative units from all the military forces on the Allied side present – English, Scottish, Welsh, Irish, New Zealand, Australian, Indian – together with the French and Italian commanders of their detachments with him. This event was, in fact, dictated by the British Foreign Office, even the entry of Allenby on foot into the Holy City as a deliberate contrast to that of the Kaiser twenty years before (he rode in on a white horse, through a specially made gap in the city wall). But this was only the third act of a sequence, equally carefully arranged. The first had been when the mayor of the city had ceremonially handed over the keys of the city to the British – after he had found someone willing to accept them. The second had been the appointment of Brigadier-General Borton, formerly Postmaster General in Egypt, as Military Governor of the city.

To any who paid attention this was a clear statement that the British were in command, not just of Jerusalem but of Palestine - and that they intended to remain so. It was here that one of the casual promises of the past raised its head. Lloyd George had promised the French Foreign Minister, Aristide Briand, that Sykes and Picot would head the civil administration of the region, probably jointly. It is likely that the Prime Minister was thinking of the whole of Syria and Palestine, and meaning that it would operate only until the definitive partition and allocation of territories at the end-of-war peace conference. But it is always the weaker party to an agreement who has to assert himself and insist on the letter of an agreement, while the stronger has the option of acquiescing or insisting on changes – or even making changes without discussion. At Jerusalem, the day after the ceremonial entry, but two days after General Borton's appointment, Picot, who had entered the city with Allenby, adopted the style of High Commissioner. But then he found that Allenby was quite adamant that he might have the style, but there were to be no duties attached to

---

the appointment.[8] Palestine was, he stated firmly, still a military region – the Turkish forces on 11 December were no more than three or four miles north of the city, and attempted to retake it a few days later – but to the French this looked very much like a pre-emptive strike to exclude the French permanently. And so it may well have been: Allenby was supported in his decision by Lloyd George.[9] It was also incontestable that it was British troops who had done the greater part of the fighting, and that the forces of France and Italy in the region were minimal.

In the circumstances, Picot in Palestine and the government in France could do little to change the situation, other than keep a man close to Allenby – who found Picot thoroughly annoying – waiting for the moment to assert French 'rights'. The size of the British forces in Palestine could not be rivalled by anything the French could possibly send there while a large swathe of France was under enemy occupation – it was suggested that France should send a full division, but the Premier, George Clemenceau, refused.[10] Over the next months, however, the French contingent in Palestine was quietly and gradually increased, until it was 8000 strong by March – these were mainly colonial troops, in fact.[11] This was in addition to the French contingent with the Arab Army.

The disruption of the British forces from March to July 1918 prevented any further successful advances. No doubt the French feared that this might signal a closing down of the Palestine front. After all, the front in Mesopotamia had been shut down more or less when the area was that which the British wanted. To suspicious French minds – and diplomats are trained to be suspicious – it might have seemed that the British, having conquered what they themselves wanted, were prepared to stop, thereby leaving the 'French areas' in enemy hands. Unless further conquests were made, there might not be a case for the Allies to demand more than southern Palestine in any peace agreement, and so the Ottoman Empire would lose only part of its Arab lands. The French colonial ambitions in the Near East would be thwarted – as would those of the Arabs as well, of course.

Alternatively there was the issue of where the British would stop their advance if they did attack again. An advance similar to that which had followed

8   Hughes (ed.), *Correspondence*, p. 94, Allenby to Robertson, 25 January 1918.

9   Tanenbaum, 'France and the Arab Middle East', in *Transactions of the American Philosophical Society* 68, 1–50 at 20.

10   Ibid., 20–1.

11   Porte, *Du Caire à Damas*, pp. 253–60.

the breaching of the Gaza-Beersheba line, about sixty miles, would just about reach the line of the Turkish railway from Haifa to the Jordan bridge, Jisr ed-Damieh, south of the Sea of Galilee, and would take in such towns as Nablus and Jenin, perhaps Haifa and possibly Nazareth. This in fact was roughly where Allenby was suggesting his next line would be in a letter to the War Office in late July.[12] This would still leave about the same distance from that line to the northern border of Palestine – 'Dan', as Lloyd George termed it – at the southern slopes of Mount Hermon. This would imply that another battle would be needed to reach the north of Palestine, yet this would still not reach into the area desired by French ambitions. If the French knew of Lloyd George's biblical definition of Palestine as 'from Dan to Beersheba', they no doubt feared that Dan would be Allenby's next target, and perhaps his last. In that case none of the lands the French wanted would have been captured.

Yet it had certainly occurred to both Allenby and the Chief of International General Staff (CIGS), Sir Henry Wilson, in London, that the British attack which was being contemplated might well reach into that 'part of the Syrian areas which are regarded of special interest to France', as the CIGS put it in a telegram to Allenby on 25 July. He recommended that the French should be reassured 'that, subject to your supreme authority, French advice would be taken and French assistance accepted' in these areas.[13] It would not be much of a concession, but it would be a sign that French claims were receiving attention.

Meanwhile Allenby had taken the French forces in hand, as part of the planned advance, which was scheduled for September.[14] He reported on their condition on 12 August. There were two battalions of a *Regiment Mixte de Tirailleurs*, composed of Algerians; three battalions of Armenians, two of them formed into the *Legion d'Orient*; some artillery and a regiment of cavalry. (The Armenians were refugees from the Turkish massacres in 1915 who had been picked up by the French navy near Alexandretta; such a force could be expected to fight very hard against any Turkish army; their discipline, however, was suspect.) There was also a Syrian force, about a company strong, also composed of refugees. The problem for the French with regard to these two groups was that both of them were more interested in freeing their respective homelands from Turkish rule rather than subjecting Armenia or Syria to

---

[12] Hughes (ed.), *Correspondence*, p. 135, Allenby to Wilson, 24 July 1918.

[13] Ibid., p. 136, Wilson to Allenby, 25 July 1918.

[14] Ibid., p. 135, Allenby to Wilson, 24 July 1918.

French rule. (There was also, of course, the French contingent, about a 1000 men, with the Arab Army and with King Husain.) Allenby noted that the artillery had guns and were training 'correctly and efficiently', but that they had no ammunition. The infantry and the cavalry were also becoming trained to his standards, and he proposed to brigade them with his own forces.[15]

Allenby's poor relations with Picot, the putative High Commissioner of France in the Levant, epitomized the general condition of Franco-British relations in the region. The British had arrived at a position where they felt they had a proprietary interest in the fight against the Ottoman Empire, while the French were beginning to insist on the 'letter of the law' of earlier agreements. The Sykes-Picot Agreement had been intended to obviate such tensions, but was now being increasingly ignored by the British. The ensuing attack on the Ottoman forces in Palestine would therefore sensibly increase those tensions. It was going to be necessary for Allenby to make some territorial concessions to Picot if a full-scale quarrel was to be avoided.

[15] Ibid., p. 141, Allenby to Wilson, 12 August 1918.

CHAPTER 6

The Plan

IN December 1917, as soon as Allenby had reported the capture of Jerusalem and thereby the completion of the main task assigned to him by the Prime Minister, he was asked what he would now do to exploit his success.[1] He was then asked to think in terms of first conquering the rest of Palestine, and then of campaigning as far north as Aleppo.[2] He stated in reply to the first enquiry that he felt it 'essential' to advance 'step-by-step',[3] and then pointed out in a later letter, after Aleppo as a target was restated by Robertson, that such a campaign would require large reinforcements.[4] Along with the need to send away many of his experienced troops to France, a process which began in March, this effectively meant that any serious ambition for the conquest of all of Syria dropped out of the discussions for the time being. It did not necessarily drop out of Allenby's mind, however; a seed had been planted, if it had not already been there.

For Palestine, Allenby suggested in a letter of 20 December that he might, six months later, be able 'to place force of my present strength north of Nazareth–Haifa line'. This he later defined as 'only sufficiently far north to afford adequate protection to a lateral road and railway. Say a base from Tiberias to just north of Acre and with right flank refused and covered by the Jordan against possible incursion from Deraa'.[5] He said nothing about how such an advance would be conducted, but his main concern was that this was as far as he could advance and still be able to supply his forces. Further, his initial estimate on 20 December was that he 'should require 16 or 18 divisions besides my mounted corps', and of course this would increase the difficulties of the supply situation even more. But it is highly unlikely that he ever expected such a huge reinforcement. A little earlier he had tentatively proposed that 'if circumstances are

---

[1] Hughes (ed.), *Correspondence*, p. 78, War Office to Allenby, 12 December 1917.
[2] Ibid., p. 81, Robertson to Allenby, 14 December 1917.
[3] Ibid., p. 83, Allenby to Robertson, 14 December 1917.
[4] Ibid., p. 85, Robertson to Allenby, 18 December 1917.
[5] Ibid., pp. 87 and 92, Allenby to Robertson, 20 December 1917 and 3 January 1918.

favourable, I may gradually push forward my left towards Tul Keram covering railway construction and perfecting preparations for offensives with naval co-operation.'[6] In this brief comment may be seen the germ of the plan which he eventually contrived. But even before March, when he expected to have his original force plus the two Indian divisions from Mesopotamia, he was still clearly thinking in terms of an advance of relative slowness, followed by a pause to consolidate and to bring up supplies.

This was clearly based on the army's experience at the Third Battle of Gaza and on the pursuit which followed. In the battle it had taken a week to break through the Turkish defences, and after another six weeks the pursuit had left the troops exhausted. The capture of Jerusalem was a very difficult operation, and it was only possible to go on the defensive from then on. On this timescale he might expect a week's battle to break through the new Turkish defence line, and then a pursuit of a similar timeframe, which would exhaust the army's available supplies. A halt at the railway would then be necessary.

It was therefore as much a logistical problem as a straightforward military matter for Allenby. He had inherited this from his predecessor, General Murray, who found he could only move a sufficient force from Egypt against the Turks at Gaza by building a double track railway from Egypt, and a water pipeline to bring Nile water to the troops in the trenches. Egypt remained Allenby's essential base, the source of food supplies, the location of his stockpile of weaponry and ammunition, and the country of origin of many of his labourers and animals. The railway had now been extended north as far as Ludd, just behind the front line, though only as a single line, but from December much work was done to improve the roads. Supplies for the troops were getting through more easily, therefore.

If the British advanced beyond the front as it was in mid-1918, it was thought that construction of more of the British railway would be required. The Turks had the use of the pre-war lines to the north, but in Palestine these were narrow gauge and single track, and so unsuitable for the standard gauge British locomotives and wagons used as far as Ludd – and the Turks would be able to remove or destroy their own rolling stock as they retired. The southern extensions of the Turkish railway as far as Gaza and Beersheba had been destroyed either by the British army in its advance or by the Turks in their retreat, and the track had been taken up and used on the new British construction. This destruction would be repeated in the north, with the addition of attacks by the

[6]   Ibid., p. 83, Allenby to Robertson, 14 December 1917.

RAF, which had now developed considerable expertise in delivering bombs accurately. It was therefore impossible to rely on capturing the enemy railway in anything like working condition.

Roads were few throughout Palestine, and metalled roads even fewer, but it is true that armies also advance across country. The land was firm enough for transporting goods and supplies in the dry season. 'The lorries used for ammunition services [at Beersheba] went straight across country, right up to the gun positions, and were often under fire.'[7] But once the winter rains began, usually in October, the 'surface broke, and in low-lying areas became an impassable swamp.'[8] This actually refers to southern Palestine, but it applies equally well to the land north of the front line. (The rains did help with the water supply in October and November 1917 but at the same time they rendered movement difficult or at times impossible.) It had been necessary to break off the offensive in late November to concentrate on road-building before a serious attack could be directed against Jerusalem.

An account of the difficulties by two RASC officers summarised the means by which the supplies were maintained, at least for a time.

> As can well be imagined, the work of Supply over this period was the most difficult of the campaign. It was successfully met by the employment of any and every means that could further a single purpose. While the weather permitted, mechanical transport replaced the railway line; a succession of rainy days, however, reduced the country to a morass, and, for a period, all wheeled traffic came to a standstill. An abundance of camels, working in three echelons along the sand dunes which fringe the coast, saved the situation, and the pursuit was able to continue. In places camels sunk up to the girth in mud and many had to be abandoned. The wastage in animals and even in drivers was high, but the troops were enabled to go forward. The Divisional Trains themselves, at this time and throughout the advance, were so heavily handicapped that they could do little more than serve as first line transport.[9]

Part of the answer was to utilize the small ports along the coast, but all were awkward and none was large enough to provide much relief. Nor were local

---

7   Badcock, *Transport Service*, p. 189.
8   Elliott and Kinross, 'Maintaining Allenby's Armies,' in *RASC Quarterly* 13, 114–28 at 122.
9   Ibid., 123.

supplies available: 'The country itself was bare; no stores could be requisitioned; and the enemy had destroyed whatever supplies he could not carry away with him.'[10]

The pause after the capture of Jerusalem therefore enabled roads to be repaired and constructed, railways to be built and doubled in length, and the general supply system to be eased and developed. The main depot remained at Kantara on the Suez Canal in Egypt, the nearest port at which seagoing vessels could unload, and where there was sufficient wharfage to unload and store the supplies. The ports available in Palestine were inadequate; only Jaffa was really usable, and that only on a small scale. From Kantara sub-depots at Ludd and Jerusalem were supplied, and from there the supplies were sent forwards to the front line for distribution to the fighting units.

All this provided a wealth of experience for the planners of a new advance. The trans-Jordan operations had in part failed because of transport difficulties and the poor roads which had to be used, not to mention the bridging difficulties. On the other hand, the Turks' improvement of the road from Amman to Shunet Nimrin was a direct consequence of the defeat of the es-Salt attack. They were clear lessons here: it was necessary either for the troops to carry supplies sufficient for a slow advance, or that the attack should operate in such a way that supply ceased to be a restraint on movement. It was also necessary to avoid the rains, which had so slowed the pursuit after Gaza. It followed that Allenby had a fairly narrow period of time within which he would be able to attack and conquer enemy territory. The rains would come in October, and would rapidly reduce the country in which his troops would have to move and fight, and over which their supplies would have to be moved, to the condition of 'an impassable swamp'. The coastal area and the hills were likely to be reasonably passable in the rainy season, but neither area was blessed with decent roads. Further north there were hills and ridges alternating with low lands; the former had few roads or passes, the latter was liable to collapse in wet weather. The ridge which stretched south-east from the coast at Mount Carmel was awkward to pass over, and there were few routes across it. An alert enemy would be able to block an advance with relatively few forces; and if the Vale north of that ridge was not reached until the rains began, travel and supply would become very difficult and slow. To the north were the Galilean Hills and the Lebanese mountains, again with few roads. Geography was clearly a major problem.

[10] Ibid., 124.

It was not until July that Allenby could be reasonably confident that he had a large and stable army, which was unlikely to be disrupted again by having to send troops elsewhere suddenly. By July it was therefore evident that he was able to make serious plans. Even then the Chief of Imperial General Staff (CIGS) seemed to suggest that he might be able to send three or four divisions to Palestine for the winter.[11] As surely Allenby understood, and expected, Wilson then withdrew the idea. Such bright ideas, typical of the mercurial Wilson, scarcely helped Allenby's planning.

After this little to-do, Allenby explained that he wanted to 'make a move in September', and that his aim was to reach 'the Nablus-Tul Keram line', and so gain control of the cross-country railway and road route the Turks upon which were heavily dependent. (The railway connected with the Hejaz line at Deraa, and reached south to Tulkarm and westwards to the coast at Haifa.) He expected this to net him a large number of prisoners, and to allow the Arab Army to come north. A reference to 'es-Salt' in the letter implies that he expected to attack towards the east as well as the north, but not to stay there.[12]

This would be an advance of no more than fifteen or sixteen miles. It would certainly inflict a solid defeat on the Turks, capturing considerable quantities of men and guns, and presumably demoralising the survivors. It would gain a defensible line and deprive the Turks of a major east-west transport route. If a new attack was also made across the Jordan, the Turkish IV Army there would be unable to intervene to assist VII and VIII Armies. An advance north along the Jordan Valley would probably secure the major crossing point at Jisr ed-Damieh. It was a plan which, given the British superiority in guns and men, would provide a clear victory, one which, if achieved on the Western Front, would have everyone cheering.

Once again geography imposed constraints on possible action. The attacks against Amman and es-Salt had shown the difficulty of moving eastwards, in part because of the lack of roads, but also because of the steep scarp on either side of the Rift Valley, which made the transfer of supplies extremely difficult. The fighting to gain Jerusalem in December, and later attacks in the hills, such as that at Tell Asur, made it clear that progress in the centre of the line would be slow – and again the reliance on a single road would hinder supply. It followed that the only practicable offensive, one where a decisive blow could be struck which would destroy the Turkish army, was in the coastal plain. This

---

[11] Hughes (ed.), *Correspondence*, p. 132, Wilson to Allenby, 4 July 1918.
[12] Ibid., p. 135, Allenby to Wilson, 24 July 1918.

was something which Allenby had decided early on, so far as we can see. But how far his thoughts had gone beyond the general idea of an attack there is not clear.

On 1 August Allenby issued instructions to his three corps commanders which allowed them to begin developing their own plans of attack.[13] It is easy to assume that he had already mapped out in his mind the overall scheme which was put into effect in September,[14] but, according to several letters and telegrams he sent in the next two or three weeks, it seems that he had not yet gone beyond his aim of reaching Tulkarm and Nablus. So the plans being made by the staffs of the three corps must have been based on that aim. The Desert Mounted Corps in particular was at that time mainly located in the east, and was concentrated on events in the Jordan Valley. So we must assume that the plans being made were based on each corps launching an attack from the area in which it was stationed during August and using the troops it had under its command at that time.

Presumably the procedure would be for the plans to be made in some detail at the corps' headquarters. These would concentrate on attacks on the enemy line directly in front of each corps; it would be up to Allenby to plan for the exploitation. These plans would then be sent to Allenby for his comments. He would then be certain of the impracticability of attacks in the Jordan Valley and the Judaean Hills, so, as he had long assumed, the only place where a smashing attack was possible was in the coastal plain. Bulfin's XXI Corps would therefore be the force which would make that attack. On 14 August, by which time he had presumably received the corps' plans, he was writing to Wilson and outlining his aim of reaching 'the line Jisr ed-Damieh-Nablus-Tulkarm', and perhaps using his cavalry to get to Haifa.[15]

A week later a new plan had been made. He wrote to Wilson that 'I propose to use my cavalry very boldly, and to park 3 Divisions thereof round to Afule, and thence to raid and catch the bridge over the Jordan – Jisr el-Mejamie'.[16] This he explained to his corps commanders on the next day at a meeting.

---

[13] Falls, *Official History* Vol. II, p. 448.

[14] Capt. Falls in the *Official History* Vol. II suggests that Allenby had developed the idea in March, and Chauvel also believed this (see Hill, *Chauvel of the Light Horse*), but there is nothing from Allenby himself on this, and it seems we can trace the plan's development from the hints in his correspondence, and that that development took place only from July onwards.

[15] Hughes (ed.), *Correspondence*, p. 142, Allenby to Wilson, 14 August 1918.

[16] Ibid., p. 144, Allenby to Wilson, 21 August 1918.

According to Falls in the *Official History* Vol. II, Allenby says he 'startled' them with this idea.[17] The plan was executed a month later. So, rather than being a long-nurtured idea, Allenby's plan had developed from being a set of local attacks along the front to a narrow attack near the coast, followed by the cavalry exploitation designed to capture most of the Turkish forces. And this was decided in the week before his meeting with the corps commanders.

The main event would be an infantry assault by XXI Corps, commanded by Lt-General Sir Edward Bulfin, in the coastal region. This was the sort of operation Bulfin was particularly good at. He was a leader-from-the-front type, capable of swift emergency decisions. He and Allenby had both fought in South Africa and on the Western Front and Bulfin had commanded the 60th London Division in France, Salonika and Palestine before Allenby promoted him to command the corps.

The other infantry corps, XX, was to attack to the north on the plateau, along the line of the top road which led from Jerusalem to Nablus. This was more difficult, since there were easily defensible ravines and hills along the route. A strong and speedy advance in this area was almost impossible, but such attacks would prevent the Turkish VII Army from helping at the coast. The corps commander was Lt-General Sir Philip Chetwode, an officer remarkable for his imaginative schemes, but not always capable of that final risky push which brings success at the last in a balanced situation. He and Allenby had been colleagues in South Africa, and were both cavalrymen. His talent in command was swift movement, which is why Allenby did not choose him for the hammering and bludgeoning role in the planned breakthrough attack.

The third corps, the Desert Mounted Corps, was to go through the gap in the enemy line which Bulfin's infantry would open up. The horsemen would then turn east and cross the Carmel ridge. Using the route of the road and the railway, they were to capture el-Afule, and cut the Turks' communications at Sebastiye and Nablus, so blocking the retreat of the forces facing XX Corps. XX Corps would then attack them from the south. The Desert Mounted Corps was commanded by Lt-General Sir Harry Chauvel, an Australian cavalryman who had fought in South Africa, and at Gallipoli, always refusing alternative commands which would take him from his Australians. He had shown dash and high competence at Gaza-Beersheba, and was as conscious of the difficulties of fighting in the desert as Chetwode, but with perhaps a more per-

---

[17] Falls, *Official History* Vol. II, p. 449.

sonal and intimate knowledge, since his family's estate in Australia was liable to drought.

The basic scheme had been extended and elaborated into something essentially bigger, more ambitious, much bolder and potentially much more decisive, and it necessitated a substantial change in the disposition of the troops. Bulfin's push was to have an overwhelming force for his breakthrough, and, having achieved that, he would then swing the infantry round to face east, meanwhile sending some of his force along the Nablus road to cut the connection east from Tulkarm. Bulfin's corps of four divisions was increased by the transfer of the 60th Division to his command, together with the French Detachment (equivalent to perhaps two brigades) and the 5th Australian Light Horse Brigade from the Anzac Division. This brigade was the re-horsed former Camel Corps troops, two regiments; he also had the French cavalry contingent.

The Desert Mounted Corps now therefore had a new task. The Anzac Division was to remain in the Jordan Valley and the rest were to be concentrated behind XXI Corps for the coastal attack. Instead of turning east along the Nablus road or heading due north along the coast to Haifa, the horsemen would wait until the infantry had broken through the Turkish positions and then ride through the north and swing north-eastwards to capture the railway junction of el-Afule, well north of Nablus and only six miles south of Nazareth. This central position would destroy Turkish communications between their headquarters at Nazareth and the troops in the line to the south, as Allenby had said in his letter to Wilson the day before. Exploitation towards Beisan and the Jordan to the east was to follow, and/or to the port of Haifa to the west. Chauvel asked to add Nazareth to his targets in an attempt to capture Liman von Sanders and his headquarters staff.[18]

The role of XX Corps was not changed; it would still attack north along the Jerusalem-Nablus road, but it was not expected to do too much, and was reduced to two divisions by the loss of 60th Division; XX Corps' role was to pin down its Turkish opponents until it was too late for them to get away.

In addition, a rather greater role was now envisaged for the troops in the Jordan Valley, even though most of the cavalry was transferred to the coastal attack. They were now commanded by Major-General Edward Clayton, the New Zealander in command of the Anzac Division, and were designated

---

[18] Hill, *Chauvel of the Light Horse*, p. 162.

'Chaytor's Force'. His task, like that of XX Corps, was to fix the full attention of the Turkish IV Army across the Jordan on his troops in order to prevent them moving to help in the west. In particular the crossings of the river had to be guarded, and those to the north captured. It was hoped that this would prevent the transfer of any Turkish forces westwards, but Chaytor was given plenty of latitude in responding if they did, either to advance upriver, or to cross over to the east to link up with the Arab Army.

The development of the plan through several stages can be explained as the progressive revelations of Allenby's ideas, which he had had for several months. But this relies on the unproven assumption that Allenby had had such ideas earlier, and that he then chose to reveal them bit by bit. It is better to assume that he changed and elaborated his original idea under the pressure of events, availability of intelligence and revision in his thinking. His early idea, formulated in July, became elaborated into the orders to the corps commanders on 1 August. The changes after that date, however, need rather more explanation. The expansion of the roles of XXI Corps and the Desert Mounted Corps was not so much an elaboration as a conceptual leap. The eventual plan demanded that the troopers of three mounted divisions – 4th and 5th Cavalry and Australian Mounted – advance over forty miles in a day. They were to be at el-Afule within twenty-four hours of the start of the mission, arriving early on the second day of the offensive. This was asking a lot of the horses, and of the men. Chauvel is reported as having exclaimed, when presented with the new plan, 'I can do it', which rather suggests that he and the others were certainly surprised.

The explanation of these changes must be in information Allenby received or acquired in the first half of August, and in a reconsideration of the likely enemy reaction to the attack. The attack by Bulfin's corps was to be on the coast, on level ground where it was possible to concentrate five divisions into an attack without having to worry about hills and other geographical obstacles – even the wadis would be dry, or almost so, at the end of summer. The danger in such a move was that the enemy would react by attacking the flank or flanks of the aggressors (as had happened in the es-Salt raid), and if the attacks penetrated any distance into the rear of the main infantry assault, the Desert Mounted Corps might find itself cut off, or at least without support, far ahead of the infantry. The solution was to use the infantry to block any such move, hence the pinning attacks of XX Corps and the right turn of XXI Corps to face the hills where the main surviving Turkish forces would be. The other problem was that it was quite possible that the Turks would retreat northwards more rapidly than the Desert Mounted Corps could advance, and that Nablus and Sebastiye would be more strongly held than the horsemen could cope with, something which would be very likely if the cavalry concentrated on reaching Haifa. Chetwode's advance, using only two infantry divisions, might not be able to pin down the Turks in the centre successfully enough to prevent this.

These were tactical considerations, but they were also based on Allenby's estimates of the Turks' capabilities. The force he faced was about half the size of his own (though in the cavalry he had a preponderance of three-to-one), spread more or less evenly along the front line. A constant dribble of deserters escaped into the rear areas or crossed the line to surrender and reach the safety of a reasonably comfortable prison camp. (There had also been some deserters the other way, particularly from the Pathans recruited among the people beyond India's North-West Frontier; as soon as this desertion began, Allenby pulled them out of the line.)[19] The Turks escaped because of bad treatment, insufficient food, and sickness. Their commander, Liman von Sanders, was fully aware of the problem, but was unable to do much about it. When Mustapha Kemal arrived in August to take over command of the VII Army in the Judaean hills, he is said to have been shocked by the condition of his command.[20]

The deserters revealed all this to their captors, no doubt speaking between mouthfuls of food. But there was another element depressing to Turkish morale. The Turks depended heavily on German support, and this seemed to be failing. The apparent victories in France in the spring and early summer had ceased. The attack by German troops at Abu Tulul in the Jordan Valley in July had been defeated suspiciously easily and with much loss by the Australians and the Indians. News of this no doubt spread rapidly amongst the Turkish soldiers, who did not much like the Germans they had come into contact with, and cannot have been polite when the Germans blamed the Turks for the defeat. Then on 8 August came the 'Black Day of the German Army', as Ludendorf described it, when the British attacked on the Western Front and comprehensively trounced the Germans. Again the news of this no doubt rapidly arrived in Palestine. Even if the result of the fighting in France did not become known to the Turkish rank and file, the commanders clearly knew, and they would understand that any more support from Germany was now very unlikely.

---

[19] Hughes (ed.), *Correspondence*, p. 134, Allenby to War Office, 7 July 1918.
[20] Liman von Sanders, *Five Years*, p. 264.

These are the developments which would have influenced Allenby and led to him changing and expanding his plans. But there is another aspect which must be considered. On 14 August he wrote to Wilson outlining his ideas, and his mention of Haifa as an objective implies that he was considering the role of the cavalry. But he also discussed his problem with the Arabs. The dispute between King Husain and Ibn Saud might, he thought, divert Faisal's Northern Army southwards to assist his father. He wanted that army to take part in his own attack, but he was clearly uncertain as to whether or not it could be relied upon.[21] He wanted the Hejaz railway to be cut; he would also need a strong flank guard. In the orders of 22 August he opted for Chaytor's Force as his flank guard, not the Arab Army. At this stage he clearly did not expect the Arabs to contribute much. He had already written to Wilson on 21 August explaining his new plan without referring to the Arabs at all.

Even before the new strategy of battle was revealed Allenby had told Lawrence what he expected of the Arabs, though he did not necessarily believe it would happen. One of the preparatory moves had been the raid by the Camel Corps on Mudawwarah which effectively pushed the Medina Army 200 miles south to Madain Salih, leaving General Fahr ed-Din unable to escape, even if he had wanted to. The raid on the viaduct near Amman which followed might have led to the fall of Ma'an but the Turks were alert and prepared. This was August, and it was known among the British officers with the Arab Army that Allenby's attack must happen soon in September.

Despite the semi-failure of that raid it did in fact serve Allenby's overall purpose in drawing the Turks' attention to the east once more. On the other hand August saw a serious dispute within the Arab higher command. King Husain accused Jaafar of setting himself up as Commander-in-Chief, a position he regarded as his own. He had in fact misunderstood the situation but did not find it possible to apologise. Jaafar resigned and sat in his tent, like Achilles. He was supported by most of his officers, who also resigned, and by Faisal and Nuri es-Said, leaving the king effectively isolated and increasingly obdurate. Lawrence and Joyce, by intercepting, toning down, and even blatantly altering enciphered messages between Husain and Faisal, smoothed things over, and the officers resumed their posts.[22] But the whole affair took a fortnight and distracted the entire Arab command at a time when the British and the Arabs

---

[21] Hughes (ed.), *Correspondence*, p. 142, Allenby to Wilson, 14 July 1918.

[22] Lawrence, *Seven Pillars*, pp. 461–4; Barr, *Setting*, pp. 267–70; Hughes (ed.), *Correspondence*, p. 145, Allenby to Wilson, 11 September 1918, and p. 146, Allenby to War Office, 12 September 1918.

were preparing for another northern anti-railway operation, which, for once, Allenby had asked to be completed by a specific date, 16 September. The target was the railway junction at Deraa, where the line from Damascus to Amman was joined by the line from el-Afule and Haifa and Tulkarm.

The corps commanders had been set their tasks on 22 August, and at that time or thereabouts Lawrence was also given his role. Probably the date for the main attack was set at that time. Detailed plans could then be made. This involved a decision on force levels in each of the four corps, since only when the corps commanders knew what they could use could they plan accurately. In other words Allenby's instructions on 1 August had been a practice run, and now they became the basis for the real thing. A large set of detailed preparations had to be made before the attack, and a timetable was laid out.

CHAPTER 7

Preparations

T HE date of the great attack had been settled by August, but the preparations for it, in various ways, had already been going on for months. The attack was generally expected, of course, and anyone who thought for any length of time about conditions in Palestine could have worked out that it would be launched in the coastal plain, and in the autumn, preferably earlier than the end of October. The Third Gaza battle had begun on 31 October and the pursuit was soon bogged down by mud and rain; therefore an attack at least a month before the end of October would be suggested, while any part of the front away from the coast was geographically much more difficult to fight in.

The arrival of so many new units – new both in the sense that they were unfamiliar with conditions in Palestine, and, in some cases, that they had only just been constituted as battalions, or that they included raw recruits – meant that a fairly intensive programme of training had to be organized. This, in fact, did not merely apply to the new arrivals and new recruits, but for different reasons was applied to the existing units as well. These were brought out of the line regularly, given a break, then given further training. Officers were sent on courses which imparted the latest tactical ideas, and these were then translated into fairly realistic training for the rank-and-file, ranging from lectures and demonstrations right up to action on the front line.[1]

The procedure was two-fold: one was to rest and refresh the experienced units and to bring them up to date with the latest methods; the other was to give raw units, some of whom were only recently recruited and had not seen combat, the necessary training and experience to fit them for the attack. These two procedures were linked. Before the incoming inexperienced Indian battalions arrived and allocated to their brigades, officers from the British battalion of that brigade were given special training. They selected and trained some of their own men, who could in turn train the arriving rank-and-file. Rather

---

[1] A compact account of the training regime is in Erickson, *Ottoman Army Effectiveness*, pp. 135–40; scattered details are in Falls's, *Official History* Vol. II, Chapters 19–21.

more was involved than simply military effectiveness. Language training in Hindi and Urdu was needed, particularly for officers, and extra signallers had to be trained and allocated to the Indian battalions. The whole programme was organized by the divisions, and in many cases it was supervised in detail by the divisional commander personally.

The inexperience of the Indian battalions ranged from recruits who had never even handled a rifle, right up to old lags who had managed to avoid active service for most of their recruitment service. Elementary drill and weapons training could be done by the senior NCOs, but it was clearly necessary to give the troops experience in being shelled and fired at, and in attacking enemy positions. In some cases the experienced British battalion would pretend to be the enemy and indulge in mock combat, but eventually the new battalion had to make a real attack. This was done usually after a fairly extended period of vigorous training, perhaps lasting a month, then the battalion, often stiffened by contingents of British soldiers who had worked with and trained the Indians, could execute a raid on the enemy trenches.

The divisional commander had to agree that the new battalions were battle-fit, and since it was in his interest as a commander to ensure that they were, they had to be honest about it. The older Indian battalions, those who had served in France and Mesopotamia, were quickly inspected and passed, so long as any new recruits were properly trained. The inexperienced units were inspected and reported on by Brigadier-General A.B. Robertson, who was in charge of training for the whole army. His reports were blunt and to the point, identifying gaps in training, and pointing out what still needed to be done, while at the same time dispensing praise. Two of his reports are noted in Falls's *Official History* Vol. II. For the 2nd Guides he wanted further practice in bombing, greater numbers of Lewis gunners, and more signallers. For the 2/30th Punjabis, on the other hand, although its progress was satisfactory, new recruits had not yet undertaken a musketry course, no bomb throwing had been practised, there were too few Indian machine gunners, and not enough signallers. The Guides he considered would be ready after a fortnight, the Punjabis would need a month. This was in July; they both fought in the great battle in September.[2]

Regiments' accounts of these months are sparing with regard to training, and few go into any detail, noting it usually in no more than a couple of words or a phrase. One which is a little more expressive, is that of the 53rd Sikhs,

---

[2]   Falls, *Official History* Vol. II, p. 419, note 1.

which noted that they sent candidates to the Imperial School of Instruction at Zeitun near Cairo, where each 'cycle of courses' – such as Lewis Gun training, bombing practice, coaching for platoon commanders, musketry training – lasted a month.[3]

Most of the infantry battalions which were due to perform the initial assault were taken out of the line for a time during August and early September for specialized and specific training. 'Every detail of the attack was rehearsed in rear of our lines on defences constructed from air photographs', is a footnote in the history of the 8th Gurkhas.[4] Equally vague is the Manchester Regiment's history which merely records: 'training of all kinds and making preparations',[5] but these two examples show that the practice was normal and widespread at the time.

The regimental history of the 124th Baluchis is a little more informative: 'training was pushed on rapidly … [with] ten days intensive training in full marching order.' This battalion received a reinforcement of 180 men as late as the beginning of September, men who were from a 'robber tribe' in the Punjab. The tribe had not furnished recruits for the army before; they had never carried packs, some had never fired a rifle, and all were minimally trained. These men were a replacement for a company sent to India to form a cadre for recruitment, but the battalion thought them a bad bargain. The battalion was quickly sent to a hilly part of the line held by the Meerut Division, in order to inculcate rapid training.[6]

Even battalions which were long established in Palestine went through the mill:

Our work started gradually with ordinary Company training, leading up to Battalion exercises, and this meant training for what everyone thought was some 'big stunt' that was to come off in the near future. We would go out with tapes and flags which were placed to represent trenches; we would 'jump' off from these and 'attack' others. This was done first of all by Companies, then by the Battalion, and finally by the

---

3   Anon., *53rd Sikhs*, p. 244.
4   Huxford, *8th Gurkhas*, p. 109.
5   Wylly, *Manchester Regiment*, Vol. 2, p. 195.
6   Chaldecott, *The 1st Battalion*, pp. 68–9.

Brigade. We would go out at night and march by compass bearing on our position, and then do the attack from our 'dummy trenches'.[7]

This is an account from the history of the Wiltshire Regiment, and it may stand in its unusual detail for the rest. The attacking army was to be as well prepared as the staff could devise. The 1st Gurkhas spent over three weeks at it.[8]

These are all accounts of experienced units, and even these brief references suggest that they were impressed by what they went through, though as several of them mention, the training only became relevant when they realized it had been undergone in preparation for the coming attack – the Wiltshires' 'big stunt'. The less experienced units have rarely left accounts of their work, though the experience of the 124th Baluchis, noted above, may stand for their work.

The new units were 'blooded' by a short stint in the front line, often sending patrols to capture a Turk or two, or simply to keep the enemy awake. They needed to be subjected to rifle fire, machine-gun fire, and above all, shellfire, if they were to be useful in the attack. The stiffening of these battalions by the presence of older British soldiers was salutary,[9] and those who panicked at first, as did the Indians who were training with the 1st Leinsters, became more blasé as the time for the great attack approached.

The lessons of the Western Front were imported. The sheer intensity of the fighting experience in France had stimulated much tactical innovation in the British forces. This was the foundation for the sustained and successful offensive undertaken in the autumn of 1918 and which broke the German army. The new methods were distilled into succinct booklets which were distributed to the Palestinian divisions, whose staff officers then lectured on them to the officers down to battalion level. Demonstrations of attacks by companies, rather than battalions, were laid on, and so the Western Front experiences were spread through the army, if in a rather academic way at first, though they did penetrate to all the divisions. Allenby himself took part in this, through the conferences with the senior officers, who then passed on the word to the battalion and company commanders in their own meetings and discussions.[10]

Part of this revitalization process was the acquisition of new and better weapons. There were major increases in the number of Lewis guns, trench

7 Black, *Wiltshire Regiment*, p. 118.
8 Petre, *1st Gurkha Rifles*, p. 176.
9 Johnston, *Orange, Green, and Khaki*, p. 403.
10 Erickson, *Ottoman Army Effectiveness*, pp. 137–40.

mortars, and grenade-firing rifles in every unit. All of these also required men to be trained or retrained in their use and maintenance – which meant more work and more training. This even extended to the cavalry, which was not subjected to the same sort of intensive pre-battle training as the infantry. The Indian lancers were re-equipped with lances, at their own request, to good effect as was seen in the fight at the bridgeheads east of the Jordan. The Australian mounted troops had always carried rifles and bayonets since their main purpose had been to approach on horseback and fight on foot. But the men tended to ride directly into battle anyway, and from the back of a horse the rifle was difficult the fire and the bayonet was of little use. There were cases of men using a bayonet-tipped rifle as a club, unable to either fire it or bayonet his enemy. These troops were now equipped with swords, and were given a fortnight's training in their use.

As usual, the addition of a new weapon required other changes as well as training in its use. Nine brigades acquired swords (the New Zealanders refused). An expert in their use, Brigadier-General Charles Gregory of the 19th Lancers (an Indian Regiment) took on their training, which involved not just how to hold and wield the weapon, but meant a change in tactics from mounted infantry to cavalry, requiring them to charge in a body – this was regarded as shock tactics.[11] It was no longer practicable to sling the rifle over the shoulder, where it would impede the use of the sword, so a cavalry 'bucket' was added for the rifles. The newly organized 14th and 15th Regiments took up swords as well. These had been formed from the disbanded Cameleers, some of whose men had never ridden a horse, having volunteered for the Imperial Camel Corps from the infantry. Colonel Olden of the 10th Light Horse explains the enjoyment the men had:

> The cavalry thrusting sword was ... to make such a wonderful addition to the tactical repertoire of the Light Horsemen, with no less wonderful results. The men, attracted by the introduction of 'something new' in their make-up, and inspired by the suggested breakthrough of the Turkish defence, which would give them the opportunity using it, turned to the new weapon as a child to the light. Casting their weariness aside, they set to with enthusiasm to make themselves proficient in its use and in the assimilation of a modified form of cavalry shock tactics specially adapted to meet the occasion. Cavalry double rank formation and drill

[11] Anglesey, *British Cavalry*, p. 223.

was substituted for that of the Light Horse, and from daylight to dark through those long, hot days of a dying summer, the open spaces in the vicinity of Ludd, were made to be appear alive by the vista of trotting and galloping troops of a Division.[12]

On the other hand, a view from closer in is that of Private John Davidson of the 14th Light Horse, former cameleer. He pointed out that handling swords for the first time was dangerous to anyone nearby; so was an ex-infantryman on a horse, holding reins with one hand and a sword in the other. Bad or inexperienced riders might drop their swords and cling to the horse's neck. The 'neddy' interpreted this as a signal to increase speed; horse and rider would go off at a gallop, generally ending with the unseating of the rider; the horse galloping back to the lines.[13]

This new training was in part the outcome of experience in the Palestinian theatre, but most of the training originated from the replacement of British by Indian battalions, and the move to Palestine from other theatres of fighting. The need for training was forced on the army by this new chaos, but also by the huge variations in experience, by the new weapons, and perhaps by Allenby's developing ambition, which grew from simply defeating the enemy army to totally destroying the Turkish forces. This ambition was clearly imparted to the senior officers, and transmitted itself successfully right down to the private soldiers, bringing forth new reserves of energy from soldiers who were often very weary, particularly those who spent time in the debilitating Jordan Valley. General Barrow comments that the 4th Division was 'a very tired formation' when it moved from the Jordan Valley to the coast, but 'the exhilarating nature of the manoeuvre in which it was engaged and the will to victory' kept it going for a little longer.[14] By September all had undergone a heavy training programme, a shared experience which no doubt they ruefully acknowledged to each other.

The intensity of this training programme does not seem to have been realized by the Turkish command. Liman von Sanders did know in general terms about the exchange of British for Indian units, but the training they were undergoing is never referred to in his memoirs.[15] One reason for this was

[12] Olden, *Westralian Cavalry*, p. 254.
[13] Davidson, *Dinkum Oil*, p. 100.
[14] Barrow, *Fire of Life*, pp. 191–2.
[15] Liman von Sanders, *Five Years*, pp. 238–9.

the ubiquity of British air power. During the three months or so before the September attack the pilots gained experience in co-operating with ground forces, and became more expert at attacking enemy ground forces, but their main task was to prevent enemy aircraft from seeing what was going on south of the front line, and at the same time to discover as much as possible of what was going on to the north.

The patrols of the 1st Australian Squadron were particularly relentless at hunting out the German aircraft, chasing them to their landing grounds and then shooting them up even on the ground.[16] This was a dangerous practice since they were then in range of ground weapons, even rifles and pistols. In the air the quality and quantity of the rival air force's machines tended to dictate tactics and results. The British and the Australians, confident in the superiority of their airplanes, charged at the enemy aircraft as soon as they were seen, but the Germans avoided a fight if they possibly could. The contrast, of course, meant that the British pilots were usually successful in shooting down the enemy aircraft, or at least in driving them away.

The British also developed their expertise in ground attack. This had become the practice first in the fighting east of the Jordan in March and April, but was also used successfully in assisting in the raids by the Arab Army, as with the bombing of the last redoubt at Mudawwarrah. Because of the achievement of general air domination by the British aircraft, in the summer of 1918 attacks were extended to enemy units, camps, trains, airfields, and stations. This meant that the fighter bombers were constantly practising their skills, and this resulted in increasing the effectiveness of the operations.[17]

The preliminaries to the German-Turkish attack at Abu Tulul in July were instructive. It was known from prisoners that an attack was planned, but not precisely where or when. The 142 Squadron, based in Jerusalem, was operating with the Desert Mounted Corps in the Jordan Valley and was alerted to keep watch for enemy activity. For several days before 12 July the pilots reported 'minor activity'. Next day they reported none at all, and the attack went in on the 14th, at night, presumably after the attacking troops had rested up the previous day. It seemed, therefore, that air reconnaissance could detect troop movements, even 'minor activity', and when that ceased it could be assumed that the attack was imminent.

[16] Jones, *War in the Air*, p. 201.
[17] Cutlack, *Australian Flying Corps*, Chapter 12.

Turning that insight around, it followed that it was necessary to prevent German air reconnaissance over the British positions in and behind the line for several weeks before an attack in order to hide the necessary movements of units, and the training they were undergoing, both of which would be strong indications of Allenby's plans. The only way to do this was to establish complete air supremacy, though measures could also be taken on the ground which might hide the evidence of movements and troop concentrations.

The air campaign took time to have its effect, but, by persistently intercepting German aircraft as they approached the front line and then pursuing them relentlessly, dominance in the air was achieved during the summer of 1918. Jones's *Official History of the War in the Air*, written in 1937, cites some figures: in one week in June a hundred enemy aircraft crossed the line; in late August only eighteen crossed in a week; in the first three weeks of September only four altogether are recorded.[18] While these figures are necessarily only approximations – some aircraft were surely not seen, some would not be reported, and some were probably reported more than once – the point is made. Indeed in one area the domination was such that it was possible to allow German aircraft to get across the line when it was desirable that they should see something.

What had to be concealed was the progressive concentration of British forces in the narrow coastal plain. XXI Corps and DMC packed five infantry and three cavalry divisions into an area of less than ten miles by five. This, had the Turks discovered it, would have made it clear that a great attack was imminent and where. So both the concentration itself, and the movement of the units to the coast, had to be hidden. At the same time, the absence of these units in the rest of the rear areas had also to be concealed – that is, their continued presence had to be implied in their former stations, in the Jordan Valley above all. It was the cavalry divisions, which were normally in the east and were now in the west, which had to be demonstrated not to have shifted.

To achieve this concentration without the Turks suspecting what was going on therefore required much clandestine movement, concealment and deception. This was something Allenby enjoyed. He had employed deception aplenty in the preparations for, and the conduct of, the battle at Gaza, and now he did the same on a much bigger scale. The major problem was to move the horses and men of the cavalry. The bivouacs of the three mounted divisions of the Desert Mounted Corps in the Jordan Valley were left standing in their former stations, and were even apparently increased by the addition of

[18] Jones, *War in the Air*, Vol. 5, pp. 209–10.

old tents. The troops and their horses moved away at night – though this was normal anyway, at least in the summer, in order to avoid the day's heat. When they reached their new camps the men and animals were kept out of sight in the daytime, and when they got near the coast, they were concealed in orange groves. The men and the horses could be hidden by the trees, and the irrigation channels could be used to water the horses. Apparently it was so well done that even the local inhabitants did not realize what was going on, or so it has been claimed.[19]

The mounted forces moved out of the Jordan Valley in succession, usually taking four days on the march to the coast – or rather four nights. All the units camped in the same places, in succession, so that if spotted the move would not be realized.

> The well-known road to Talat-ed-Dumm was climbed for the last time, and the famous 'Halfway House' was reached shortly after midnight [on August 22]. Resting by day – not to speak of grooming and watering of horses – and marching by night, the regiment passed in succession through Jerusalem, Kuryet Enab, Deir Eyub, and arrived in the olive groves of Ludd early in the morning of August 26th.[20]

This was the move of the Western Australians, but it was also the same moves followed by the other regiments.

At the same time, the engineers were employed in maintaining the pretence that the offensive intentions of the British lay eastwards. So it was not merely a matter of hiding the movement to the west, but of implying that yet another eastward attack was intended. Dummy bridges were made of cordage and hessian and the approaches to them cleared of vegetation. Pretend horses were lined up, made of wooden frameworks covered by blankets, apparently ready to be fed and groomed. Men marched about, kicking up the dust which would be expected by a much greater number. Units of horsemen travelled back and forth, implying much greater numbers; infantry marched down to the valley one day, and back up again the next, then again and again. The aim, of course, was to allow them to be seen and to be photographed, and the Royal Air Force duly obliged. Their pictures showed that, from the air, the camps seemed authentic, so the odd enemy plane was allowed to get through and see the

[19] Falls, *Official History* Vol. II, p. 462.
[20] Olden, *Westralian Cavalry*, p. 254.

'evidence'. How deceived the enemy was is not clear. From the air 'in comparing them with the bridge proper one could hardly tell which was the dummy', but it would only take one low-flying plane or one man to get close enough on the ground to detect the deception. Active patrolling deterred enemy investigations both on the ground and by air. When enemy aircraft were allowed to see anything they were forced to stay at a high altitude.[21]

A great deal of energy was also poured into other methods of deception. A major hotel in Jerusalem was taken over and converted into a dummy General Headquarters, complete with sentries, staff officers, masses of paperwork, and busy signallers. In the new camps the movement of troops during the day was banned. If an aircraft approached, police would blow whistles and everyone would stand still. Fires were not to be lighted and cooking was done in field kitchens using smokeless solidified alcohol. One item the troops no doubt appreciated amid all this great inconvenience was that visits by staff officers to units were kept to a minimum. At Jaffa a general made rather obvious inquiries about securing a house for himself and his wife for the coming winter, all in the confident assumption that this would be relayed across the line to the Turkish intelligence officers. Bridges were needed across the Nahr el-Auja (the western one); to conceal preparations bridging schools were established where bridges were repeatedly built and then dismantled, but would be available when the time came. All this supposed, of course, that there were spies in such places as Jaffa and Jerusalem, who would either see what was going on or pick up gossip, but would not be able to move about freely, spotting, for example, the hidden camps in the olive and orange groves.[22]

Infantry divisions also had to be shifted, again marching at night. These foot soldiers had to be right at the front, ready to attack first, and four of the divisions lined up from the coast inland in a space of only five miles. The section of the line that had been held by the 7th Meerut Division alone was now held by the 60th London Division, on the coast, and the 7th, the 75th, and finally the 3rd Lahore Divisions. There was even a thinly held gap between the Londoners and the Meerut Division, and a wider gap between the 3rd and the 54th East Anglians further along. The latter then held a stretch of the front almost

[21] Aston, *Secret Service*, pp. 276–9.
[22] A detailed survey of all these matters is in Massey, *Allenby's Final Triumph*, Chapter 7.

as long as the other four put together. It was flanked by the French contingent to the east.[23]

Further, these infantry forces were supported by the densest concentration of artillery yet achieved in the Palestine war. Each division had its own allocation of three brigades of the Royal Field Artillery, and these in total amounted to sixty 18-pounders and twenty 4.5 inch howitzers; but each division was also supported by the heavy guns of the brigades of the Royal Garrison Artillery. All these guns were 'registered', that is, they were taken to the positions they would occupy in the bombardment, then they were fired at specific targets to note the orientation, elevation, and so on, for their particular targets. A representative reminiscence is in the account of the history of 'A' Company of the Honourable Artillery Company, attached to the 5th Brigade of the Australian Mounted Division:

> On August 23rd one section was ordered up to the front line and took over a prepared gun position just north of Arsuf, about one mile from the sea. On the 25th/26th they registered numerous points that were indicated in the first three lines of Turkish trenches. The fact that sections of other batteries were engaged on the same task and that apparently there was a steady stream of sections or even single guns and batteries coming up to this neighbourhood, registering, and returning to their unit again, was the first clear indication of what was impending.[24]

This had to be done gradually so that no abnormal increase in the regular bombardment would suggest a major attack was preparing. The gunners of the Desert Mounted Corps were to take part at the beginning under the orders of the Corps headquarters, and were to revert to their division's control once the gap had been opened up. In total Allenby had amassed over 380 guns for the attack, along with 35,000 infantry and 9,000 horsemen. The Turks they faced had only 8,000 infantry and 180 guns.[25]

In the preparations for the assault the RAF's balloon companies reconnoitred the Turkish lines day after day, while its aircraft repeatedly photographed the Turkish positions, all with the aim of producing accurate plans – 'mosaics',

---

[23] *Advance*, plate 41.

[24] Goold-Walker, *Honourable Artillery Company*, p. 148.

[25] Falls, *Official History* Vol. II, pp. 452–3; Erickson, *Ottoman Army Effectiveness*, pp. 146–8.

they were called, composed of several photographs – of the enemy trenches, strongpoints, gun positions, stores, and so on, and in detecting any changes. For a month before the attack the artillery, guided in part by the air reconnaissance information, fired repeatedly at the Turkish guns, but in such a way as not to imply any particular plan, and the intensity of the firing was kept at 'normal' levels while registering targets. Similarly, although it was suggested in the discussions with the Air Staff that a preliminary bombing campaign against selected important targets such as railway lines, and headquarters, be launched, it was decided that nothing extra should be done, for fear of alerting the Turkish command. Indeed, attacks on enemy headquarters were deliberately avoided, though they were located. Thus when the time came the surprise air attack would be all the more startling and effective; this was called 'fattening-up' the enemy headquarters for slaughter; an indication of the agricultural mindset of the British staff.[26]

The one exception to all this was raids along the Hejaz railway, first Dawnay's destruction of Mudawwarah in August, and then on 16 and 17 September when Lawrence attacked Deraa, but such activity would help keep the attention of the Turkish command eastwards, and so help to conceal western preparations and activity.[27]

Elsewhere on his front Allenby was taking a considerable risk. In order to achieve the dense concentration in the coastal plain, he had thinned out his line everywhere else, so that not only did the Turks have an overall numerical superiority elsewhere than on XXI Corps' front, but there were three sections of the front which were wide open if the Turks chose to attack. One of these gaps was that section between the 3rd Lahore and the 54th East Anglian Divisions near the coast. A second was at the steep scarp down into the Jordan Valley, which was effectively unscalable except at the tracks which already existed. Neither of these gaps was a serious problem, being either too small to matter or exceptionally difficult. The third, however, was astride the Nablus road, between the two divisions of Chetwode's XX Corps.

The reason was Chetwode's plan of attack.[28] The Turks had fortified the road and the land to either side of it to the extent that this was now the strongest part of the whole line. There had been British attacks in this area back in the spring, and the road was the most obvious place. Chetwode had no inten-

---

[26] Aston, *Secret Service*, p. 276.
[27] Jones, *War in the Air*, pp. 220–1.
[28] Falls, *Official History* Vol. II, Appendix 25.

tion of attacking such a strong position, and had covered the approach to it with only a small force of odd units – the Worcester Yeomanry from the corps troops, two pioneer battalions (1/155th and 2/155th) from his two divisions, and a scratch force brought up from the corps reinforcement camp. The whole was under the command of Lt.-Colonel G.B. Watson of the pioneers - hence 'Watson's Force'.[29] This group of heterogeneous units could not possibly hold the seven-mile gap against a determined Turkish attack, but Allenby and Chetwode were confident that no such attack would come.

In the Jordan Valley General Chaytor had put his infantry battalions in the line facing northwards. These were two battalions of the British West Indian Regiment, the first time they had been involved, and the two Jewish battalions, the 38th and 39th Fusiliers. These had been in the valley longer, but were scarcely more experienced than the West Indians. In other words Chaytor, like Chetwode, had to put his least experienced troops forward into the line in order to pretend to have many more troops than he had. These troops were fairly closely backed up, even supervised, by the mounted troops of the Anzac Division, plus the 20th Indian Infantry Brigade at the el-Ghoraniyeh crossing. The southern crossings at el-Hinu and Hijla were held by the 2nd Light Horse Brigade.[30] This was quite sufficient, together with the deception techniques, to persuade the Turks on the scarp top five miles away that an attack eastwards was possible, even likely.

[29] Ibid., pp. 465–6.
[30] Ibid., p. 463.

CHAPTER 8

Preliminaries

T HE decisive defeat of the Turkish army in Palestine is collectively known as the Battle of Megiddo, which is something of a misnomer since there was very little fighting in or near that place; its selection, however, did allow the British to link their victory with the Bible and Old Testament fights. Every account on the British side makes these links, and even Falls's *Official History* Vol. II devotes two full pages to a discussion of the place of Megiddo – 'Armageddon' – in military history. The initial fight, on 19 September, also has a separate name – the Battle of Sharon – from the name of the coastal plain in which most of the fighting took place. This was an infantry fight: 'Megiddo' which followed was a cavalry action which was spread over much of central Palestine. There were also a number of distinct subsidiary encounters, each of which might be called a battle in itself.[1]

Allenby had consistently tried to keep expectations of results from his attack low. Repeatedly he said that his target was to disrupt the enemy line and secure a new line passing east and west through Nablus. It was only at the end of the planning process that he raised his sights, and even then he carefully refrained from stating a particular geographical aim, instead focussing on the destruction of the two Turkish armies west of the Jordan.

The main attack in what became the battles of Sharon and Megiddo was due to be launched just before dawn on 19 September, but many preliminaries were undertaken before then. The attacking battalions had to move into place, having sorted out where they should be in the previous days. And there were three fairly major operations in other parts of the battlefield which must be seen as integral parts of the whole scheme. One was an attack by the Arab Army and its associates on the Hejaz railway at and about the town of Deraa; a second was an apparently major offensive in the central hill area of Judaea; the third was a major air attack. All this was intended to prepare the way for an exploiting manoeuvre to follow the main attack in the coastal plain. None of these attacks was wholly successful.

---

[1] See the classification in Falls, *Official History* Vol. II, Appendix 1.

The first move in the great battle was a series of Arab attacks on the railways around Deraa. In the same way that the divisions west of the Jordan were moving up towards the posts from which they were to attack, so the much smaller and slower Arab units were gradually moving to their target. They consisted of one Arab force of 450 men on camels, the Egyptian Camel Corps, a detachment of Gurkhas, also on camels, and the French mountain gun battery commanded by Capt. Pisani. Lawrence travelled in a Rolls Royce armoured car driven by Lord Winterton, who had been second in command of Buxton's Camel Corps, and who had now attached himself to the adventure, in the usual independent style of British aristocratic warriors; there were two other armoured cars and all three cars had their trailers filled with petrol and other supplies.[2] Allenby had indicated to Lawrence that he wanted the Arabs to attack the Hejaz line on 16 September. This was not the date for the main attack, so the Arabs were once again being used to pull the Turks' attention to the east – and indeed Liman von Sanders did send reinforcements to Deraa as soon as the Arabs' attacks began.

Lawrence and Faisal and the rest had all been delayed by the problem of Jaafar and his command status which had been raised so suddenly and inconveniently by King Husain, but the parties finally set off in several separate groups between 3 and 5 September, mainly departing from Aqaba, though some had come from Egypt. The rendezvous was the oasis of Azraq, well to the east in the Syrian desert where there was an extensive lake. From there the Egyptian Cameleers and the Gurkhas, commanded by Capt. Frederick Leake, rode to attack the railway at Mafraq south of Deraa, while Lawrence and the main force headed to sabotage the track north of the town. At Mafraq the Beni Sakhr prevented Leake from attacking the railway. They felt that they would be blamed by the Turks, and an agreement over supplies they had would then be broken, leaving them without access to water. Leake joined Lawrence instead. Lawrence laid on attacks which destroyed a bridge, then both groups moved along a stretch of the line northwards wrecking it as they went.

The Turks retaliated with an air raid, which delayed the railway destruction for a time; two British aircraft which attempted to intervene were shot down. The raiders then split up. Col. Joyce attacked the line closer to Deraa; Lawrence attacked the depot at Mezerib on the line towards Nablus, and wrecked a stretch of that line; the Arab Army contingent attacked Nesib, the station next south from Deraa. This Nesib garrison was large enough and alert

---

[2] Lawrence, *Seven Pillars*, p. 581; Barr, *Setting*, pp. 270–1.

enough to fight hard, and it took some time to capture the place. A nearby bridge was then blown up.

This was all very satisfactory, and Lawrence and the others greatly enjoyed playing with explosives and blowing things up. But the first bridge which Lawrence 'destroyed' was repaired within two days, and the Turks reacted strongly, while the local Arabs were annoyed and began sniping at these outsiders. The line's rupture was only over relatively short distances; on the rest of it the Turks could move without hindrance. Liman von Sanders had also reacted quickly. He brought a German engineering unit south from Damascus to help the engineers at Amman repair the line, and another small German force came across from Haifa to help defend Deraa itself. Neither of these forces would have been decisive in the great battle to the west, nor is there any evidence that Liman could have brought any more extra forces along the line to reinforce his main army. Retreating along the line, however, was to be another matter. These measures kept the lines operating for several days even though they were repeatedly cut. Liman was level-headed about all this and does not seem to have been too disturbed.

This activity may have warned Liman and his generals that a major attack was imminent, though it was no more than a larger Arab attack than usual. In fact they did not need such a warning. On the same day he heard of the Deraa attacks, a deserter from an Indian unit, a 'sergeant' as Liman called him, came over, and explained that he had not wanted to be involved in the big fight which was about to begin. On the British side his reason is given as religious, that is, a Muslim unwilling to fight other Muslims, which is perhaps more credible than fear.[3] This information could have effectively nullified the effect of the Arabs' attacks in the east, but it was far too late and unspecific for the Turks to be able to pre-empt the British attack, even if the Turks could find out any real details – the 'sergeant' cannot have known much, other than that extensive preparations were underway.

Liman claims to have 'realized at once' that a major attack was coming, and he certainly took measures to reinforce the Turkish forces in the coastal region.[4] He was not operating in total ignorance, though his air reconnaissance had effectively ceased two weeks earlier, when the German air com-

3 Liman von Sanders, *Five Years*, p. 274; Falls, *Official History* Vol. II, p. 468; Massey, *Allenby's Final Triumph*, p. 160.
4 Liman von Sanders, *Five Years*, p. 274.

mander stopped flights to prevent a further collapse of pilots' morale.[5] (On the British side this was reported as a great reduction in enemy penetration across the front line.) Liman put some of his best units into the coastal area, because it was the obvious place for the British to attack, but not from foreknowledge. Then on 18 September, and as a direct result, he says, of the Deraa attack and the Indian deserter's information, he moved the 46th Infantry Division to et-Tire from its reserve position at Tulkarm. Even earlier the 2nd Caucasian Cavalry Division's destination had been changed to Tulkarm.[6]

Liman knew that his army was more or less immobile. He mentions in his memoirs that some weeks before he had considered pulling back to a better defensive line, but decided not to do so. He cites his own preference for holding on to territory, and Enver Pasha's prohibition of retreat, but more immediate was the physical difficulty the army faced in actually moving. The Turkish soldiers were badly shod and weakened by underfeeding, their animals were weak and underfed, and the use of bullocks as draught animals, all meant that the army would only be able to move slowly.[7] Any removal from the trenches they now occupied would have given the more mobile and fit British an opportunity to launch their cavalry to break up the Turkish forces in detail. The Turks were therefore fixed in position until attacked. Liman's method of defence was thus to stand and fight, using above all machine guns to break up attacks, meanwhile attempting to gather forces together in the rear for a counterattack.

The second preliminary move by the British was made by the 53rd Welsh Division. This was one of Chetwode's XX Corps' divisions, and the aim was to seize control of a position to outflank the main Turkish defences astride the Nablus road. The division's role in the main attack was to cut the escape routes the Turks could use east of Nablus, notably along the Wadi Fara, but if they waited until the main attack to the west began their opponents would be alert. So the attack went in the night before the main event. The news might further distract the Turkish high command.

Allenby's method in the planning of the great attack had been to lay down the general outline to the Corps commanders, who would then organize their staffs to do the detailed work. It was up to the Corps commanders to decide the work to be done by each division, and the divisional commanders had then to devise the detail. It was clearly therefore at divisional level that the timing

---

5   Ibid., pp. 272–3.
6   Ibid., pp. 274–5; Erickson, *Ottoman Army Effectiveness*, pp. 145–7.
7   Liman von Sanders, *Five Years*, pp. 273–4.

and objectives for each unit, down to the company level, was arranged. The work of XX Corps in the Judaean Hills is a particularly notable example of this. Chetwode as Corps Commander laid down that the main Turkish positions defending the Nablus road should be ignored and that his two divisions should attack to either side of it, with the 53rd attacking first. It was then up to the divisional commanders to devise their plans of attack. The 53rd Division commander, General Hon. Stanley Mott originated the plan of attack by his two brigades which seized the Samieh position on the night of 18/19 September.

Two brigades, the 159th and the 160th, were to be used.[8] They were to capture an area of high ground across the Wadi Samieh. The wadi flowed through a wide basin 2000 feet below the hills, three miles long and over four miles wide. The Turks held most of the hills to the north, the British those on the south side, and some of the lower hills on the north; much of the basin was unoccupied by either side. The Turkish defences consisted of posts occupying hills and the tops of spurs. These spurs stretched out from a watershed ridge which curved round behind them and had very steep sides. Each post had been identified and given a name. Sometimes the local name was used, where it was known; more often one was given by the observers.

An attack directly on the Turkish positions would probably be detected and defeated, so that was never considered – except to dismiss it. (This may well have been Chetwode's decision; he liked indirect attacks, fully appreciating their generally lower costs.) If the watershed ridge could be taken many of the posts on it and on the westward spurs could be attacked from the rear, and the Turks' positions between the ridge and the wadi basin outflanked. So the two brigades were to make separate attacks, but were to converge at the end at a hill called Hindhead, having secured the ridge to the east and the hills to the west, and so the spur positions as well. At that point the division would have achieved a position from which to attack northwards when the time came to assault the retreating Turks in the Wadi Fara and the Nablus area.

The 160 Brigade went in to the attack first, its target the curving watershed ridge. The brigade included four battalions: 1/7th Royal Welch Fusiliers, 1/17th Indian Infantry, 1/21st Punjabis, and the 1st Cape Corps. They were to attack successive posts, in a manoeuvre described as a 'leap-frog' attack. They gathered on the afternoon of the 18 September in olive groves to the south of the Wadi Samieh, which hid their concentration. They were also protected by two

---

[8] Falls, *Official History* Vol. II, pp. 471–2; Ward, *53rd (Welsh) Division*, pp. 230–5; Ward, *Royal Welch Fusiliers*, Vol. IV, pp. 184–6.

patrolling aircraft from any German aerial view. The approach and the attack were to begin soon after dusk, the noise of the march hidden by the slow bombardment of a Turkish post.

The 17th Infantry led. They were detected partway, but the Turkish response was slow and their firing was wild. By moving faster they avoided casualties and arrived at their first objective early, and had to wait until the timed 20-minute bombardment battered their targets. Then, with no difficulty they captured Wye Hill. The Cape Corps came through and seized a series of small posts along the ridge as far as Square Hill and Khirbet Jibeit, leaving picquets along the way to detect any movement from the north or west by other Turkish forces. The Royal Welch Fusiliers came through, guarded by the Cape Corps picquets on their right. The 21st Punjabis tackled Valley View, one of the more important Turkish spur-posts. The Turks fled, but into the hands of the advancing Fusiliers, who then pushed through to capture Boulder's Boil and el-Mugheir, where a battalion headquarters complete with battalion commander was captured. The operation, which was over by 3 a.m., took almost 450 prisoners, two howitzers and fifteen machine guns, all for only thirty casualties.

To the west the 159th Brigade (the 4/5th Welch Regiment, and the 3/152nd, 1/153rd and 2/153rd Indian Infantries) waited to attack until 160 Brigade had moved into position. Its objectives were a series of hills each held by a Turkish garrison. None could be taken in rear or in flank, or by surprise. The first posts, on Forfar Hill and Bidston Hill, were on either side of a steep valley, and were captured by the 3/152nd and the 1/153rd respectively with little difficulty. The latter battalion then went on to attack the next hills to the north, Sekub and Kew. The Turks, however, were now fully alert and resisted strongly. Sekub was taken, but the Indians had suffered considerable casualties by then, and could not go on alone; the Welch battalion came up to help and together the two finally took Kew well after midnight. They were joined by most of the 2/153rd which had occupied Cone Hill on the way. The Turks were now fully alert and the next objectives were several particularly strong positions.

The 2/152nd Infantry attacked Abu Malul hill. This was garrisoned by a larger force than any of the rest. There were caves where the troops could shelter and so they had escaped any serious damage from the bombardment. The Indian attack was met by determined and successful resistance from well-manned machine guns. Three attacks failed; it was not possible to organize a new bombardment to provide assistance. A supporting attack, by the 3/153rd Infantry on loan from 158 Brigade to the west, also failed to capture Fife Hill and Amunieh. On the other hand the Welch battalion at Sekub and Kew, when it was clear that the 160th Brigade had succeeded to the east, was able to move quickly against Hindhead and capture it. The operation was thus not wholly successful, with the formidable Abu Malul still under Turkish control. Fresh attacks later, after the troops were rested, would probably succeed. Allenby's choice of attacking in the coastal plain was plainly correct, for in the hills in the centre, and in the Jordan Valley, and on the eastern plateaux, the countryside worked for the defence.

While the 53rd Division was attempting to break the Turkish positions in the hills (and her sister division waited to exploit that attack and the fighting in the plain), the forces in XXI Corps were moving to their final positions for the main attack. Allenby's overall plan was essentially very simple, even traditional. It was what the high command on the Western Front had always wished to achieve – a break in the enemy line through which the cavalry would move to disrupt the enemy rear areas. It was the very method later used in France in 1940 which the Germans arrogantly called *blitzkrieg*, though the exploitation, by tank columns, was no greater or faster or more decisive than what Allenby achieved in 1918 (or than Napoleon or Alexander the Great had achieved in the past). Briefly, the infantry was to assault the Turkish infantry, push them out of the way, either by destroying them or pushing them into the hills to the east, and so permit the Desert Mounted Corps to ride through the Turkish defences without having to fight. This was crucial, and the mounted men were ordered to avoid fighting and to evade any formed Turkish units, for their main purpose was to get into the rear of the Turkish line and disrupt any organization there; capturing towns, severing railways, attacking fortifications, were their main tasks.[9]

The men finally received their detailed orders on the evening of 18 September. Their commanders, brigade and battalion, had only been told the plan two or three days before, by Allenby personally: the divisional staffs had laid down the objectives of each battalion, the routes to be taken, the timing of each march. Many of the infantry battalions had trained for their specific roles during the previous month or so, though largely in ignorance that this was so.

The individual elements in the plans were regularly revised in the light of more up-to-date information. Much of this came from air reconnaissance, which claimed to be able to detect the movement of Turkish forces, but sometimes it was the result of patrols on the ground. For example, the 5th Bedford-

---

9 Falls, *Official History* Vol. II, Appendix 23.

shires, of 54th East Anglian Division, sent a patrol out on the night of 9/10 September, which found that the Turkish position on a ridge they faced was more strongly held than they had thought; another, larger patrol the next night confirmed this. As a result the plan was altered to include the ridge in the main attack. (The Turks counter-attacked the second patrol as it was retiring, but this was foiled by a single private, Samuel Needham, who charged the Turks alone, bayoneting several of them. The patrol made its escape; Needham was awarded the VC.)[10] In the end, in the main attack, it was found that the ridge was not strongly held after all, but this is an example of the constant rearrangement of forces on both sides.

In general, the Turkish positions and strengths were well known, their guns had been located, and their aircraft largely deterred from crossing the line. The Turks occupied a slight ridge which gave them command over the land to the south. Behind that they had formed three successive lines close to the coast, the trenches interspersed with strongpoints and lined with barbed wire – but the wiring was not regarded as done well by the British, especially those with experience in the Western Front. In most cases it was only a single roil of wire, easily cut and pulled aside; nor were the trenches continuous. The whole system was three miles deep, but the third, rearmost, line was more an aspiration than actuality, though some posts were formed and manned. Some parts were better arranged than others. In front of the 8th Gurkhas in the 7th Indian Division, the 'system … ran along a low sandy ridge, and had a depth of 3000 yards. They were well constructed and formed a continuous line. A rear system of defences near el Tireh was situated three miles behind the front system'.[11] On the other hand, the coastal part of the system to be attacked by the Kumaon Rifles in the 60th London Division had gaps so that they were able to get into the midst of the system before the Turks realized their approach.[12] To the east, the 5th Essex had to attack over a rocky, hilly area, seamed with wadis, and their objectives were not so much lines as fortified posts, villages and hilltops, rather like the positions the 53rd Division had attacked.[13]

The battalion commanders had been told, in conferences often attended by Allenby in person, of their specific tasks a few days before the attack was to be made. They had had time to prospect the precise Turkish positions and to

[10] Maurice, *16th Foot*, p. 212.
[11] Huxford, *8th Gurkhas*, p. 110.
[12] Overton, *Kumaon Rifles*, p. 11.
[13] Gibbons, *1/5th Essex*, p. 139.

design their own particular operation. The men were informed during the day before, and moved stealthily to their starting positions in the last hours. And each battalion made its own particular preparations.

These preliminary arrangements tended to be individual to each battalion. The Kumaon Rifles were pulled back out of the line on the evening of 18 September to give the men a rest and make the final preparations for combat, which included a 'stirring' speech in Urdu from General Shea – an odd beginning for a 'London' division.[14] Equally curious and eccentric was a decision by the 5th Essex to go into battle in shorts, which 'gave greater freedom of movement and was cooler, but the nature of the rocks and wiry grass we were to attack over was very rough on bare knees, as we found to our cost'.[15]

All battalions disposed of accumulated extra items of kit. In the 53rd Sikhs officers were allowed 12lbs of kit, and 'other ranks none over and above that carried in packs'.[16] 'Haversacks were left behind and everything was carried in the pack', the Essex history says, and points out that

> This was sound as haversacks carried at the side were very uncomfortable, and it made more room for two water battles, which were considered a necessity and proved a great boon. In the pack were 50 rounds of extra S.A.A. [small arms ammunition], cardigan, cap comforter, washing and shaving kit, two iron rations and a pair of socks. Each man had a triangular tin disc sewn on the back of his pack, which, flashing in the sun, let the artillery know where we were.[17]

By contrast, in the 7th Gurkhas 'on the way up each man was issued with a jersey and a second water bottle; useful things, but not a convenient moment to receive them'.[18]

The pioneer battalions had particularly dangerous preliminary work to do. The Bombay Pioneers' history gives an example: 'The night of 18th/19th September was somewhat noisy, with a good deal of machine-gun and trench mortar fire coming over. During the night both battalions of Pioneers removed

[14] Overton, *Kumaon Rifles*, p. 11.
[15] Gibbons, *1/5th Essex*, pp. 140–1.
[16] Anon., *53rd Sikhs*, p. 247.
[17] Gibbons, *1/5th Essex*, p. 141.
[18] Mackay, *Gurkha Rifles*, p. 76.

stretches of our own wire along the front; they also filled in shell holes and improved tracks in rear of our fire trench, the 2/107th having one man killed.'[19]

The noise of the guns helped to hide the sound of the pioneers' work, and of the troops moving up to their attacking positions, and during the night the British artillery very carefully made only the same sort of bombardments as had been happening for the previous month. All along the line the assault troops moved close, and then closer, to the Turkish line. The 3rd Gurkhas were given a final drink of water so as to begin with full water bottles. They were woken from a short, rather disturbed sleep at 2.30 a.m. and moved forward at 3.15 a.m. The British wire had been gapped by the pioneers and the battalion passed through and lined up 'on the tape line at 4.20 in two lines of half-companies'.[20] The 7th Gurkhas were already in position by 4 a.m., and the author of the regiment's history remembered that 'everything was very quiet', which can only be a trick of his memory since others recall a continuous racket of gun and rifle fire.[21] The two leading battalions of the 21st Brigade in the 7th Division had to attack a well-fortified village, Tabsor, 600 yards from the British lines; they therefore moved into no man's land between the opposing lines before the time of the assault. This was 'a fortunate thing for the battalion, as when the Turkish counter-barrage came down, their shells passed over [to hit their former positions], causing only a few casualties'.[22] The Turkish artillery had been registering targets as well.

The Kumaon Rifles did much the same. The three companies which were to make the initial attack lined up to the east of the coastal road. 'B' Company was to tackle a strongpoint perhaps 300 yards from the British line, but 'C' and 'D' Companies were to move up east of 'B' and then turn sharp left *behind* that strongpoint, then right to attack a series of trenches directly behind it. 'B' Company's commander Capt. J.E.T. Catron had personally scouted the Turks' situation and selected the positions from which they would begin the assault, which was an area right in the midst of the Turkish posts. The three companies moved forward five minutes before zero-hour, at 4.25 a.m. This had the same advantage as noted by the 7th Gurkhas, in that this move took them away from the Turks' artillery target. Several hundred men loaded with equipment

[19] Tugwell, *Bombay Pioneers*, p. 326.
[20] Woodyatt (ed.), *Own Gurkha Rifles*, p. 219.
[21] Mackay, *Gurkha Rifles*, p. 76.
[22] Huxford, *8th Gurkhas*, pp. 11–12.

cannot possibly have avoided making some noise, but the Turks did not detect them.[23]

The Kumaons were in 60th Division, with two other battalions on their left in the space between the road and the coast. On 75th Division's front, the 3rd Gurkhas also moved early, by four minutes, when 'the first wave of the first line stepped forward into the darkness'.[24] (The moon had set at 3.55 a.m., the sun would rise at about 5 a.m., so some light was available by about 4.30 a.m. – zero-hour.) In 7th Division both the 8th Gurkhas and the 2nd Black Watch moved forward into no man's land so as to begin the attack without delay – no doubt avoiding Turkish artillery retaliation was again in their minds.[25] None of these preliminary moves were noticed by the Turks.

The men of 5th Essex in 54th Division had a more awkward territory to attack. They would need to march forward almost two miles before reaching an enemy position, and their main target was twice that distance further on – an advance over rough ground of about six miles. It was essential to begin moving in the darkness, but also essential to ensure they went in the right direction, otherwise everything would go wrong. The Royal Engineers had laid out a tape to mark the start line and make the way forward clear, but it had been laid on the forward slope of a ridge which was being intermittently shelled by Turkish artillery. 'The enemy was evidently apprehensive and expected something was going to take place, but there is no doubt he was deceived as to the point of the main attack.' The noise of the Welsh Division attack in the hills was clearly audible; this would have alerted the Turks in front of the Essex Battalion. So the Essex men lined up behind the crest on the reverse slope, hopefully out of sight of the Turks. Their colonel remembered, 'I knew the ground better than any part of my parish, and officers and men who had been on patrol knew it far better.' The men lay down in safety (like the squares at Waterloo); the danger they avoided was illustrated when the commander of 161 Brigade, Brigadier-General H.B.H. Orpen Palmer, who was observing events from a hilltop with his staff, became the target for an accurately aimed Turkish shell.[26]

The 5th Essex was at the front by 2.30a.m. At 3.50 a.m. the men began to move forward and had advanced 5000 yards by the time of the British bombardment signalled zero-hour. They and all the other battalions then waited

[23]   Overton, *Kumaon Rifles*, pp. 11–12.
[24]   Woodyatt (ed.), *Own Gurkha Rifles*, p. 219.
[25]   Huxford, *8th Gurkhas*, p. 111.
[26]   Gibbons, *1/5th Essex*, pp. 141–2.

just below or in front of, or in some cases, in the middle of the first Turkish objective for twenty minutes while the British shells screamed over them.

The third of the actions before the main attack was a series of air raids on specific enemy targets. The aim here was less conquest than disruption, which was intended to hinder the response to the infantry attack. It was, therefore, apart from the attack by 53 Division on the night of 18 September, the air force which began the attack, with several bombing raids.

The concentration of the infantry and the cavalry close to the coast was to a large extent mirrored by that of the air force in the same general area. 113 Squadron and 142 Squadron were based at Sarona, close to Jaffa, just behind the line; 14 and 144 Squadrons were at Junction Station; 111 Squadron, one flight of 145 Squadron and 1 Squadron of the Australian Flying Corps were at er-Ramleh, near Ludd, between Sarona and Junction Station. Since there was only twenty miles between Sarona and Junction Station, this was a strong concentration of air power – a hundred aircraft, if all were present and operational. (Part of 142 Squadron was based also at Jerusalem.)[27]

The air force was involved in several activities. They needed to keep enemy aircraft away from menacing the troops on the ground. The British aircraft had certainly established dominance in the air in the previous six months or so, but it was still possible for enemy aircraft to create surprises. The sudden appearance of several German aircraft to menace Lawrence's activities around Deraa had led to the destruction of the only two British aircraft in that area – in other words, it was always possible to bring about a sudden concentration of aircraft for a particular task no matter how outnumbered the whole air force might be – and such a thrust might just be sufficient to reveal moves or inflict crucial damage.

The planes were to be used for bombing, an operation in which the skills of the pilots had greatly improved in recent months. A series of targets was devised, and this was to be one of the crucial tasks for the aircraft. In order to prevent the enemy from interfering, or getting any clear information, the main Turkish airfield at Jenin was to be subjected to a constant patrol by relays of SE5a aircraft of 111 and 145 squadrons. These were to prevent any German aircraft from taking off. This standing patrol suppressed much German air activity. There were always two aircraft over the airfield, armed with bombs which they were to drop to prevent any aircraft from taking off. When relieved by the next patrol, the pilots were then free to drop any remaining bombs where they

[27] *Advance*, plate 41.

wished. Jones's *Official History of the War in the Air*, notes dryly: 'no German pilot left the ground.'[28]

Aircraft were also to be used as observers, to report the progress of the ground troops back to division and corps headquarters, and to act as reconnaissance vehicles, particularly for the advancing cavalry. Elaborate methods of communication between the troops, the pilots, and the corps headquarters and the artillery were devised, and some of the bombers were assigned to act as supporting artillery, especially tasked with dropping strings of smoke bombs to blind the enemy, or indicating targets for the British ground artillery.

These tasks were devised for action in daylight once the fighting had begun. Other measures were also used that were designed to destroy as much of the enemy's means of communication as possible. At el-Afule the Turkish army had its main telephone exchange. It was attacked by the great Handley-Page aeroplane of the Australian 1 Squadron, piloted by Capt. Ross Smith, carrying sixteen 112lb bombs. He took off in darkness and dropped its bombs on el-Afule at dawn, just as the bombardment of the Turkish front line was beginning. It was soon followed by five planes of 144 Squadron and then eight more, which targeted the military headquarters and the airfield. The raids were highly successful in destroying the exchange and other targets. Other raids attacked the headquarters of the VII and VIII Armies at Tulkarm and Nablus.[29] Liman von Sanders also says that 'land lines had been cut in the early morning hours by the Arabs.'[30] He was out of touch with both armies from 7 a.m., but the German signal engineers restored telegraph communication with Nablus within three hours. By that time the situation at the front had drastically changed and the British cavalry was into the back areas, and the army commanders had been unable to react except locally to what was happening.

---

[28] Jones, *War in the Air*, Vol. 5. pp. 214–21.

[29] Cutlack, *Australian Flying Corps*, pp. 151–2; TNA, AIR/2262/209/60/9, War Diary of 1 Squadron AFC, 19 September 1918.

[30] Liman von Sanders, *Five Years*, p. 275.

Chapter 9

The Infantry Battle

Zero-hour for the attack, 4.30 a.m., was anticipated by many of the attacking units. In fact 'zero-hour' was the start of the artillery bombardment, whose timing was integrated with the infantry advance. The aim was to stun the Turks with a sudden shelling, then to advance the infantry just behind the shells. They would then occupy the shattered enemy trenches. This is in the main what happened, at least in the plain of Sharon where the rival lines were fairly close together.

Many of those who wrote accounts of these events remembered the sudden beginning of the bombardment. 'Every gun on our side was fired as though by the pressing of an electric button,'[1] creating 'a veritable inferno of noise and dust. Many of our guns were so close behind, and the screaming shells passed so closely overhead, that the effect was bewildering. Momentarily the whole line was checked from sheer amazement at the astounding din.'[2]

The Turks had been 'apprehensive' all night, and had been firing at the British lines rather more actively than usual.[3] This was in part because of the noise of the fighting in the hills. When the British bombardment began, 'from the Turkish lines hundreds of Verey lights and much machine-gun fire' replied,[4] but 'It was some time before the Turkish guns came into action'[5] though Falls's *Official History* II claims that 'the Turkish artillery replied promptly'.[6] The main point, however, was that the British infantry had either already come close to the Turkish lines or were moving forwards as the guns fired. So the Turks' reply tended to hit empty positions.

The bombardment was a moving thing, beginning with ten minutes of shelling of the Turkish front line, then moving on to positions behind, so that the infantry could advance immediately into the areas just blasted. The explo-

---

[1] Black, *Wiltshires*, 124.
[2] Woodyatt (ed.), *Gurkha Rifles*, p. 219.
[3] Gibbons, *1/5th Essex*, p. 141.
[4] Chaldecott, *1st Battalion*, p. 70.
[5] Ibid.
[6] Falls, *Official History* Vol. II, p. 472.

sions threw up enough 'dust as to make a dense fog', and the many smoke-shells meant that 'Direction had to be checked by compass'.[7] The rate of the barrage's advance is variously stated as seventy or a hundred yards per minute, but its effect was to stun or kill the Turks in the front line, and destroy or heavily damage their positions. In several cases the damage was less than hoped for or intended. In front of the 3rd Gurkhas 'the wire had not been cut. This was an unpleasant moment, for machine-guns were chattering on either flank. But the wire was cut through at once by means of the special cutters fixed on the rifles, and the entrenchments were rushed with hardly a pause'.[8] However, in most cases the wire was well cut, so it is never mentioned. Repeatedly units describe the first advance as being without difficulty. 'The enemy's defences' were 'now an infernal mass of fire and smoke ... we found the enemy absolutely panic-stricken'.[9] 'Most of the [first] line had been evacuated. Some five officers and fifteen men were captured in a dug-out',[10] that is, they had not had time to climb out to man the line between the end of the barrage and the arrival of the infantry. Sometimes no conflict happened: 'Advancing close behind this [barrage] the Black Watch were quickly in occupation of the enemy front line.'[11] 'As the guns lifted ... the Dorsets had captured the first line objectives.'[12]

Close to the coast was a Turkish redoubt and a sequence of trenches which, facing westwards, were clearly designed to resist an attack from the sea. Here the 2/19th London and the 2/97th Deccan Infantry faced the redoubt, which was presumably the strongest element of the defences. These two battalions also had the 2nd Guides on their left, actually on the coast, and the Kumaon Rifles on their right. These four battalions attacked on a front of about a mile, though in fact the attacking front was even narrower since the Deccan Infantry and the Kumaons were each attacking on a front of perhaps 200 yards. The Deccan Infantry captured their objectives 'within a few minutes', before the dust and smoke of the initial bombardment had cleared, taking many prisoners and several machine guns. All their objectives were achieved by 5.40 a.m.and the 2/19th Londons then passed through to attack the next line.[13] Their ulti-

7 Condon, *Frontier Force Rifles*, p. 85.
8 Woodyatt (ed.), *Gurkha Rifles*, p. 219.
9 Black, *Wiltshires*, p. 124.
10 Woodyatt (ed.), *Gurkha Rifles*, p. 219.
11 Huxford, *8th Gurkha Rifles*, p. 111.
12 Petre, *1st Gurkha Rifles*, p. 177.
13 Eames, *Second Nineteenth*, p. 154.

mate objective was the Nahr el-Falik, a stream which was fairly wide when it reached the sea and which was backed up by a marshy area through which the coastal road passed. This watery area could have been a major barrier, had the Turks been able to hold it, especially to the horsemen. The road and the ford across the *nahr* and the marsh were essential captures.[14]

The aim in most parts of the attack was the same, that one battalion would break into the Turks' front line, and after making progress would halt and a second battalion following close behind would take up the advance. The fear, obviously, was that the first attackers would have suffered heavy casualties in attacking the most heavily fortified sections of the Turkish line, and would have used up much of their ammunition, but that the back-up battalion would be fresh and fully armed. The rearward Turkish positions were also likely to be better prepared and alert than those in the first line where the men were battered by the initial barrage and then immediately assaulted by the infantry. It worked very well on the coast, where the full breakthrough as far as the crossings of the Nahr el-Falik were reached soon after 7 a.m. – an advance of four miles (in a direct line) in less than three hours.[15]

Next to the London and Deccan Infantry, the Kumaon Rifles had a complex attack to conduct, and did not have a second battalion as back-up. Half of 'A' Company was in reserve, but two of its platoons were placed west of the coast road to maintain contact with the Deccan and London soldiers. 'B', 'C', and 'D' Companies had moved stealthily into the area of no man's land before zero-hour, where they were confronted on two sides by Turkish positions, with a small lake, the Birket Atife, on the third. This was the plan devised and reconnoitred a day or so earlier by Capt. Catron (who was in fact wounded early on). For an hour they waited, silently, amid their enemies, and then witnessed the bombardment striking within a few yards of them. It takes quite exceptional soldiers to accomplish such an advance, in silence, and knowing that the artillerymen might make mistakes. 'B' Company attacked its objective 'a strongpoint in the enemy first line situated on a small knoll', as the barrage lifted at 4.40 a.m., and overran it. The Turks were able to put up something of a fight, but it ended with 30 of them dead and 110 of them prisoners; 8 machine guns were captured. The two platoons of 'A' Company across the road now moved up northwards and the two in reserve move forward to join with 'B'; the initial move had succeeded.

[14] Overton, *Kumaons*, pp. 11–13.
[15] Eames, *Second Nineteenth*, p. 154.

'C' and 'D' Companies moved in behind the position on the knoll which had been attacked by 'B' and turned to the right to face north. The Turkish artillery therefore missed them. They moved north beside the road and a Turkish communication trench which was laid out as part of the defences against an attack from the sea. They moved too quickly and reached their objective in advance of the barrage, but then went straight into the attack on their target strongpoint without delay, burning red flares to indicate where they were. The artillery barrage was suspended and the place was taken, resulting in the killing of 40 enemy soldiers, and the capturing of 105 prisoners and 6 machine guns. Two platoons were left in possession of the place and on guard, the artillery barrage resumed farther ahead and the remainder of 'C' and 'D' 'passed forward through dust and haze towards the battalion's third objective'. They were now once more co-ordinated with the creeping barrage. They captured the position comparatively easily. The Turks were already beginning to retreat as quickly as they could; an Austrian battery was also taken.

The battalion commander, Major Latham, now caught up with the advanced troops. He checked the situation to either flank, for it would not do to get into a situation where the battalion would be so far out in front that it could be attacked in flank. Since on both flanks the attackers were more or less at the same point he took the two 'A' Company platoons which had been in reserve 'and a number of parties of men he had collected on the way up' - men left behind for various reasons - and pushed them forward in parallel with the 2/19th London to his left. As they captured the Nahr el-Falik crossings the Kumaons occupied the land south of the *nahr* inland, and dispersed a Turkish force which was trying to retreat through them.[16]

The 13th London Battalion (the 'Kensingtons') now came forward from the reserve.

> When the order came to advance, instead of having to charge forward to support lines of trenches, they found the enemy had gone! Passing rapidly over the Turkish line, with hardly a moment to look at the terribly efficient work of our guns, they were met by no determined counterattack, such as had been anticipated, and soon they were over the three lines of trenches, without seeing a Turk other than the casualties and prisoners.[17]

[16] Overton, *Kumaon Rifles*, pp. 12–15.
[17] Bailey and Holler, 'The Kensingtons', pp. 366–7.

There was a lightly guarded space of a few hundred yards to the right of the Kumaons, then two brigades of the 7th Indian Division were to attack, with a third in reserve. The 2nd Black Watch led the attack of 21st Brigade, and rapidly seized control of the Turkish first line, and the 8th Gurkhas moved through to capture the remaining trenches. They met little resistance; the Gurkhas captured 340 prisoners and 15 machine guns, for the cost of fifteen casualties. By 6.30 a.m. less than two hours after the bombardment began, all objectives had been achieved.[18]

The 19th Brigade had the other half of the attack. This time the four battalions of the brigade were joined by two borrowed from 21st Brigade. Before them was a formidable strongpoint, the fortified village of Tabsor; they then were to pass two other strongly held villages, Miskieh and et-Tire, the objectives of 75 Division to the east. It was, however, always possible for the enemy garrisons to fail to realize this division of responsibility so they would attack those passing by. The main target of this reinforced brigade was in fact beyond Tabsor, an area of marsh, the Birket Ramadan, and the crossing point at Zerkiyeh. This was an extension of the marsh connected with the Nahr el-Falik which was one of the targets of 60 Division. The main point to be seized was Ain el-Basse. The third brigade of the division, the 28th, was to follow up, being particularly attentive to the needs of the 19th. Tabsor was clearly being taken seriously.

19th Brigade formed up in two columns, on a frontage of one battalion, almost as in a French revolutionary battle. The left column was headed by the 28th Punjabis, followed by the 125th Rifles, with the 20th Punjabis (borrowed from 21st Brigade) in third place; on the right the 92nd Punjabis were followed by the 1st Guides and the 1st Seaforth Highlanders. As in almost every case the first Turkish line was quickly seized once the barrage had moved on. In the event, Tabsor fell just as rapidly, overwhelmed by the barrage and the infantry's numbers and speed. Miskieh and et-Tire were passed by the Seaforths and 125th Rifles without difficulty, for the 75th Division to the right was mainly engaging the garrison's attention. At the Zerkiyeh position, a trench line was taken by a small party of the 125th, and the Seaforths gained Ain el-Basse. Zerkiyeh itself was then taken partly by the 125th attacking from the east and partly by the Seaforths who got behind the main Turkish position. Guns and prisoners in plenty were taken. This had all been achieved by 9 a.m. when the 1st Guides and the 20th Punjabis were returned to 21st Brigade.[19]

---

[18] Huxford, *8th Gurkha Rifles*, p. 111.
[19] Ibid.; Anon., *53rd Sikhs*, pp. 247–8.

The infantry had thus, on a front of perhaps five miles, destroyed the Turkish defences totally. Even the first attackers found that the Turkish defenders in the first line were incapable of fighting, and the second line was almost equally unable to resist. The men of the 60th Division had secured the crossings of the Nahr el-Falik and the nearby marshes by soon after 7 a.m. The success of the infantry assault had been so obvious that the 5th Cavalry Division had been told the way was clear to ride along the coast in the 60th Division's wake even before the Nahr el-Falik crossing had been seized.

The cavalry divisions had moved up behind the infantry as the fighting went on, so when General Shea of 60 Division decided a way had been cut through the enemy line, Major General Macandrew brought the 5th through.[20] Shea had made his decision by 7 a.m., but the cavalry had four miles to go, so the infantry had plenty of time to complete the capture of the crossing. The *nahr* was crossed by the leading cavalry regiment, Hodson's Horse,[21] almost an hour later. At the start line the division's artillery component was handed back by 60th Division, and joined the march. After crossing the Nahr el-Falik their next objective was the Nahr Iskenderun. This was the decisive moment, for the cavalry were clear through the Turkish positions. At 8.40a.m., even before the Seaforths and the 125th captured the crossing at Zerkiyeh, General Fane of the 7th Division gave General Barrow permission for the 4th Cavalry Division to ride through,[22] collecting their Royal Horse Artillery batteries on the way. By 11.15 a.m. both cavalry divisions were across the Nahr Iskenderun.

The infantry, however, was still fighting. In 7th Division there was a pause at Zerkiyeh while 21st Brigade was reassembled – it took some time to find all the various parties and gather them together – and while 28th Brigade came up from reserve. Meanwhile the neighbouring 75th Division had a much more difficult task than most at et-Tire. This large village was garrisoned by the recently arrived Turkish 46th Division, commanded by Major Tiller, a German officer who had been a determined opponent at Gaza a year before; it was also the headquarters of the Turkish XXII Corps, commanded by another tough and determined soldier, Colonel Refet Bey. This strength was one reason why 21st Brigade to the west had been so strong; and similar strength was needed for

[20] TNA, WO 95/4515, War Diary of 5 Cav. Div., 19 September 1918; Falls, *Official History* II, 522.

[21] TNS, WO 95/4515, War Diary of 5 Cav. Div., 19 September 1918, '0810' hours; Cardew, *Hodson's Horse*, pp. 200–1.

[22] TNA WO 95/4510, War Diary of 4 Cav. Div., 19 September 1918; Barrow, *Fire of Life*, pp. 194–6.

the actual assault on et-Tire. The main attack was to be by 232nd Brigade, 4th Wiltshires and the 2/3rd Gurkhas leading, and the 72nd Punjabis in reserve. To the east 234th Brigade with 152nd (Indian) Infantry and 58th (Indian) Rifles was joined by two companies of the 5th Somerset Light Infantry.

The 75th Division's task had all along been rather more difficult than that of the 7th. The 3rd Gurkhas met considerable opposition in the second Turkish line where three strongpoints had to be captured. One of these had to be directly assaulted by two of the battalion's companies, both of whose commanders became casualties.

> At this moment the rising sun, appearing huge and crimson through the dust and smoke of battle, disclosed an army broken and defeated. To the north the whole rolling plain was plastered with its fragments. In one area was transport, feverishly limbering up; in another stranded hospital wagons; here, a gun-team, caught in a storm of bullets, lay around the piece they would never drag again. Men, on horses or on mules, galloped wildly away; men on foot, singly or in bunches, plodded slowly northwards – too tired to hasten, as their victors were too tired to pursue.[23]

The battalion was reunited at the third Turkish line, and then advanced intermixed with men of other units, including the 152nd Punjabis, 123rd Rifles, and parts of the 234th Brigade on the left. Resistance was encountered briefly at two strongpoints; more prisoners were taken; the advance continued.[24]

The 4th Wiltshires, as every other unit, found no opposition at the first Turkish line, and 'advanced on and on, always keeping just a safe distance behind our barrage, and being led, as was always the case in action, by our Little Colonel' – Lt-Colonel A. Armstrong. 'The farther we advanced the more obvious were the traces of the completeness of the surprise. We found machine-guns, trench mortars, ammunition dumps untouched, stores of every kind overturned and disordered. We also came across field kitchens in which breakfast was being prepared.' Miskeh was captured, where they 'surprised and took prisoner nearly 100 Turks, some of whom had only just been awakened from sleep, and the personnel of a Field Ambulance, complete with patients.'[25] It was still only just after dawn.

---

[23] Woodyatt (ed.), *Gurkha Rifles*, p. 220.
[24] Ibid.
[25] Black, *Wiltshires*, pp. 124–5.

The battalions had fought separate fights until then, but joined up as they approached et-Tire. The size of the garrison, the relative freshness of the Turkish soldiers, the presence of determined commanders, and the time which had elapsed since the attack began, all meant that et-Tire was well prepared. The Wiltshires reached a trench 400 yards south of the village and there became stuck, suffering casualties every time a man became visible – including Colonel Armstrong, leading from the front for the last time. To their left the 3rd Gurkhas were similarly blocked. Their position was not helped by the British artillery mistakenly shelling their supports in the rear for a time, but they did gain the help of the 1st South African Field Artillery Brigade, which galloped up rather more quickly than expected, and whose commander managed to stop the 'friendly' shelling.

Et-Tire was surrounded, as were many Palestinian villages, by cactus hedges, very difficult to penetrate, and by a comprehensive system of trenches. This was what stopped the two battalions, and the arrival of the 72nd Punjabis, the brigade's reserve, did not really improve the situation. The difficulty here had been to some extent foreseen, and more reinforcements arrived. The 3rd Kashmir Rifles, an Imperial Service battalion, was brought up by its British Senior Special Service Officer, Major R.A. Lyall; there also arrived, brought up by Brigadier-General Huddleston in person, a squadron of the Corps Cavalry Regiment, and a Light Armoured Car Battery, also from the Corps reserve. So et-Tire was now to be attacked by four battalions plus armoured cars and cavalry. This quantity of manpower enabled the cars and the cavalry to begin a turning movement round the right flank of the village, while the infantry menaced the town from their position to the south. 'The right' of the 3rd Gurkhas

> worked its way gradually forward, and after a prolonged and severe fight, the enemy's last position on the west of Et Tireh was finally captured by a mixed force of Gurkhas and some 100 of the 152nd and 72nd Punjabis … under the leadership of Capt. Barter, V.C.
>
> This position was captured at 10.30, and consolidation was started at once. Lieut. Middleton, with sixty men, worked his way through the gardens, which surrounded the western side of the village, to secure a defensive position on the northern side. As this party arrived level with the northern boundary of the village they met with heavy machine gun fire from a redoubt about 500 yards in front of them.

The redoubt guarded the Turks' line of retreat. 'About 1 p.m. … everyone was astonished to see some 400 Turks issuing from these works and advancing with great bravery to make a counter-attack. They were quickly dispersed by an extremely accurate fire of the 4.5 howitzers of our S.A.F.A. friends and three machine-guns of No. 229 M.G. Company, under Lieut. Statham.' This had been one of the more expensive parts of the overall offensive. The Wiltshires had 87 casualties, and the Gurkhas 132. (Colonel Refet Bey, however, escaped, and spent a week bluffing his way through British units until he reached Tyre and safety.)[26]

With et-Tire captured by early afternoon, it was possible to begin the next strategic move. The 75 Division was withdrawn into corps reserve and left at et-Tire. The 7 Division now turned to the right and advanced into the foothills to the east. The division's reserve brigade, the 28th, had moved forward, but it had not been involved in any of the morning fighting. The 21st Brigade swung to the right through et-Tire, and the 28th passed beyond it, north of the village, to a position north of the 21st on its left flank, both facing east. The 19th Brigade now went into reserve. The division moved east across the Turkish railway to block any Turkish counter-attack, so holding open the route north for the cavalry. The Turks who got away from et-Tire had retired in that direction as well and the 56th Sikhs were held up by a rearguard of machine gunners at about 2 p.m., a mile and a half north-west of et–Tire, suffering forty or so casualties. The 56th was reinforced by the 53rd Sikhs and the 2nd Leicestershires, and they pushed this rearguard back. By 6 p.m. the division had occupied the village of Taiyibe. The delay in taking et-Tire had allowed the Turks to recover their balance. The afternoon fighting was much more difficult everywhere.

To the south 21st Brigade advanced in parallel, but was also confronted with serious opposition. The 20th Punjabis led, aiming for the village of Felamah, but they were stopped about 5 p.m. by fire from several well placed machine guns in the hills below the village, which caused over thirty casualties. As darkness fell, the battalion stopped where it was. The machine gunners were probably from the German 701st Regiment, but they were pulled out during the night.[27]

The 7th Division was the middle division of three facing east by the end of the day. To its south was the 3rd, and to the north 60th Division came across

[26] Falls, *Official History* Vol. II, pp. 479–80; Woodyatt, *Gurkha Rifles*, pp. 221–2; Black, *Wiltshires*, pp. 126–8.

[27] Anon., *Brownlow's Punjabis*, p. 45; Huxford, *8th Gurkha Rifles*, p. 111; Anon., *53rd Sikhs*, p. 248; Wylly, *Leicestershire*, p. 193.

from the Nahr el-Falik. The 60th Division's two brigades had advanced five miles to cut through the Turkish defences as far as the Nahr el-Falik and the nearby marshes, followed by the third brigade, the 181st, 2/22nd London, 130th Baluchis, 2/7th Deccan Infantry, and 2/152nd Indian Infantry. Attached to the 181st were the two regiments of the 5th Australian Light Horse Brigade which had the French cavalry element brigaded with it, and the brigade's field artillery batteries. This was a strong force which was designed for a specific purpose - to seize control of Tulkarm, a railway junction, which was at the western end of the routes (road and rail) leading towards Nablus. So while the two brigades, totalling four battalions, held the Nahr el-Falik crossings, and thus the northern end of the main position, a single brigade of four infantry battalions and one of cavalry swung right.

An hour before the crossing of the *nahr* was secured, 181 Brigade set off. The 97th Deccan Infantry had already been involved in the earlier attack and now joined in the exploitation of victory. Crossing the bridge and the causeway over the marsh, the 130th Baluchis captured a ridge to the north and the entire force swung round to face east. Then they, with the 22nd London, moved first to cut the routes to Tulkarm and then to attack Tulkarm itself.

The instructions to the 5th Light Horse Brigade had been similar to those given to the other cavalry formations – avoid getting involved in fights, but concentrate on cutting Turkish communications. This worked well enough, but one squadron of the 15th Regiment had to be sent to disperse a large body of Turks so that the rest of the brigade could manoeuvre around the north of the town. The Baluchis had a hard fight to capture the village of Qulunsawe, and the squadron of the 15th Light Horse helped out, so it was out of the main cavalry operation.

The remainder of the 15th, together with the whole 14th Regiment, moved round to the northeast and east of Tulkarm, and found that a combination of RAF bombing and infantry attacks had convinced many of the Turks in the town to leave. The horsemen spent the afternoon capturing prisoners, and an Austrian battery. 'The whole brigade was engaged several miles along the Nablus Road, preventing the enemy's escape.'[28] Some of the 14th became involved with an attack on the town and were beaten back. The Baluchis' difficult fight at Qulusware, however, prevented any Turks from moving north to help to defend Tulkarm (or to escape). The 152nd Infantry was brought up

[28]   AWM E 54/3, War Diary 14 ALH, 19 September 1918.

to assist the 22nd Londons at Tulkarm, and the latter reached and took the place at about 5 p.m., and at much the same time the Baluchis took Qulusware. With the infantry in the town, the horsemen were also able to enter. 'The town was eventually entered just after dark, and all opposition ceased.'[29] Some of the escapees headed north, thereby cutting through the rear of the Australian Brigade, who sent the French *Regimente Mixte de Marche de Cavalerie* after them. Altogether in the town, in that pursuit, and on the eastern road, several thousand prisoners were taken, the majority by the cavalry.[30]

The French and Australians had not intercepted all the escaping Turks, for considerable numbers of them had got further away by the time the cavalry-men arrived – and the Australians, having cut the route, turned to assist in the fight for the town. Other Turks had got as far as the Anebta defile, through which the railway and a road ran in a narrow, hill-enclosed pass. There they were subjected to attack from the air. The RAF had already located this as a likely place at which to launch an attack, and when, at about noon, it was reported that the defile was crowded with retreating Turks, all available air-craft were armed and sent in. For several hours the fugitives were bombed and machine-gunned from the air. The wrecking of vehicles repeatedly blocked the route. Despite clearing the way at least twice, in the end the victims had to escape by climbing out of the defile, losing cohesion and discipline in the process.[31]

Returning to the initial attack, the 3rd Lahore Division was in the line east of the 75th, and faced particularly difficult conditions in its attack. There was a mist covering the sight of the Turkish posts before them, made worse in terms of visibility by the initial darkness and then by the dust thrown up by the artil-lery bombardment and the smoke-shells which were included in it. In addition the division had an awkward manoeuvre to accomplish right at the start. It was the rightmost of the four divisions in the coastal plain, and there was a lightly patrolled area to its right, separating its main strength from that of the 54th Division. This gap of four or five miles was deliberately left so that the 3rd Divi-sion could turn to the right as soon as it began its attack, for it was to form the southern end of the new line facing eastward towards the hills. It was to link up with the 54th on its right and the 7th on its left, the 75th being pulled out

---

29 AWM E 41/4, War Diary, 5th Brigade, 19 September 1918.
30 Ibid.
31 Jones, *War in the Air*, pp. 218–19; Falls, *Official History* Vol. II, pp. 487–8; Cutlack, *Australian Flying Corps*, pp. 153–4.

into reserve at et-Tire. The overall line to be held by the four divisions when facing east at the end of the day was thus longer but more thinly held than at the start. This manoeuvre is often likened to a door swinging open, but the 3rd Division was to be part of the 'door' and the 'hinge' as well – the hinge was in fact an almost empty space. And, of course, it was nothing like as innocuous as opening a door.

Four of the division's eight battalions were in the initial assault and the others soon became involved. On the left the 1st Gurkhas and the 27th Punjabis of 7th Brigade were to be followed by the 1st Connaught Rangers. On the right 9th Brigade put the 7th Gurkhas and 124th Baluchis in the front. The turn to the east would mean that the front of advance would widen out, so the following battalions would move into the gaps. The turn would also separate the 1st Gurkhas on the left of the division from the rightmost units of the 75th Division, who had a much shorter line, but had a much tougher target at et-Tire. Gaps would naturally open up between the divisions and between the individual battalions. To the east of the 7th Gurkhas, the 8th Brigade held a lengthy section of the line and was in reserve at first, but with the widening of the division's front it was soon called into action. Indeed a company of the Manchester Regiment was involved from the start.

The first target was the Turkish first line, which included the fortified village of Sabieh and an associated trench system. Beyond were two other villages, Kalkilieh to the north and Jiljulieh to the south; the latter was protected by a strongly fortified ridge called the Railway Redoubt, a hill position about 1000 yards long. Seizing these places quickly would sever the main Turkish communications between their forces to the south and Tulkarm.

The first move was apparently made by 4 Company of the Manchesters, which moved forward towards a Turkish picquet post at about 2.30 a.m., and seized it five minutes after zero-hour, at the cost of firing two rifle shots. The company then moved forward, so that when the Turks replied by shelling the picquet position they were safe.[32] The 1st Gurkhas and the 2nd Dorsets were able to capture Sabieh on the left of the Division's line with ease, but the Gurkhas soon faced more determined opposition. The 93rd Burma Infantry came up to assist, though they were technically part of 9th Brigade, as did some of the 27th Punjabis.[33]

[32] Wylly, *Manchester*, p. 197.
[33] Petre, *1st Gurkha Rifles*, p. 177.

The 9th Brigade attack did not have full artillery support, so the 124th Baluchis made do with a bayonet charge at the Turks' first line.[34] The 7th Gurkhas groped their way through mist and smoke and dust, and found that the Turkish wire had not been cut, 'but, like all Turkish wire, it was poor and no real obstacle, and we went through it all as through butter and soon had taken the last of the redoubts.'[35]

The bad visibility contributed to much confusion, with units mixed together and some left isolated.

It was very confused. A number of platoons were missing. On the other hand we had collected men from several other units, some even from the Brigade on our left. While we were trying to straighten things out the Turks opened on us with machine-guns from a village some distance away and there was nothing for it but to go on and clear them out.

We appeared to be quite alone – no one either to our right or left. Our heavies were dropping shells at about one per minute into the copses ahead and to advance was hazardous, but there was no means of stopping them. Our artillery observation party was missing, the brigade signallers were also missing and there was no telephone line to Brigade. We had sent back situation reports by carrier pigeon, but there was no way of telling whether they had got through. We received no orders.[36]

The Turkish artillery was more active in this part of the attack than elsewhere.

The morning was dull and cloudy which, with the addition of the dust and smoke of the bombardment, made it very easy to lose direction, and very difficult for officers to control beyond a very short distance. The Turkish barrage had begun soon after the British, but did surprisingly little harm. This was perhaps due to the Turks using H.E. [high explosive] shells instead of shrapnel. Nevertheless one section of the 1st Gurkhas was hit and lost every man but one. This one unwounded man picked up the Lewis gun belonging to the section and carried it, as well as three hundred and seventy-six rounds of ammunition till he joined another section.

---

34 Chaldecott, *1st Battalion*, p. 70.
35 Mackay, *Gurkha Rifles*, p. 76.
36 Ibid., p. 77.

The 1st Gurkhas, as was to be expected, had an exposed left flank, having separated from the 75th Division, but a timely charge by 'D' Company and the Headquarters party broke up Turkish preparations to intervene. The bad visibility also left Turks in the rear, overrun by the advance. The 1st Gurkhas 'met a good deal of resistance from Turks overrun by the Dorsets. In one instance a Gurkha, seeing his platoon held up by a machine-gun, worked round on his own initiative till he was behind the gun, jumped into the trench, killed two men with his "kukri" and took the rest prisoner'. Later 'they captured six field guns, four 5.9 inch, and one 4.1 inch. They had passed the guns without noting them in the smoke and dust'.[37]

By 7 a.m. these Gurkhas, despite confusion and distractions, had almost reached their main objective, the village of Kalkilieh. They were well clear of the earlier fighting, and the defence that the Turks put up was tougher. There were machine-gun posts to be tackled and flanks to guard. 'They took the post and killed many Turks with their kukris, besides taking twenty and exterminating with Lewis-gun fire those who attempted to escape', in the bloodthirsty words of the regiment's historian. Progress now slowed, and the 1st Gurkhas became a flank guard while the 93rd Burma Infantry pushed on. Finally the Turks realized that the 75th Division's units were approaching from the left, and retired to avoid themselves being taken in flank. This late resistance underlines just how necessary the early surprise attack had been. 'In trying to work round the flank of these machine guns the 1st Gurkhas lost more heavily than they had done during the rest of the day.' The Gurkhas were actually short of the final objective they had been set, the village of Jiyus.[38]

To their right the 124th Baluchis had tackled the Railway Redoubt. They were in position soon after 9 a.m., but the artillery bombardment had been timed for 10.10 a.m. and they had to wait. 'The battalion was ready for the attack by 9.15a.m., and every endeavour was made to get into communication with the supporting artillery, without success. The battalion's and the forward observation officer's wires had both been cut by the enemy's artillery fire, and they were repaired too late to make any alteration in the programme worth while.' In the event, after a five minute barrage, 'The Railway Redoubt was captured without difficulty, together with eleven unwounded prisoners, four mules, a camel pack gun, two machine-guns and quantities of ammunition. The remainder of the garrison of the redoubt made good their escape to

---

37 Petre, *1st Gurkha Rifles*, p. 177.
38 Ibid., p. 178.

the hills'. The 'remainder' must mean, given the few prisoners taken, the vast majority of the garrison. However, these escapees ran across the front of the 7th Gurkhas and the 27th Punjabis: 'the Turks came streaming away from the Railway Redoubt and gave both the Punjabis and our men some very pretty shooting.'[39]

The Manchesters of 8th Brigade pushed forward about this time, the advanced company being joined by the rest of the battalion. They had helped at the Railway Redoubt with Lewis guns, and half an hour later captured Jilju-lieh.[40] They and the 7th Gurkhas moved on to a feature called the Hableh ridge, and were joined by the 47th Sikhs, who had passed through the Gurkhas. The Gurkhas were then halted by orders from brigade headquarters, but the Sikhs and the Manchesters went on into the dark hours. The 1st Gurkhas had not reached Jiyus, but the place was taken by the 105th Mahratta Light Infantry coming up through the Gurkhas with some of the 93rd Burmans, about night-fall.[41]

The sheer professionalism of these soldiers is evident. They were scattered, out of touch with their higher command, all mixed together, and yet they went on, combining with other units when necessary, and assisting where they could. The spectacular feats of individual Gurkhas was well matched by these informal combinations. In fog and smoke and confusion, the division's objectives were all achieved.

Between the fog-shrouded 3rd Division and 10th Division of XX Corps in the hills were the three brigades of 54th East Anglian Division and the French *Detachement Francais de Palestine et Syrie*; the latter was attached to 54th Division, in effect forming a fourth brigade. Between them these brigades faced a front as long as the four divisions to their left put together – the 54th also patrolled the lightly held section between it and 3rd Division. Their role in the attack on 19 September was not so much to seize territory as to hold the attention of the troops facing them, and in the case of the leftmost brigade, to gain contact with the 3rd Division, and so continue the new line to the north which was to be established by the end of the day.

Two of the division's brigades, and the French *Detachement*, were to take part in the attack, 161st Brigade on the left and 163rd Brigade on the right; the French were still further to the right. The territory to be assaulted was

[39] Chaldecott, *1st Battalion*, pp. 70–1; Mackay, *7th Gurkhas*, p. 77.
[40] Wylly, *Manchester*, p. 197.
[41] Ibid., pp. 198–9; Mackay, *7th Gurkhas*, p. 77.

very similar to that attacked by the 53rd Division to the east the night before: a 'series of rocky conical bumps – they could hardly be called hills – which fringed the foothills'. But this was the viewpoint of an artillery major whose unit had only recently arrived at the line.[42] To the infantry who had been there much longer, 'there was not the danger of losing direction that there was at the last Gaza battle over the sand. The hills were all known and their outlines familiar to most of us'.[43]

The 161st Brigade had the four Essex battalions plus the Hertfordshire R.F.A. battery in support. Accounts survive of the actions of both of these and show how the two worked together. The battery fired its guns as part of the bombardment beginning at 4.30 a.m., while the infantry had already moved forward to within a mile and a half of the Turkish line – though here it was a series of hills and fortified villages. It was there that the 5th Essex lay down on the reverse slope of a ridge rather than take up the position on the forward slope which had been designated for them by the engineers. In front was the Bureid Ridge which had been found a few days earlier to be unexpectedly well manned, though as a result of the bombardment '[t]he enemy's outpost had retired after firing a few shots, and white Verey lights began to go up, also green ones in pairs; the latter were signal lights to their artillery, who must have had a busy time responding to the many frantic calls for support'.

Beyond the ridge the centre of the Turkish line was anchored in the small village of Umm el-Bureid. Here again the guns had so softened up the resistance that as soon as the 5th Essex deployed in preparation to attack, the Turks left. 'The enemy ... did not wait for the bayonet and was evidently thinking about the best way back. There was no wire'. The infantry moved forward again, across the Wadi Rabah (the fourth of these steep valleys they had crossed since starting) and then stopped to sort themselves out.

'Rather more resistance was met with on Hill 479 and the spur to the left of it. The sangars contained machine guns and were protected by barbed wire. The Lewis guns did good work, pushing well forward, using the rocks for cover and bringing oblique fire on the sangars'. Up to this point, the fighting by the infantry had in fact been largely carried out by machine gunners. 'The mobility of the Lewis guns proved of great value. On three occasions enemy machine guns were silenced by Lewis guns acting alone, two of them were captured and the whole of the teams taken or killed by the bayonet men. Hardly a rifle had

---

[42] Sainsbury, *Hertfordshire Battery*, p. 85.
[43] Gibbons, *1/5th Essex*, pp. 141–2.

been fired; it was unnecessary, as the advance had never been checked. The capture of 'Sangar Hill' as the artillerymen called it – the infantry's 'Hill 479' – now brought a change. The infantry faced the more difficult hills of Jevis Tepe and Sivri Tepe, and the village of Kfar Qasim. The programme of timed artillery fire had now ended and the Hertfordshire 'batteries were moving forward. The ground across which they had to advance was in large part visible from the very enemy positions which the supported battalions were attacking, and the batteries were shelled as they crossed the Wadi Raba and from then on were subject to both shelling and machine-gun fire'.

The Turks were now resisting with some determination and effect. Their artillery was very active, though not too accurate; their machine gunners were 'giving great trouble … from Jevis Tepe and Sivri Tepe'. Major Stanley of the Herts Battery and his staff

scrambled up the steep side of the wadi and found a place from which a fair view could be obtained. From here we opened fire on the two Tepes, and, thanks to the close range, were able to hit very hard. Several heavy batteries were also turned on them, so that half an hour later … opposition was broken and we could confine our attention to assisting the departure of the Turk, pursued by the triumphant men of Essex … who … got in immediately after the barrage lifted, shewing that again the enemy had not waited for the assault.

The 5th Essex now halted, the 7th Essex came through to take the final objectives, but were unable to capture Sivri Wood (also Crown Hill), where the Turks had a strong defensive position. Their colonel asked for help from the 5th but he was only offered a single company and this was not enough. He appealed to division headquarters, and the 5th Essex was told to put forth its full strength; battalions from the 162nd Brigade were diverted to assist as well. Silvri Wood was thus about to be assaulted by two battalions from the east, and two more from the south, and the prospect persuaded the defenders to leave. The 5th Bedfords from 162nd Brigade managed to capture plenty of prisoners; the two attacks, coming from different directions, fortunately did not collide, though they did cross each other. Together, the 5th and 7th Essex went on to attack Sivri Tepe.

I had had a good view of the bombardment of the hill. Several times the enemy had been shelled out and as many times had returned to his defences. But he had not yet been threatened by bayonets, and I had little fear of the result. The artillery had a good view of the hill from the left and would be able to see our men swarming up it. This enabled them to give covering fire up to the last moment, and soon 'D' Company were cheering on the crest of that formidable hill, which had frowned down on us for so many months.... We enjoyed a picnic on Sivri Tepe, tired but happy.[44]

We do not have this sort of detail and description for other parts of the attack by 54th Division, but it does seem to have been the most important of all the work of the division. The arrival of the 5th Bedfords had been due to the advance of the 162nd Brigade, formerly in reserve, which had come forward at 8 a.m. to take over as leaders of the advance. Having assisted at Sivri Wood, its three battalions – the 5th Northamptons and the 8th Hampshires as well as the Bedfords – advanced with little opposition, other than small awkward parties of the enemy, as far as Azzur and Khirbet es-Sarae, which were reached at last early on the morning of 20 September.

To the right again, the 163rd Brigade advanced with the barrage until it became clear that the battles of the Essex men around Kfar Qasim and the Sivri Wood were in danger of leaving the brigade with an exposed flank at a time when Turkish resistance was clearly hardening. To their right, the attacks of the French *Detachement* had to be co-ordinated with those of 163rd and 162nd Brigades. The French attacked a set of hills, sending the *Legion d'Orient* (two Armenian battalions and a company of Syrians) against a section of high ground west of Rafat, while two battalions of Algerian *Tirailleurs* attacked two hills to the west, called Scurry and Three Bushes Hills.

The *Legion* was the first to succeed, then the *Tirailleurs* captured Three Bushes Hill after a fierce struggle, and went on to seize Scurry Hill by about 5.45 a.m. From there a company of the *Tirailleurs* spotted a Turkish force about a company strong about to attack the 5th Suffolks of 163rd Brigade in flank as they advanced. The *Tirailleurs* instead took the Turks themselves in flank, firing from their hilltop position, so allowing the undamaged Suffolks to move on. (The French *Detachement* guarded a front of more than three miles with only four battalions, so its objectives were necessarily limited.)

So the 163rd Brigade was guarded on its right by the French, but had to wait until the Essex battalions, assisted by the Bedfords, captured Sivri Wood on

44 Ibid., pp. 142–4; Sainsbury, *Hertfordshire Battery*, p. 85.

their left before they could advance further. This had been designated as the southern end of the new infantry line, which stretched northwards – and so, presumably, the actual 'hinge'. But the brigade, freed by the capture of Sivri Wood, went on to gain control of Khirbet Sirisia and then Mesha, with little fighting on a large scale. However, like 162nd Brigade, which came up to fill the gap on their left, the battalions were delayed by the resistance of small nimble enemy parties.[45]

More than one account of the events of 19 September from the infantry units comments that this was the end of their work in Palestine. This was so only in that it was the end of fighting Turks and Germans. What was perhaps the bigger surprise was that the major fighting, at least by the infantry, was completed in a single day. It was thus rather traditional, like an old pre-machine-age battle. The exhaustion of the men who had fought indeed explains why these old-time battles were over relatively quickly. The infantry had succeeded in effectively destroying the major part of the Turkish forces, but there were still substantial groups left who had no intention of giving up. These were the targets of the airmen and the cavalry.

---

[45] Falls, *Official History* Vol. II, pp. 473–4.

CHAPTER 10

The Cavalry Battle

THE infantry could crush the Turkish forces immediately before them, and did so on 19 September, but only the cavalry could properly exploit that victory by rampaging through the Turkish rear areas, capturing and scattering unsuspecting Turkish units, and destroying any immediate prospect of the revival of resistance. The 4th and 5th Cavalry Divisions had got through the old Turkish defences very early on the 19th, and once past the Nahr Iskenderun, there was little in the form of resistance to their 'great ride'.

From the crossing of the Nahr Iskenderun they intended to swing right into the Plain of Esdraelon to sever the road and rail communications that the Turks relied on. The ultimate target for both the 5th and 4th Divisions, was el-Afule, the main railway junction of the Turkish railway system. This was a manoeuvre fraught with danger, since the precise Turkish intentions and strength in the region were unknown. Some possibilities could be anticipated. Thus the 5th Division was to detach some troops to meet any attack which might come out of Haifa, which was to be left on its flank. It was also to leave a force at the Abu Shushe Pass, since if the Turks recovered control after the division went through it would be in serious danger. A third detachment was to be sent against Nazareth, north of el-Afule, where the headquarters of the whole Turkish force was located, 'with a view to capturing influential persons and important documents' – the prisoner everyone wanted was Liman von Sanders, of course.[1]

The 4th Division was to advance in parallel with the 5th but inland of it. It was to reach el-Afule by the Musmus Defile across the Carmel ridge and not to leave any substantial detachments anywhere – and it was explicitly forbidden to pay any attention to the Turks in and about Tulkarm, where the plan was that the infantry of the XXI Corps and the 5th Australian Light Horse Brigade would keep them busy. It must have gone against the military grain to obey that instruction. From el-Afule the horsemen were to head further

---

[1] Falls, *Official History* Vol. II, Appendix 26. DMC Operation Order, 12 September 1918.

east towards Beisan, but also to send a detachment to seize the bridge at Jisr el-Mejami, the crossing of the Jordan south of the Sea of Galilee, which should block any serious Turkish reinforcements arriving from IV Army.

The Australian Mounted Division was the Desert Mounted Corps reserve. It was to follow the other two divisions as far as the Nahr Iskenderun. This division was the weakest of the three, since its 5th Brigade had been detached to ride with the 60th Division and then cut the railway east of Tulkarm. The only latitude the division had was that a brigade might be sent further on, but not without permission from the corps.

The overall aim was to sever Turkish communications to ensure the capture and destruction of the Turkish armies west of the Jordan, the VII and VIII Armies. Occupation of territory was not the object, but gaining control of node-points such as el-Afule and Beisan and the Jordan bridge was central; this would enable the routes to be controlled as well. (Nazareth was not in itself an important point; it was added at the express wish of General Chauvel, who had captured a general at Gaza and wanted to bag another – Liman would do very well.)[2]

The targets of the cavalry were a long distance from their starting places, a ride of sixty miles at least, and the timing they were set was tight. The geography of the country ahead of them imposed severe limitations. From the Nahr Iskenderun, itself only reached after a ride of over fifteen miles, the horsemen swung round to the north-east, heading for el-Afule and its neighbourhood. There were two passes which had to be seized before the enemy did so, the Musmus Defile, which was on the route designated to the 4th Division, and the Abu Shushe route for 5th Division north of the Musmus Defile, and which meant that the men and horses of the 5th had farther to travel. Not only that, no one knew the routes, there were no maps other than rudimentary ones covering the whole of Palestine, and the routes were no more than rough tracks which had to be negotiated in darkness. Officers had been given a lecture on the geography of the area in the training period but it clearly did not include anything specific on these routes.

Hence the earlier start of the 5th Division, and hence the unusual speed with which the leaders set off. This was Hodson's Horse, a lancer regiment in 13th Brigade, which was given the order to ride at 7 a.m. They rode along the beach, which was bounded on one side by the sea and on the other by a low cliff which provided protection from any firing still going on inland. Hodson's

[2] Hill, *Chauvel of the Light Horse*, p. 162.

Horse rode rather faster than General Macandrew thought was sensible; he set off after them to restrain the leaders, but was unable to catch up. The going was bad: 'For two hours the going along the sand of the shore was very heavy and when the Nahr el-Falik was reached at 8 a.m. the long trot had taken a good deal out of the horses.'[3]

Only after crossing the stream did they meet any opposition, and only then from small groups:

> Fire was opened on [the leading squadron] by some Turkish cavalry dismounted. Two machine-guns returned the fire while Major Vigors moved round amid the sand dunes to turn the position; at the same time the Commanding Officer ordered C Squadron (Captain Stevens) to attack direct in column of troops widely extended and at increased distances. The enemy did not await the attack but made off in haste pursued for some distance by C Squadron. Major Vigors now received a warning message dropped from an aeroplane that about 200 Turkish troops with two guns and some transport were in an orchard and farm some 400 yards to the right front. The advanced troops under Risaldar Nur Ahmad had already come under the fire of this party. Major Vigors at once brought up the remainder of the squadron and without any delay delivered a mounted attack with complete success, capturing three officers, fifty or sixty men, two guns and twelve wagons with teams.[4]

From 4 a.m. two Royal Navy torpedo-boat destroyers, *Forester* and *Druid*, had bombarded Turkish positions in the area of the Nahr el-Falik. At 5 a.m. *Druid* sent its whaler on shore for information and got in contact with XXI Corps headquarters. As a result the two ships then moved north, bombarding the coastal area, presumably wherever they saw a likely target; they remained off the coast for another day 'bombarding [the] coast between Caesarea and Cape Carmel'. None of the horsemen seem to have noticed any of this, but they were moving away from the coast by then.[5]

This was the pattern throughout 19 September. The instructions to the cavalry to avoid combat were clear, but the Turks had not received the same message. They were retreating, but clearly going fairly slowly. They were always

3   Cardew, *Hodson's Horse* p. 199; Falls, *Official History* Vol. II p. 523, note.
4   Cardew, *Hodsons' Horse* pp. 200–1.
5   TNA ADM 53/40220, 41999, logs of *Druid* and *Forester*.

surprised to be attacked by British cavalry so far to the north of the original front line. The fighting was in fact done by only one of the squadrons of Hodson's Horse as far as the Nahr Iskenderun, then 'B' Squadron took up the lead. Once across the Nahr el-Falik, the going was better: 'after turning into the plain the country was mostly turf and the cavalry simply cantered on, taking in their stride every obstacle that the retreating Turks tried to set up and sending huge batches of prisoners back with the smallest of escorts.'[6]

At Liktera (also called Hadera) on the Nahr el-Mafjir, another five miles on, the division halted, partly to let the rear elements close up, but mainly to rest and feed the horses. There was a German depot in the area: 'a patrol of 'A' squadron [of the 24th Poona Horse] captured five motor lorries with their German drivers in a wood a mile and a half south-west of Hudeira.'[7]

> This transport and supply depot was chiefly manned by Germans. It was taken completely by surprise, and hardly a shot fired. Sergt. Gastle did some good work here in rounding up several motor lorries, which were escaping, filled with German mechanics. All of these men seemed astonished at our appearance, and surrendered without protest. 2nd Lieut. R.U. White and a troop were detached just before entering the supply depot to make a further search of the village, and succeeded in making an important capture of a complete training establishment, including the Commandant, several officers, and about 400 men, including many Germans.

The division now rested until the evening.[8] The pace had been very wearying for the horses; the Gloucestershire Yeomanry lost twenty-two and the 18th Lancers, fifteen;[9] at this rate well over a hundred will have been lost in the division in this march.

The 4th Division did not start off until 9 a.m., when Major-General Barrow, who had stationed himself at the headquarters of the 7th Division, was told the way was clear. He had already authorized one of his brigades to move forward, and pioneers had already been busy filling in shell holes and any remaining obstacles even earlier. Barrow rode back from Tabsor, where 7th Division

---

[6] Fox, *Gloucestershire Hussars*, p. 262.
[7] Wylly, *Poona Horse*, p. 152.
[8] Fox, *Gloucestershire Hussars*, pp. 262–3.
[9] Ibid., p. 262; Falls, *Official History* Vol. II, p. 523, note.

headquarters had advanced, and ordered his first brigade, the 11th, forward. Barrow was anxious to move, based on the very good grounds that the cavalry might have only a brief opportunity of getting through the Turks' lines, on the reasonable assumption that any gap would be quickly blocked.[10]

But the Turks did not recover. One reason was the destruction of their communications and the distraction of the headquarters by the air raids. Their defence lines were cut right through by the infantry, so the horsemen were able to move into the rear areas quickly, and there was little organized opposition. This had, of course, already happened on the coast, and when the 4th Division started, the 5th was already across the Nahr el-Falik and dealing with the isolated, retreating and surprised small Turkish groups.

Much the same conditions were met by the 4th Division:

> in line of troop column we rode off through gaps in the wire and quickly passed over the Turkish trenches. The signs of battle were fewer than would be supposed. Here and there the loose huddled body of a dead Turk, or one badly wounded calling for 'moyah', a few forsaken machine-guns, an occasional field piece, several dead donkeys and pack-ponies.

The leading regiment, Jacob's Horse, 'came under fire from the right flank but … galloped the position in style and captured two hundred and fifty prisoners. Our regiment [the Middlesex Yeomanry] encountered no opposition and we rode rapidly on to reach Kakun, a position well behind the Turkish lines, by nightfall.'[11] The division had crossed the marshes by the Zerqiyeh causeway, one of 7th Division's main objectives, and had then advanced on a three-brigade front, heading north more or less parallel to the Turkish railway.

The long halt by 5th Division at Liktera allowed the gap between it and the 4th Division to be narrowed. General Barrow seems to have been much more concerned to speed up his advance than Macandrew, but both divisions would be going through the passes in the dark. At Liktera the commander of 13th Brigade, Brigadier-General P.J.V. Kelly, an Arabist, questioned locals about the pass, and finally secured two men as guides, at £5.00 each.[12] At 6.15 p.m. the 5th Division, led by Kelly's brigade, resumed its march. At Kerkur, where the

[10] Barrow, *Fire of Life*, p. 195.
[11] Hatton, *Yarn of a Yeoman*, p. 249.
[12] Anglesey, *British Cavalry*, p. 269, quoting Osborne, 'Operations of the Mounted Troops', *Cavalry Journal* XIII, 27.

4th Division gathered between 8.30 and 10.00 p.m., there was a delay when horses were watered; Barrow ordered the advance to be resumed, but his '10.00 p.m.' start had become 11.30 p.m. at the head of the column;[13] this delay widened the gap between the divisions once more, but both were crossing the ridge into the Vale of Esdraelon during the night, and well before the Turkish command realized where they were.

The Australian Mounted Division had a long approach march before reaching the front line, and so it had travelled 28 miles that day by the time it bivouacked at the Nahr Iskenderun in the evening of 19 September. The division had already detached the two regiments of its 5th Brigade, and now another regiment was detached as escort for the corps headquarters which had come up to the Nahr Iskenderun; then the 11th Regiment was detailed to escort the divisional transport. Finally the last regiment in the 11th Brigade was ordered to find and escort 5th Division's transport park, which had become detached – such were the tasks of the reserve. When the division moved on to tackle the Musmus Defile in rear of Barrow's 4th Division, Major-General Hodgson commanded only a single brigade. It began to move forward at 1 a.m.

There was a good deal of surprise and some relief on the British side that 'everything', as they frequently said, 'had gone to plan'. Of course it had not, but enough had gone right that those who didn't actually know could claim so. One presumption was that the deception activity had succeeded in pointing enemy attention away from that part of the front which was attacked. In fact the Turks did not react to the deception by moving any of their troops, and certainly none into the Jordan Valley, which was supposed to be hinted at as the intended attacking point. Liman von Sanders says nothing in his memoirs to support the idea that he was surprised. The only surprise would be the date, and perhaps the weight, of the attack. His doctrine of defence was to instruct the troops in the line to fight where they were, and to not give up. There was to be no retreat, no manoeuvre. In part this derived from his own experience, above all at Gallipoli, but it was also a response to the condition of the Turkish army troops in Palestine, who were low in morale, sick, unfed, and with mangy and weak transport animals. He clearly understood that his army was not fit or mobile enough to sustain a campaign of manoeuvre, which would have to be, given the disparity in strengths between the rival armies, a fight-

---

[13] Barrow, *Fire of Life*, p. 197.

ing retreat. Standing fast and fighting until death, was really the only Turkish option available.[14]

The threat of an attack in the coastal plain was so obvious that General Jevat Pasha, commander of the VIII Army, which would be the object of the British attack, had suggested a few days earlier that he should move his forces back, so unbalancing the attackers.[15] Liman refused, but he did reinforce Jevat's army with the 46th Division. Turkish army intelligence was fully aware of the strength of the British forces facing VIII Army. At Nazareth the British found a map which purported to show what was believed at Liman's headquarters about British dispositions, and it was gleefully reproduced to show that the British deception measures had been successful. But Turkish records indicate that VIII Army knew full well that it faced five British infantry divisions, and VII Army in the hills knew that it faced two.[16] Where Turkish intelligence was seriously mistaken was over the location of the cavalry, believing that two divisions were in the Jordan Valley. This was a vital misapprehension since the cavalry would be the decisive branch in any exploitation. It seems best to accept this as evidence of what Liman knew, and hence Jevat as well; the map from Nazareth will have to be discarded as evidence – unless it is simply wrongly dated.

Liman's communications with his subordinate armies were, of course, partly disrupted, but he would hardly have been able to do very much to affect the situation even if he could talk to his generals. Virtually all of the Turkish armed strength was in the line, and once that was broken there was little or nothing to fight back with. Falls's British *Official History* Vol. II claims that Liman was 'completely in the dark', but then explains that 'communications with Tul Karm ceased at 7 a.m.', which was two and a half hours after the attack began.[17] He must have learned a good deal before then. Soon after that time Colonel von Oppen, in command of the Asien Korps east of VIII Army, began sending some of his forces westwards to help out. Their presence before Qalqilye and north of Azzur effectively blocked a British advance by 54th Division and the French *Detachement* for some time. Oppen was fully aware by 9 a.m. that the coastal defences had been destroyed, and he began preparing for the expected

---

[14]   Liman von Sanders, *Five Years*, p. 273.

[15]   Erickson, *Ottoman Army Effectiveness*, p. 143.

[16]   The German map is reproduced in *Advance*, plate 40; for the contradiction cf. Erickson, *Ottoman Army Effectiveness*, pp. 144–6, which is largely based on the Turkish Official History written in the 1970s.

[17]   Falls, *Official History* Vol. II, p. 495.

attack into the hills. He reacted in fact as Jevat Pasha had suggested to Liman, and withdrew his forces to a better line. They had skilfully avoided destruction, as the relative lack of prisoners in that sector showed. As Oppen's forces withdrew, the VII Army, commanded by Mustapha Kemal (the later reviver of Turkish pride, the dictator Kemal Ataturk), retreated to the east. This was partly in order to maintain the line, but also because of the pressure they were under.

Liman's real area of ignorance was in the actions of the British cavalry. His contact with VIII Army at Tulkarm ceased and VIII Army's contact with et-Tire was also lost. Jevat Pasha was cut off by the afternoon by the actions of 60th Division advancing from the west and the 5th Australian Brigade cutting the railway to the east. By the time darkness fell Jevat had moved his headquarters to avoid capture, and this inevitably disrupted any further contacts he still had with his troops.[18]

By that time the 5th Cavalry Division had been resting at Liktera/Hadera for several hours; the 4th Cavalry Division was soon at Kerkur, north of Tulkarm; the Australian Mounted Division was camped at the Nahr Iskenderun. All three British cavalry divisions were therefore north of Jevat's headquarters before he left Tulkarm, and he apparently knew nothing of it. But Liman was aware of the destruction of the coastal forces. Attempts were made to shore up the position by moving some of Oppen's and Mustapha Kemal's forces westwards. Liman also took special measures to hold the choke-points where British forces might break through into the Plain of Esdraelon. He sent a regiment from Kemal's division to hold the defile at Anebta through which the railway from Tulkarm to Nablus passed – his loss of communications with Tulkarm clearly warned him that such a move was likely. This would block any advance on Nablus, a command centre and airfield. He also ordered that the Musmus Defile be blocked at el-Lejjun by the 13th Depot Regiment from Nazareth, and any other troops which could be found.[19] He does not seem to have considered the Abu Shushe Pass, no doubt assuming it was too distant for the British to use. It is clear from these measures, however, that, even if he did not know where the British cavalry was, he understood the menace it presented.

Liman ordered the move to el-Lejjun soon after noon on 19 September. General Barrow had ordered that the 4th Cavalry Division should begin its

[18] Erickson, *Ottoman Army Effectiveness*, pp. 148–9, based on Turkish army war diaries inaccessible or unknown to Falls when writing the British *Official History*.

[19] Liman von Sanders, *Five Years*, pp. 278–9.

march towards the Musmus Defile soon after 11 p.m. The 2nd Lancers formed the advanced guard and set off to seize the crossroads at Khirbet Arah, at the western end of the pass, at about 10.45 p.m. The advanced guard moved a troop at a time, about 100 yards apart. Then the main body followed in column for it was found that movement off the road was impossible. They crossed the railway line at Tel el Asawir, and caught up with a column of retreating Turkish transport and stragglers which surrendered without fighting. The prisoners were sent to the rear with small escorts. Khirbet Arah was reached by 11.30 p.m., and it was learned that another Turkish column had recently passed through.[20]

General Barrow decided to change the Lancers' orders and drove up in person, giving orders that they should push on to seize the exit from the pass. He ordered two armoured cars of the 11th L.A.M. Battery to go ahead of the Lancers to ensure that the narrowest part of the defile at Umm el-Fahm was clear.[21] They all set off again at 11.45. Meanwhile Barrow looked for the remainder of his division, which had missed the route. Two of his brigades had headed off northwards before he found what had happened. He put the 12th Brigade, originally the third in the line, on the right route, then got the others turned round to follow, but there was considerable delay.[22]

The War Diary of the 4th Division records, as the first entry for 20 September, that 'A report was also received at this hour (0100) that an enemy party, strength unknown, was advancing on the Lejjun from el-Afule at dawn'. This, of course, was the force ordered off by Liman at noon, thirteen hours before. Barrow's source for this 'report' is not stated, but it is most likely to be from prisoners. Turks were being captured all the time by the advanced parties, including the men in the armoured cars. It is curious that the report was already current, while the troops themselves had still not occupied the pass. Barrow's reaction was to order the 12th Brigade 'to push on as rapidly as possible through the pass and gain the heights at el-Lejjun commanding the entrance of the past before dawn'.[23]

This was done. The 2nd Lancers got through the pass and reached el-Lejjun at 3 a.m., and captured a hundred or so Turks who were 'sitting round a fire with their arms piled', at the exit of the pass. This party was probably the

[20] Whitworth, *2nd Lancers*, p. 135.

[21] Ibid., 236.

[22] Barrow, *Fire of Life*, p. 196.

[23] TNA WO 95/4510, War Diary of 4 Cav. Div., 20 September 1918.

advanced guard of Liman's force sent to hold the pass, the main body of which was encountered later in the morning.'[24] It had clearly been a fairly close thing. Had the 13th Depot Regiment moved more quickly, it is unlikely that the Lancers would have been able to gain control of the exit. 'A couple of machine-guns could have sufficed to hold us up for hours.'[25] The narrowness of the defile could have seen a long traffic jam. But the head of the 12th Brigade arrived at about 4.30 a.m. to reinforce the Lancers, and this ensured that the whole division would be able to get through. Barrow's frantic concern to hurry was thereby fully justified.

The slowness of the German 13th Depot Regiment is uncharacteristic of the German army. A day later Liman met the officer who had commanded the move but received no explanation. It looks as though there was no sense of urgency at Liman's headquarters, and that this had transmitted itself down the military hierarchy.

The 5th Division had much the same experience of the physical difficulty of its route, but found no enemy opposition. The Musmus route had actually been improved by the Turkish army, and this at least allowed the armoured cars to get through, but the Abu Shushe route used by 5th Division was in its original unimproved state, suitable for animals and men, but scarcely for motors; the divisional transport was diverted to go by the Musmus road. One brigade was left at Liktera as escort, and no doubt to help the divisional artillery get across, though this lightening and shortening of the column did not help much. The lead was now taken by the 18th Lancers, with Hodson's Horse and then the Gloucestershire Yeomanry following. The Lancers set a pace which the rest of the division could not match, just as Hodson's Horse had done on the beach earlier.

> The column turned northeastwards and at once became involved in a tangle of rocky hills. The track was so bad that for miles the men had to march on foot leading their horses, and in the uncertain light it was difficult to keep to the road or indeed to distinguish it at all. In these tiring circumstances the situation was saved by the special qualifications and aptitude of Brigadier-General Kelly, whose thorough knowledge of Arabic and experience in traversing almost trackless country enabled

[24] Whitworth, *2nd Lancers*, p. 136.
[25] Barrow, *Fire of Life*, p. 197.

him to obtain all possible information from the stray Arabs encountered during the night, and to follow their vague directions with success.[26]

As instructed in the original orders two squadrons of Hodson's Horse were left at Jara, at the crest of the pass. Falls's *Official History* II criticizes this, arguing that they should have been detailed from the last units to go through.[27] However, their purpose was partly to guide later units, and in part to act as a flank guard. The head of the column, the 18th Lancers, arrived at Abu Shushe, the east end of the pass, at about 2.30 a.m.

Behind the leaders the situation was almost as bad as that of the 4th Division in the Musmus Defile. The leading battalion, chivvied on by Kelly, moved confidently forward, but behind it the column was in single file so any delay resulted in those in the rear losing touch. The pack animals at the rear of Hodson's Horse the pack animals were being recalcitrant in the dark and on the uncomfortable ground. The column broke, and the battalion, the Gloucestershire Yeomanry, which was following behind was delayed while scouts went out in search of the right track. This was finally determined, and a lost section of Hodson's Horse was found.[28] But this sort of friction common in war delayed the rear part of the column.

All this happened in the dark, but enterprise and common sense – sending out scouts – brought the whole column into the Vale of Esdraelon by dawn. The 13th Brigade had halted at the exit, allowing the 14th to catch up. This was a notable achievement. Despite moving at night over unknown territory and without roads, the division had covered thirty miles in darkness and was ready to attack both Nazareth and el-Afule soon after dawn. And to the south, the 4th Division was also through the pass and ready to attack its targets.

The much depleted Australian Mounted Division, reduced to the 3rd Light Horse Brigade, followed the 4th Cavalry Division through the Musmus Defile at 1 a.m., and reached el-Lejjun late in the morning. 'Water was obtained from a good stream, and during the short halt all ranks enjoyed a refreshing bath and rest.' Evidence of the early success of the other cavalry divisions was that 'Portions of the road in the Pass were strewn with stores and ammunition evidently hastily abandoned by the enemy', and there was a 'steady streams of prisoners.' 'Two thousand Turks and Germans, a force who had been speedily

---

[26] Cardew, *Hodson's Horse*, p. 203.

[27] Falls, *Official History* Vol. II, p. 524.

[28] Fox, *Gloucestershire Hussars*, pp. 263–4.

despatched by the German high command in a desperate effort to seize the pass, and so doing delay our advance, were now prisoners in our hands on the very ground they had been sent to hold'.[29]

This had been the work of the other two cavalry divisions. The 5th Division had reached the Haifa-el-Afule railway soon after setting out across the vale, and engineers had blown up a section of the line. This led some to believe that the explosions had alerted the Turks to their approach, though in fact when they did encounter Turks they showed no evidence of having been aware of the bangs. The cavalrymen were close to Nazareth by dawn, having twice stumbled on villages which were at first assumed to be the town. In each case numbers of Turks were captured, and men from the 18th Lancers had to be left to guard them. As they approached Nazareth the Lancers were therefore distinctly under strength, and the Gloucestershire Yeomanry were detailed to the attack, and the 18th Lancers were sent south to block the road from el-Afule.

The Gloucesters charged up the main street, looking to capture Liman von Sanders, or at least his staff. He did in fact manage to get out of the town by car, reportedly still in his pyjamas – though most German accounts insisted he had left the previous day (the pyjamas being a picturesque, possibly Australian, invention). His staff had burnt many of their most important papers earlier. Altogether it is clear that he was not so surprised as the British have always supposed. The Gloucestershire Yeomanry had the advantage of making a surprise attack at dawn, and managed to take a large number of prisoners, but it was not long before resistance developed, particularly once the Germans and Turks appreciated just how few attackers there were. The Gloucesters were soon defending rather than attacking, and the fighting was in the streets and in the houses, not the best environment for cavalry.[30]

Air reconnaissance early on 20 September showed that the British cavalry were through the hills and into the Plain of Esdraelon, but it also showed that large numbers of Turks were retreating towards el-Afule and Nazareth by way of Jenin.[31] This was the place whose airfield had been overflown and bombed during the previous day. Now the town itself became the target. The Handley Page of the Australian 1st Squadron bombed the railway station during the night. The morning reconnaissance located large numbers of Turks retreating along the road north from Nablus towards Jenin. These were attacked all day

[29] Darley, *9th Light Horse*, p. 148.
[30] Fox, *Gloucestershire Hussars*, pp. 264–6.
[31] TNA AIR 1/2262/209/60/9, War Diary of 1 Sqn AFC, 20 September 1918.

and no doubt this contributed both to the Turks' casualties and to the slowness of their retreat. One result was that el-Afule was captured by the British cavalry before many of the Turks could reach it. The Desert Mounted Corps headquarters knew that 5th Division was attacking the place by 8.10 a.m.[32] Similarly when the Australian cavalry reached Jenin, a good deal of damage had already been done to the stores, and the airfield had been largely put out of action – all the aircraft had been destroyed or damaged, some by the bombing, others by the German technicians.

Soon after dawn the 2nd Lancers of 4th Division had ridden out of el-Lejjun with the 11th Light Armoured Car Battery and the 17th Machine Gun Section, heading for el-Afule. Almost at once they met the 13th Depot Regiment and others, which Liman von Sanders had ordered forward the previous day to block the Musmus exit. In a classic action the armoured cars and the machine gunners pinned down the Turks while the Lancers rode wide and took them in the flank and rear. Yet again the sight of turbaned warriors riding hard at them and pointing long sharp lances at them wholly unnerved their enemies. Forty-seven of the Turks were killed, many of them speared; 400 were captured.[33]

The 2nd Lancers continued at once to attack el-Afule from the south, arriving at much the same time as the 18th Lancers of 5th Division came in from the north. The town, its railway, its station, and its airfeld were all captured intact – one aeroplane was burnt before it could be captured, but another landed soon after, its pilot unaware of the change of control; he landed right into captivity.[34]

Some of the 18th Lancers, and those of Hodson's Horse who were close enough, went into Nazareth to assist the Gloucesters. But the three together were not enough. The 14th Brigade had come up to el-Afule by this time, but Major–General Macandrew was conscious that his forces had many other tasks that day. He had received orders to 'move as quickly as possible to el-Afule and support 4th Cavalry Division towards Beisan with one brigade, and reconnoitre towards Jenin for fugitives moving north.'[35] He decided that the brigade was not in a fit state to join in an assault on what was apparently a well-defended town, nor was street fighting a suitable task for cavalry. By this time the noise of the fighting would have alerted Liman and his headquarters

[32] AWM 4, War Diary of Desert Mounted Corps, 20 September 1918; TNA WO 95/4514, War Diary of 5 Cav. Div., 20 September 1918.

[33] Whitworth, *2nd Lancers*, pp. 136–45; Anglesey, *British Cavalry*, pp. 279–85.

[34] Whitworth *2nd Lancers*, pp. 146–7; Jones, *War in the Air*, pp. 220–2.

[35] AWM 4, War Diary of Desert Mounted Corps, 20 September 1918.

staff to get away if they were still in the town. Macandrew ordered the 13th Brigade forces to withdraw to el-Afule, which they did, carefully and competently, bringing with them their prisoners.[36] The consolation was the further disruption of the Turkish command system, which had, after all, been the purpose of the raid on Nazareth. General Chauvel wanted to capture the enemy commander-in-chief, but sending him in flight was almost as good. Liman claims to have directed the defence, and went back into the town as the British cavalry withdrew, but he then left altogether, pulling out his remaining forces as well. So Nazareth fell to the British without further fighting next day, and without further casualties.[37]

El-Afule had been captured by mid-morning, and the rest of the 4th Division came up by noon. By that time the 5th Division had relinquished its feeble hold on parts of Nazareth, and the Australian Mounted Division had reached el-Lejjun. Breathers were taken, horses were watered, and the soldiers slept when they could. But many of them had to watch their prisoners, and more kept being brought in. General Barrow's orders included directions to capture Beisan, and he got the Dorset Yeomanry moving from el-Afule towards the town by 1 p.m. They were followed by a machine gun section, the Berkshire battery of the Royal Horse Artillery, the 2nd Lancers, and the ambulance train. These were under a new brigade commander, Brigadier-General W.G.K. Green, since Barrow had dismissed Brigadier-General Howard-Vyse from his command.

The Dorsets found that the ground off the road was poor.

> An ordinary advance guard, with parties flung out on either side of the road, was found to delay the pace, for the ground was cotton soil, with dry hard cracks, which compelled the horsemen to move at a walk, and so, judiciously casting drill-book precepts aside, and mindful only of the major object, these flanking parties were drawn in, and all, with the exception of the Brigade flank guards, proceeded along the one road.[38]

The 19th Lancers had been left to hold el-Afule until the 5th Division had recovered sufficiently to organize a garrison. (Brigadier-General Kelly was to be

[36] Fox, *Gloucestershire Hussars*, p. 266; Hudson, *19th Lancers*, pp. 230–3.

[37] Liman von Sanders, *Five Years*, pp. 282–5.

[38] Whitworth, *2nd Lancers*, pp.147–50; Barrow, *Fire of Life*, p. 202; Thompson, *Dorset Yeomanry*, pp. 103–5.

another brigade commander to be dismissed by Allenby some time later – he had left himself with too few troops to take Nazareth after detaching so many parties to hold villages and guard prisoners, which his orders had forbidden him to do.) The Lancers could not rest as they had to collect the disorderly retreating enemy forces heading for el-Afule from Jenin. The enemy had to be disarmed and then detained, and there were so many of them that the whole regiment was involved. 'By the evening we had about two thousand of them collected and were heartily sick of them.'[39]

The 5th Division was even more strung out than the 4th, so it was not until dark that the 19th Lancers were relieved at el-Afule and began their next exploit – the capture of the Jordan bridge at Jisr el-Mejami. The march was a series of guesses, as the roads tended to peter out, and they had to make 'a difficult and strenuous march over an almost impossible country.'[40] At one point they met 'a colossal nullah about two hundred feet deep, in and out of which we had to scramble in single file. It took the regiment two hours to cross it.' The regiment finally captured the bridges (road and rail) at about dawn, and by 8.30 a.m. the bridges had been prepared for demolition if necessary. The regiment marched about a hundred miles in two days and nights. 'The men were dog tired. Some fell asleep as they rode until they fell off; then slept where they lay until prodded up and put on their saddles.' The route was so poor and rocky the horses had to be led for much of the way.[41]

Meanwhile the Australians at el-Lejjun were alerted by aircraft to the movement of large numbers of Turks northwards across their front, heading for el-Afule and safety, or so they must have presumed. They had already been bombed and machine-gunned from the air,[42] and some of these men were being collected at the same time by the 19th Lancers in el-Afule. At 3.30 p.m. the Australian 3rd Brigade, with armoured cars and a machine gun section, was sent to block the escape route by taking Jenin. The 10th Regiment led the way. It was quickly realized that to reach the town before dark the normal speed of advance had to be increased. Once again the drill book was discarded and the 10th rode on ahead. Similarly the general instructions had to be adapted to particular circumstances. Near Kfar Adam 'a large body of enemy numbering upwards of 1,000 were observed in an olive grove adjoining the vil-

[39] Hudson, *19th Lancers*, p. 242.
[40] TNA WO 95/4510, War Diary of 4 Cav. Div., 20 September 1918.
[41] Hudson, *19th Lancers*, pp. 242–3.
[42] TNA AIR 1/2262/209/60/9, War Diary of 1 Sqn AFC, 20 September 1918.

lage. Lieut. Doig's troop, acting with great boldness and gallantry, immediately deployed, drew swords, and charged right into the Turks, wounding several and taking the whole force prisoners. Lieut. Doig methodically formed them up, and marched them to the rear.' Given that the Australians were only two regiments strong, this enemy force could not be ignored and left behind; it had to be driven off – or in this case largely captured.

A troop captured a convoy of enemy lorries on the road north out of Jenin; and the other routes from the town were cut. 'Two troops ... charged with the sword into masses of the enemy comprising Germans and Turks, who were formed up, apparently ready to move.' 'Machine-gun fire was directed on the town from the right flank, and the enemy was immediately thrown into a state of great demoralisation, after which no organised resistance was offered, though desultory sniping was continued throughout the night.' The Turkish Commandant surrendered the town, and this was the signal for the inhabitants to loot the military stores; the Australians made attempts to stop this, but without much success. Reading between the lines it seems likely their attempts were at best perfunctory. And they did have 3000 prisoners to guard. The Germans in the town had already set fire to much of the stores, and some had been set on fire by bombing raids earlier. The Australians did capture the local pay-chest and a quantity of champagne. It is clear that the Germans, and probably the Turks also, were by no means so demoralized as Colonel Olden claims. Sniping and destruction went on for some time by his own account; no doubt quite a few men escaped as well.[43]

These exploits happened so quickly that large numbers of escaping soldiers were still at large. Some of the German officers refused to believe that the cavalry had ridden so far, and assumed they had been landed by the navy at Haifa. Many of the Turks were so surprised and confused that they simply gave up when, if given time to think, they could have made a successful fight. Several stories demonstrate Turkish loss of nerve and demoralization. The twenty-three men of the machine gun section captured a column of 2800 Germans and Turks on the Nablus road;[44] at el-Afule Trooper Reeves of the Staffordshire Yeomanry, riding alone to go to hospital (he had sunstroke), met and charged an enemy group, which at once surrendered to him – eight German officers and seventy-two Turks.[45] The Middlesex Yeomanry, in 4th

[43] Olden, *Westralian Cavalry*, pp. 263–5.
[44] Gullett, *Official History of Australia*, p. 708.
[45] Kemp, *Staffordshire Yeomanry*, p. 72.

Division, had been left to hold the Musmus Defile exit, and Colonel Lawson rode out alone to examine the surroundings, but was captured by an enemy force after only a few minutes. He then explained the situation to the Turkish commander (each man using bad French) and the Turks then surrendered to him; he returned to his regiment with 800 prisoners.[46]

By the evening of 20 September, the British had occupied el-Afule, Beisan, and Jenin, and had blocked the Jordan bridge at Jisr el-Mejami. The raid into Nazareth had persuaded the enemy headquarters to remove itself. VIII Army had been destroyed and mainly captured, but there were plenty of enemy forces still at large, and much of VII Army and all of IV Army were able to fight on. Yet the cavalry had completely disrupted the Turkish rear areas, and the surviving Turkish units were confused and without either direction or information.

[46] Barrow, *Fire of Life*, p. 203.

1 *Allenby.* Allenby is shown in his field marshal's uniform as High Commissioner in Egypt in 1922. By this time it was unusual for him to be wearing a uniform.

2 *The Allenby Bridge.* The crossing of the River Jordan at el-Ghoraniyeh was taken from the Turks at the beginning of the 'Amman Raid' in March 1918. The British then constructed these bridges as a means of maintaining access to the east bank. These bridges, though intended to be temporary, remained in existence and in use until they were destroyed after the Israeli conquest of the West Bank in 1967.

3 *Prickly Pear.* Throughout the campaign in Palestine and Syria attacking forces were hampered at every village by hedges of prickly pear, deliberately established as protection against raiders and bandits. It was even more effective than barbed wire: wire could be cut and dragged aside; prickly pear had to be cut through, and was often several feet thick. This photograph is of an example at the archaeological site of Zipori in Israel. (Author's own)

The Kia Ora Coo-ee

SECOND SERIES Nº 6

CHRISTMAS NUMBER

4 *The* Kia Ora Coo-ee. This was a magazine for the New Zealand (Kia Ora) and Australian (Co-ee) troops in Palestine. The cover of the last edition, December 1918, gives a romantic view of what the Australians and New Zealanders felt they had achieved. The magazine, edited by the future author of the Official Australian history, W.F. Gullett, very largely wrote out accounts of the rest of the British imperial forces, British, Indian, and others.

5 *Dummy Horses in the Jordan Valley*. In this photograph the 'dummi-ness' of the 'horses' is perfectly obvious, even through the haze. From above they managed to fool the few German aircraft pilots who glimpsed them. Tents, 'bivvies', tracks, camps, and so on were also laid out to fool the enemy.

6 *Megiddo*. The ancient site of Megiddo is on a hill overlooking the plain to the north and commands the ancient route through the Carmel ridge. The modern road shown here lies on exactly the same route as that followed by the 4th Cavalry Division in 1918, and many armies before. The region also has a series of ancient defensive sites; a Roman legionary base lies a mile or so away. (Author's own)

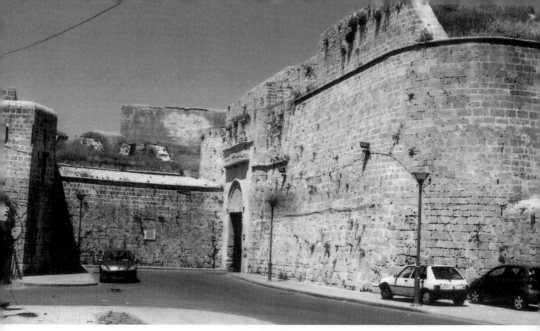

7 *Acre*. Like every other town in Palestine and Syria Acre was in 1918 surrounded by powerful fortifications. The walls were strong enough to daunt even modern artillery, and, like this gate, were cunningly designed to prevent easy assault. Yet the city fell to an Indian jemadar without resistance. (Author's own)

8 *The Jordan Valley*. A view over the valley of the Jordan from the Crusader castle of Belvoir. The valley itself is now cultivated and dotted with small lakes and ponds. In the distance through the haze can be seen the eastern scarp. At this point the drop from scarp top to the valley is about 2000 feet. It was in this part of the valley that the four fords which the British did not know about were used by the escaping Turks in September 1918. (Author's own)

9 *Sea of Galilee*. The Sea of Galilee formed a substantial barrier in front of the British forces, a barrier which extended north and south by the course of the Jordan River. Also, to either side were hills with very few routes through them. This is a view north from Tiberias, with the hills of Galilee in the distance. The only road lies along the shore. (Author's own)

10 *Golan*. When the Australian Mounted Division crossed the Jisr Benat Yaqub, it was faced with crossing the Golan area. This was dry, rocky, and virtually roadless. Liman von Sandars wanted to use this difficult country, and its Circassian inhabitants, Ottoman loyalists, to delay if not stop the British advance. (Author's own)

11 *The Yarmuk Valley*. A view looking north across the Yarmuk valley towards the Golan Heights. This was virtually the only route available from Samakh towards Deraa, the route used by the ancient road and by the modern railway. The valley sides are very steep, as can be seen by the hairpin bends of the modern road. (Author's own)

12 *Lawrence arrives in Damascus*. T.E. Lawrence is driven into Damascus in his Rolls-Royce by Stirling. Within a few days he had carried through the *coup d'état* in the city and then left for Britain. Stirling's testimony makes it clear that Lawrence used considerable force to impose his will on the city, a fact which he disguised in his memoirs. Lawrence's dress would mark him as a Bedouin sympathiser to the Damascenes, in an area where European dress was normal

13 *Aleppo: The Citadel*. Sited on a substantial rock within the city, the Citadel was the seat of the local governor. Surrounded by a moat, it was a powerful defensive position even in the days of artillery and machine guns, and, even littered with ruins, it still is. The gatehouse is here in the forefront, and a bridge crosses the moat and leads to the main building. The Arab assault in October 1918 reached about that point. (Author's own)

14 *Allenby, Faisal and Lloyd George in London*. Surely a quite inadvertent display of three men who could rarely agree. Lloyd George seems to be inspecting Lady Allenby, on the right, whose attention is on her husband and his on her. Faisal is grim, conscious of what he might consider to be British betrayal. Sometime later Allenby had to face down Lloyd George over Egypt, which he did successfully. Faisal eventually became King of Iraq, a British consolation prize.

15 *Edessa/Urfa: The Citadel*. The Citadel of Edessa is another ancient urban castle. This was one of the last French positions to be held in 1919. Its capture by the Turks signalled the decisive defeat of the French attempt to penetrate north from their later Syrian mandate into Anatolia. (Author's own)

16 *The Jebel Ansariyeh*. The mountains inland from Lattakia, the Jebel Ansariyeh, are populated by people of the Alawite sect. They objected to the French arrival and it took the French three years to suppress them, campaigning through very difficult country. This sect has formed the main backing for the Assad regime since 1970, populating the army, the semi-official militia, and the ubiquitous Syrian secret police. (Author's own)

CHAPTER 11

The East, Haifa, Samakh

T HE section of the Turkish forces primarily affected by the infantry assault
on 19 September was VIII Army, whose headquarters at Tulkarm was captured; also affected were the retreating groups and fugitives from this particular corps – they had been ravaged by the air raids at Anebta and the cavalry
raids all over the Plain of Esdraelon on the 19th and 20th. The VII Army, holding the line in the face of the 53rd and the 10th Divisions and in the Jordan
Valley west of the river, was hardly affected, except for having to retreat to
maintain a defensive position as VIII Army disappeared. The IV Army, east
of the river, was not touched at all, except by the minor attacks by the Arabs.

The capture of el-Afule, Jenin and Beisan, however, did affect VII Army,
for these were at the rear, and all were on its retirement routes. The shift of
some VII Army forces westwards had helped shore up the western flank, and
had blocked the British advance into the hills by XXI Corps, but this only
extended VII Army's area, thinned out its line, and left it in even greater danger. Mustapha Kemal, its commander, was fully aware of the danger it faced.
It had largely held its defensive line during 19 September, though some hills
had been lost to the British attack that day and the previous night. By 5 p.m.,
however (by which time Tulkarm was captured), the outflanking attack in the
west forced VII Army into a careful retreat. The two British divisions made
repeated attempts to hurry that retreat, but the Turks held on to vital hills and
even launched successful counter-attacks. But they did retreat.

The slow advance of the 53rd Division was in fact typical of the isolated
attacks which been made here and there in the hills during the months since
the capture of Jerusalem the previous December. There was no repeat, at least
for a couple of days, of the careful and subtle attack of the night before; indeed,
the failure of that attack to capture the last hill, Abu Malul, meant a lengthy
hold-up when the assault was renewed.[1] These new attacks were a reminder of
how well the Turks, outnumbered, footsore, and hungry, could and would fight
when attacked. It was a reminder also of Allenby's astuteness – his insistence

---

[1] Marden, *Welch Regiment*, p. 549; Falls, *Official History* Vol. II, p. 499.

on training and on assembling overwhelming power in the infantry assault on 19 September was correct; so too was his demand for it to be made in the coastal plain. For two days, the 53rd Welsh and the 10th Divisions pushed and prodded through the hills towards their objectives, but they only moved at the pace set by their enemy's retreat.

It became clear that the deliberate Turkish retreat was aimed at getting their forces across the Jordan, where the IV Army was untouched. There were only a few crossings of the river available and the defence would therefore have the advantage. So 53rd Division's orders were now to cut the road between Nablus and the bridge at Jisr ed-Damiyeh, which was reckoned to be the primary crossing left to the Turks.[2] This would leave the fugitives west of Nablus cut off and available for capture.

The story was the same to the west of 53rd Division. The 10th Division was repeatedly held up in its attempts to move forward into its section of the hills, and it received considerable casualties from the well placed and well used Turkish machine guns. After a day's fighting on the 20th the division had only moved as far forward as the line held by the Turks at the beginning of the day, and the Turks had established a new series of defensive posts in front of them.[3] Both divisions resumed their attacks during the night of 20/21 September and then it turned out that the Turks had largely evacuated their defences before the attack. The 53rd was now able to advance with scarcely any check. (The skill of the Turks in breaking away without detection is noteworthy.) A few Turks were found here and there, and a road-full of 'fugitives' was shelled, but on the whole the Turks got away. Not entirely though, especially in front of 10th Division, where several strategic hilltops were defended. (The 10th Division began its attack a little earlier than the 53rd, which may have made the difference.) But now it was possible to evade these posts, for the Turkish line had been thinned out. By the morning the leading battalions had reached the plain in which Nablus sat, and were able to see the Wadi el-Fara road. It was in such a state that it was not necessary to reach it.[4]

During these advances the Turks had been evacuating their forces from Nablus eastwards, aiming to cross the Jordan. Their main route was along the Wadi el-Fara, which provided a route from Nablus to the crossing at the Jisr ed-Damiyeh. The road ran along the hillside above the stream, in effect another

---

2   Ward, *53rd Welsh Division*, pp. 237–9.

3   Geoghahan, *Royal Irish Regiment*, pp. 99–100; Falls, *Official History* Vol. II, p. 493.

4   Falls, *Official History* Vol. II, pp. 499–502.

narrow passage. This movement was spotted soon after dawn by the patrol of two aircraft from the Australian 1st Squadron. This provided the same sort of target as that found at Anebta two days before, and a mass air attack was ordered.

Every British air force unit in Palestine took part, usually sending its planes repeatedly to bomb and machine gun the retreating column in its narrow road. Fairly early on, the bombing caused a block at one point, and the whole movement ceased, leaving the vehicles, animals, and men stationary and so even more vulnerable. It seems that no one was able to enforce control, and as the raids continued the men tried to escape, either up the hillside or down the slope into the stream. The real answer would have been to concentrate fire on the approaching aircraft, especially from the higher land, and at least two planes were brought down by such fire. But most men simply wanted to get away.[5]

This scene of stationary confusion and panic was the reason neither the 53rd nor the 10th Division commanders felt it necessary to push on when they came in sight of the road along the wadi. On the next day they did move in, leaving some men to salvage what they could. They spent a week collecting material – perhaps a thousand vehicles, lorries, guns, and wagons were counted, mainly not worth saving, and a hundred guns. But the number of human casualties was much less than the pilots assumed, or than was expected. Many of the men had actually got away.

This was also the case elsewhere. Some fugitives, now from VII Army as well as VIII, moved north from Nablus towards Beisan, where they found the British already in control. They tended to be captured, but others headed along narrow roads and tracks more or less due east towards the Jordan. There was a string of minor river crossings, fords, between the two main bridges at Jisr ed-Damiyeh and Jisr al-Mejami (the latter held by the British by the 20th, of course). The existence of these crossings was not appreciated by the British for some time.

The Turkish withdrawal to the east and north was partly involuntary, the result of defeat, and partly intended. Liman von Sanders had ordered Nazareth to be abandoned in the afternoon of 20 September, and had himself moved to Samakh at the southern end of the Sea of Galilee. This was one of the key railway locations, where there were workshops and a station. It was east of the Jordan and to the north of the bridge at Jisr el-Mejami, which was seized by

5   Jones, *War in the Air*, pp. 224–6; Cutlack, *Australian Flying Corps*, pp. 159–61.

the 19th Lancers later that day. His aim was to reconstitute a line of defence stretching along the Jordan from Samakh north to Lake Huleh, and he gave orders for the bridge south of the lake, the Jisr Berat Yakub, to be defended. The Turkish forces at Haifa were to abandon the town and move east. The new centre of defence would be Tiberias. Liman himself would operate from Damascus.[6]

The southern part of Liman's projected new line was from Samakh south along the Jordan River, which would mean controlling the several other crossings. Behind that line was the eastern scarp of the valley, an excellent defensive position. If that line was pierced, there were several lines north of Amman he could use if the British broke through across the river. In fact it soon became clear that he needed to shorten his projected line, for, thanks to the capture of a large part of the VII and VIII Armies, he did not have enough men to control a long position. At once he began to plan in terms of a new line from Samakh east along the Yarmuk Valley, and ordered IV Army to pull out northwards.

Liman clearly felt he could re-establish a line and fight on. Part of his calculation was that the swift movement of the British forces would have exhausted their men and horses, and sapped their supplies. And indeed every account from the British side of the events of these days mentions anxieties about finding water and fodder for the horses, and complaints about having to live on iron rations. It was quite reasonable for Liman to assume that the British would be almost as exhausted as his own troops. He perhaps did not take account of the basic difference: the British were exalted by victory; the Turks were depressed by defeat.

For the British, therefore, it was necessary to prevent Liman from consolidating a new defensive line. To weaken the possible Turkish defensive plans, Liman's manpower had to be reduced as much and as soon as possible. The VIII Army had been destroyed, and large numbers of its men were prisoners (there were far fewer fatalities), but much of VII Army had survived, though in retreat, and IV Army across the Jordan was intact. Hence the importance of the ineffective pursuit of VII Army by the 53rd and 10th Divisions, and the vital intervention of the RAF at the Wadi el-Fara. Even though the human casualties in that action were relatively few, the survivors were scattered and demoralized. In addition the actions of Chaytor's Force on 21 and 22 September should have provided another opportunity to disrupt Liman's plans.

---

6   Liman von Sanders, *Five Years*, pp. 285–92.

Major-General Sir Edward Chaytor had under his command his own Anzac Mounted Division of two Australian brigades and one of New Zealanders, nine regiments in all. In addition he had four Indian infantry battalions, two West Indian infantry battalions, and the two Jewish battalions of the Royal Fusiliers. His artillery was similarly various, one Royal Field Artillery battery from 10th Division, two Indian mountain batteries, a Heavy Battery of the Royal Garrison Artillery and three sections equipped with captured enemy guns.

This heterogeneous force had the task in the first place of making sure that the Turkish IV Army did not intervene in the fight on the west. But it also faced part of VII Army in the western Jordan Valley. The two Turkish armies did not necessarily co-ordinate with each other, so even if IV Army was deterred, this did not necessarily apply to others. The IV Army commander was Djemal Pasha (the Lesser). Liman claims that he suggested as early as 20 September that IV Army should prepare to retreat, and that a new defence line be established on the Yarmuk. It is in fact highly unlikely that Liman did so as early as the 20th, but he does also claim to have given orders – not a suggestion – to do so next day.[7]

Chaytor had done his best to confuse Djemal by making minor attacks, but since these were all west of the river it seems unlikely that Djemal paid much attention. The 2nd West Indians made an attempt to capture a ridge on their front on the 19th, but achieved only a partial success. Next day the Turks withdrew, just as other VII Army units were doing to the west. The 38th Fusiliers, on the other hand, were defeated in an attack on the Turkish positions on the Wadi Mellaha closer to the river, and a cavalry probe east of the river found no weakening in the IV Army's defences. That is, the Turks were blocking any move against the Jordan crossings, the most important of which was the Jisr ed-Damiyeh, but that at Mafid Jozele was also being defended. The Auckland Regiment of the Anzac Division located a new Turkish defence line on the 21st which was blocking the approaches to both these crossings. Chaytor ordered an attack by the three New Zealand regiments, the two West Indian battalions and the artillery for the next day, the troops moving into position during the night.[8]

There was a complicated fight for the Damiyeh crossing on the 22nd, and during that day the Mafid Jozele ford was captured. Partly as a consequence,

7   Ibid., p. 291.
8   Falls, *Official History* Vol. II, p. 549.

the Turkish forces in the Wadi Mellaha withdrew. Turkish soldiers withdrawing along the Wadi el-Fara were intercepted (despite the air raids the previous day, they were clearly still able to use part of the Fara route). The Turks held on to the Damiyeh bridge for most of the morning, and managed to evacuate considerable numbers of men.

It was during this day, 22 September, that Djemal Pasha finally ordered IV Army to retire. It is generally assumed that he should have done so earlier, even though Liman's order was issued only the previous day. The garrisons along the railway south of Amman were in fact already being withdrawn and he clearly hoped to save the 4000 men there. His forces were also involved in defending the Jordan crossings, and so were able to receive considerable reinforcements by taking in the men from VII Army. He had faced and repelled several probing attacks by Chaytor's forces at the southern end of the river line, where Chaytor controlled the el-Hinu and Hijla crossings. It does not seem unreasonable that Djemal should have waited until the 22nd to withdraw northwards.

What he may not have anticipated, any more than the British, was the reaction of the local Bedouin, particularly the Beni Sakhr of the area around and south of Amman. This tribe had been jostled and taxed and promised things by both sides for the past year. It was clearly anti-Turkish, but could not act alone. When it was clear that the Turks in Ma'an were pulling out, that was the signal for the Beni Sakhr to rise. The Ma'an force was thereby beset.

Chaytor, having secured the crossings from the Jisr ed-Damiyeh south, arranged that his forces would use them the next day. They found that IV Army had already gone. Skilfully placed Turkish rearguards and demolitions delayed the advance, so it was not until the afternoon of the 25th that Amman was reached. The rear guard in the city was captured, or at least some of it, though most of IV Army had already escaped to the north. The exception was the Ma'an force, which was now cut off. It was finally persuaded to surrender on 29 September, and even then had to be allowed to keep its arms to prevent a massacre by the suddenly enthusiastic Bedouin. Turks and Australians cooperated in the defence. The Turks finally became formal prisoners of war on 30 September.

The operation of Chaytor's Force, like those of 53rd and 10th Divisions, had therefore been almost entirely determined by the actions of the enemy, and their advance was regulated by the pace of the Turks' withdrawal. That withdrawal had been deliberate and carefully conducted. Of course, a fair number of prisoners were taken by all the attacking forces, but, apart from the 4000 men of the Ma'an force, the numbers were not particularly large.[9] Indeed, the need to deal with the Ma'an force preoccupied Chaytor and his troops for nearly a week.

In the fighting carried out from 19 to 21 September Allenby does not seem to have intervened anywhere, though he was active in supervising. He wrote several letters. Those he sent to his wife, who was in Cairo, were of such a length that he evidently had leisure time. He also sent letters to Faisal, and to King Husain, and his report of progress delivered to London included the significant comment: 'I am building up communications in order to exploit my success.' At the same time he was constantly moving about to see for himself what was happening.[10]

By 22 September he was being provided with suggestions of ways to 'exploit my success'. A 'cavalry raid to Aleppo' was one, but Allenby did not like the idea, though he was favourable to the idea of 'sending three divisions of cavalry as soon as I can, to Damascus'.[11] Indeed, the day before he wrote this he had visited Chauvel and tentatively put the suggestion of reaching Damascus to him. Chauvel was interested,[12] but it was clear that some preliminary actions would need to be undertaken in the territory the cavalry had reached, and that a proper plan would need to be made. This was the programme for the next few days, while Chaytor's Force cleaned up east of the river and Chauvel's and Allenby's respective members of staff laid plans, and preliminary attacks were made.

By nightfall on the 22nd the British forces were scattered over central Palestine from the old front line as far as Nazareth and the Jordan. The 75th Division was at et-Tire, and the 54th Division was in its old station, both more or less on the old line. The 60th Division had spread its brigades from Tulkarm along the railway to the east, and the 7th Division was at Samaria. But these were all infantry forces, and their task in the next days was to round up prisoners, collect loot, develop roads, and generally establish control. Chetwode's two infantry divisions were similarly employed, partly in the Nablus area, and partly looking east, where the unforeseen problem of the possible escape of much of VII Army was developing. Chaytor's cavalry were busy for several days secur-

---

[9] Ibid., pp. 550–8.

[10] Hughes (ed.), *Correspondence*, pp. 148–56.

[11] Ibid., p. 155, Allenby to Wilson, 23 September 1918; p. 158, Wilson to Allenby, 23 September 1918.

[12] Anglesey, *British Cavalry*, p. 295; Hill, *Chauvel of the Light Horse*, p. 172; Falls, *Official History* Vol. II, p. 501.

ing Amman and the Hejaz railway and what it could reach of IV Army. None of these forces were therefore available for the suggested dash for Damascus.

Chauvel's three cavalry divisions would have the assigned assault, as Allenby had suggested, together with any other cavalry units which could be collected. For the moment these were even more scattered than the infantry. They were also in need of rest and refreshment, and the preliminary measures had to be undertaken. The 4th Division was at Beisan, having brought up the rest of its brigades, and still faced having to cope with the Turks who were retreating in its direction. Others were escaping across the river, and the 19th Lancers had begun to move south from the Jisr el-Mejami bridge along the east bank to assist in the capture of the crossings the Turks were using. The 5th Division had similarly gathered itself together at Nazareth, and had its attention drawn to Haifa. A Turkish battalion had been met by the 18th Lancers as they patrolled the road towards Haifa and Acre on the 21st. This was presumably a force moving east in response to Liman's earlier order. The Lancers defeated the Turks, said to be about 700-strong, but did not take many prisoners.[13] The enemy forces in and about Haifa were thus of some strength and resolve, and would need to be eliminated before any move northwards could be undertaken. The brigades of the Australian Mounted Division were scattered along the railway from Jenin to el-Afule.

In effect, therefore, the British had thrust an advanced guard, the 5th Cavalry Division, north as far as Nazareth, but this was only the point of a triangle whose base was between Tulkarm and Nablus. None of the coast north of the Nahr Iskenderun was yet under control, and much of the Jordan Valley was still in hostile hands. Allenby cannot have known of Liman von Sanders' tentative plans to re-establish a line based on the Jordan and the Yarmuk valleys, but to anyone with a map and basic military expertise the possibility clearly existed; this was obviously the explanation for the attempt to gather together the Turkish forces in the east. So the immediate tasks, before any cavalry attack towards Damascus could be launched, was to secure the flanks of the occupied triangle. Unluckily for Liman, this meant attacking Samakh, one of his designated strongpoints, and Haifa, whose forces he had ordered to come east.

It was urgent that the attack on Damascus should be made as soon as possible, for the longer the Turks were given to recover, the more difficult the task would be. Allenby was conscious that in France and at Salonika the Allies were

---

[13]   TNA WO 95/4515, War Diary of 5 Cav. Div, 21 September 1918.

defeating other enemy armies; Austria had already made approaches for an armistice, Bulgaria was about to give in. It was obvious that the war was coming to an end, so politically it was essential to occupy as much Ottoman territory as possible. If an armistice was arranged it could well be that the two sides would simply stop where they were, and the armistice line might then become the new international frontier. If the Turks still controlled Damascus and the land to the north, that might well be left to them at the peace. The repercussions within the Allied councils would be grave, since that was exactly the territory assigned to France in the carve-up arranged years before. Then there were the Arabs. The city of Damascus, with its large oasis, had always glittered in the Arabs' eyes as a great prize. It had been the capital of the caliphal empire for a century during the Arabs' great conquests. It was agriculturally rich, its waters were plentiful and perennial, and its fruits were legendary, so to the desert Arabs it was a vision of paradise. For the Arabs it was inevitably one of the great prizes of the war.

However, Haifa was a more urgent target for Allenby before a new advance could be made. It was a port, which would be useful for bringing in supplies and advantageous as a naval base. An aerial reconnaissance had suggested that the town was being evacuated by enemy troops, but the defeat of the Turkish force by the Lancers had clearly halted that movement. A sortie by a general in a Rolls-Royce with armoured cars ran into resistance.[14] The 5th Cavalry Division was given the task of taking the town.

There were in fact two objectives. North of Haifa was the old city of Acre, whose capture would give the division control of another port and of the coast road to the north, and if any of the Haifa garrison tried to get away via those routes they could be caught. Haifa itself was at the foot of Mount Carmel, between the hill and the sea. Along the northern foot of the Carmel Ridge, between the ridge and the Nahr el-Muqatta, ran the road and railway. The river wandered in loops and curves through swampy land to the sea, and was to prove a major obstacle, even though it was no more than a stream. The 5th Division, considerably reduced in numbers since the start of the campaign, advanced along the road. The 13th Brigade was detached to attack Acre, and 14th and 15th Brigades moved against Haifa.

The defence consisted of machine gunners and riflemen concealed among the vineyards on the slope of the Carmel Ridge at a narrow point between the ridge and the river, and riflemen and artillery on the ridge top. The narrowness

---

[14] Preston, *Desert Mounted Corps*, p. 227.

of the approach much favoured this defence, but it was designed for defence against a slow-moving infantry attack, not faster-approaching cavalry. The 14th Brigade stayed in reserve, while the 15th Brigade, from which one regiment had been detached earlier, rode to the attack. The two regiments involved were the Mysore Lancers and the Jodhpore Lancers, both Imperial Service Regiments. Two squadrons of the Mysores were sent to climb the ridge to attack the guns on the summit, and a third went to cross the *nahr* to attack a detached Turkish group near the coast. At 2 p.m. the Jodhpores attacked along the road, directly towards the town, and as soon as this move started the Mysores also attacked. An attempt to ride wide along the river was thwarted – the ground varied from swamp to quicksand and several horses were sucked under. The Jodhpores had to shift to a direct charge against the machine gunners and riflemen on the slope. The infantry would never have been able to have done this, but the horsemen's greater speed enabled them to get among the machine gunners very quickly. The machine gunners were speared, the riflemen took to their heels. The rest of the Jodhpores, accompanied by a group of Royal Engineers who had grabbed lances, charged into the town at a gallop.

On the ridge, the Mysores had had a difficult climb, losing horses on the way, so that they were only fifteen strong when the time came to attack. But again the speed of the cavalry, covered by machine-gun fire from the left flank, took the Turkish gunners and riflemen by surprise, and three guns and almost eighty prisoners were captured. They were supported soon after breaking through the Turkish position by the Sherwood Rangers. The detached Mysore squadron on the north faced odds as great, but again the sight of the lances rapidly approaching was too much. More guns and prisoners were taken.

One of the reasons for the success of the horsemen was that the enemy riflemen, and even the machine gunners, fired at the horses whereas the the riders were the better targets. But a horse hit by a rifle bullet, or even by several machine-gun bullets, simply went on. It might die later, but the bullet which might have killed or disabled a man had only a delayed effect on the charging horse. In this operation the human casualties numbered thirty-seven, of whom only three were killed; but sixty horses died (some drowned in the quicksand) and eighty-three were wounded.[15]

It was easier for the brigade which attacked Acre, though to them it seemed

---

[15] TNA WO95/4519, War Diaries of Mysore and Jodhpore Lancers, 25 and 26 September 1918; Falls, *Official History* Vol. II, pp. 535–8; Anglesey, *British Cavalry*, pp. 296–9. This exploit is sometimes called the 'Haifa Annexation Expedition'.

an even bigger task. The brigadier perused the place from a distance, and saw a walled town surrounded by a cactus hedge. In what normally would have been a foolish decision – for who ever heard of a walled town captured by lancers? – he ordered the 18th Lancers to 'gallop the town'. Probably to everyone's surprise there was only a brief resistance, and Acre, which 'had defied all attempts by Napoleon to capture it, had succumbed to Jemadar Munshi Singh and a patrol of 'B' squadron of the 18th Lancers'. The squadron went on to pursue the retreating Turks and captured 120 of them, 'after a short fight in which the lance was used'. Truly the lance was the British secret weapon in this campaign.[16]

The first convoy of supplies arrived from Port Said at Haifa on 28 September, only five days after its capture. It was escorted by the two torpedo-boat destroyers, *Druid* and *Forester*, which had earlier bombarded the coast to the south. They then went off to the Aegean; evidently the navy considered Palestinian waters safe.[17]

In order for the 5th Division to concentrate against Haifa and Acre, the three brigades of the Australian Mounted Division moved to take up the central position of the Desert Mounted Corps along the railway. The 5th Brigade came up from the Tulkarm area, returning to the division for the first time since the great attack began on 19 September, and took over at Jenin. The 3rd Brigade moved north to el-Afule, and the 8th took over at Nazareth; the division also took over patrolling and picquetting along the railway eastwards from el-Afule.

As this was happening, the 4th Division, concentrated largely at Beisan, and encumbered with large numbers of prisoners – 4000 by the 22nd – was given the task of gaining control of a series of fords over the Jordan. These were located between the bridges at Jisr el-Mejami and Jisr ed-Damiyeh, which were being used by the escaping VII Army survivors. Jisr ed-Damiyeh had been taken by Chaytor's Force, which then switched its attention to crossing the river in pursuit of IV Army, so there remained a stretch of perhaps twenty miles of the river where the Turks could cross by several fords to the east bank. Air reconnaissance discovered that organized Turkish forces were approaching these crossings from the west. The fact that these forces were organized meant that they were both alert and under command, and therefore all the more dangerous. According to Liman, the Asien Korps crossed on the 23rd. This shows

---

[16] Hudson, *19th Lancers*, p. 237.
[17] ADM 53/40220, 41999, Logs of *Druid* and *Forester*, 28 September 1918.

a different picture to that of panicking fugitives who had often been captured so far. Most of these groups were from VII Army, which had already retreated so competently. The 19th Lancers, from their base at the Jisr el-Mejami bridge, patrolled part of the east bank, but not as far south as the crossings.

The 11th Brigade of the 4th Division was sent to plug the gap. The first ford was at Makhadat Abu Naji, six miles south of Beisan. Of the three regiments in the brigade, Jacob's Horse was sent to march along the east bank, and the Middlesex Yeomanry and the 29th Lancers, with the Hampshire Battery of the Royal Horse Artillery, moved through the rather rough country on the western side. At Abu Naji the 29th Lancers found a large and well-sited defensive force holding the approaches to the ford from the west, and Jacob's Horse met another which had already crossed on the east and had established an equally effective defensive position. These were the rearguards of the Asien Korps, intent on holding the crossing for the fugitives still approaching.

One squadron of the Lancers moved as if to attack their enemy from the north; this drew their full attention. Meanwhile, a second squadron charged in from the west, and so suddenly that the horsemen broke into the Turkish formation and destroyed its cohesion. Most of the Turks were captured; the prisoners included the commander of the Turkish 19th Division.

The men of Jacob's Horse on the east bank were unable to copy this feat, but the two squadrons which met the enemy force were able to pin it down. The Turks had a large number of well-handled machine guns, and the horsemen could not get close enough to attack – riding from a distance would only give the defence time to fire at them accurately. A heliographed message to the brigade command, however, brought the Hampshire Battery of the RFA within range, though they had to trot for six miles from Beisan to do so. As soon as the guns began firing, they were bombarded by a Turkish battery in reply, so accurately that all their guns were damaged and the gunners driven away. In another move a squadron of the Middlesex Yeomanry had found another ford, the Makhadat Fath Allah, to the south, which was less well defended. The squadron charged across, driving through the Turks on the east side, and then charged the Turkish battery, disabling the guns. A squadron of the Lancers crossed at yet another ford, and joined up with Jacob's Horse, and together they drove the Turks back and forced their surrender – 4000 prisoners to add to those taken on the west earlier.[18]

18 Maunsell, *Scinde Horse*, pp. 228–9; Hatton, *Yarn of a Yeoman*, pp. 261–3; Anglesey, *British Cavalry*, pp. 302–5.

There still remained a gap between the positions of Chaytor's Force, now largely east of the river and approaching Amman, and the 11th Brigade at Makhadat Abu Naji, and that gap held at least three fords. A squadron of the Middlesex Yeomanry bumped into a Turkish force positioned to guard the ford, the Makhadat el-Masudi, and could see that part of that force was already across the river. A charge failed, partly because of the Turkish machine guns, and partly because of the rough ground and nullahs, which broke up the Yeomanry's cohesion. A second squadron found another much larger Turkish column to the west and detained it by attacking the head of the column until reinforcements and the Hampshire Battery arrived. Meanwhile the yeomen got across the river and were joined by Jacob's Horse to head off most of the Turks on the east bank. Exhausted, most of the Turks gave up, on both sides of the river. A patrol sent out westwards by the 29th Lancers gained contact with the Worcestershire Yeomanry, which had been part of 'Watson's Force', holding the gap between the 10th and 53rd Divisions. This meant that Turks still west of the river were now enclosed within a tightening net.[19] Combined with the men captured by the Worcesters who had been following the Turks from the west, collecting prisoners on the way, this accounted for any remaining formed and organized Turkish forces west of the river – and so the greater part of VII Army was now either captured or driven east of the river in defeat. The 11th Brigade explored southwards in the afternoon of 24 September, and found no more enemy forces. The next day Amman was taken and the Turkish Ma'an army was cut off.

The last obstacle to be taken before making a northward attack was Samakh. This was a village which had developed round a station, railway workshops, and a small port on the Sea of Galilee, and was held by several hundred Germans and Turks. Holding it would give control over the route westwards along the Yarmuk valley and the railway towards Deraa, and a large enough force there would be able to interfere with any movement north along the west side of the Sea of Galilee by way of Tiberias. Of course, it could be outflanked, but not easily, since the only reasonable road north was that through Tiberias. Both of these places, and Deraa, had been part of Liman's defensive plan formulated on the 21st. Given that the 5th and 4th Divisions were busy at Haifa and along the Jordan respectively, the capture of Samakh fell to the Australian

---

[19] Stonham and Freeman, *Middlesex Yeomanry*, p. 194; Osborne, 'Operations of the Mounted Troops', 141–2; Cobham, *Worcestershire Yeomanry*, p. 183; Maunsell, *Scinde Horse*, p. 230; Anglesey, *British Cavalry*, pp. 305–7.

Mounted Division, in particular the 4th Brigade, even though this now consisted of just one regiment (the 11th) and part of another (the 12th).

The brigade had moved to Jenin on 22 September, and then on to Beisan on the 24th. It reached the river crossing at Jisr el-Mejami after dark that day. Brigadier-General Grant was then briefed on the conditions he would meet by the commander of the 19th Lancers, who had looked at Samakh in some detail earlier. The approach was necessarily over a flat open plain between the Jordan on the left and the Yarmuk on the right. A ridge of hills filled the space between the Yarmuk and the Sea, making both routes – the one along the river and the one by the Sea – narrow. The railway came in dead straight from the bridge to the village, then curved round to run south-east into the Yarmuk Valley. The Lancers reported that there were no obstacles worse than thistles in the open plain, but that there was a semi-circle of rifle pits in front of the village, and plenty of machine guns inside it. Grant made an almost instant decision to attack that night with the force he had. To wait would only worsen the odds, or even let the enemy escape.

One squadron of the 11th Light Horse was sent to gain control of the hills to the right in case the enemy tried to escape along the lake shore; it was later joined by a squadron of the 12th. The machine-gun company was directed to advance along the railway north-eastwards, to a position where it could fire obliquely into the village; the two remaining squadrons of the 11th went across the plain to the other railway line. The 12th remained in reserve. The attack therefore was to be covered by the machine gunners until the horsemen reached the enemy positions. Just before dawn the Turks and Germans realized that they were about to be attacked and opened a heavy fire from the rifle pits in front of the village. From the left the machine gunners replied, to force the riflemen to take refuge, and from the right the 11th charged, using the railway line as a guide and shouting to let their machine gunners know where they were.

The charge, assisted by the uncertain light – it was just about dawn – broke through the defence line, and into the area of the railway buildings. The machine gunners moved up and reached the western part of the village, and a squadron of the 12th came up to attack the village as well. There followed a savage, no-quarter fight for an hour, mainly in the railway station area. The Germans fought to the last, but most of the Turks kept clear. The fighting took place in and around the railway buildings, the station and the workshops, in and around the locomotives and the rolling stock, and in the houses of the village. The number of empty bottles of spirits found after the fight suggested that the Germans had been fuelled up to recklessness before the attack. All the Germans were killed or wounded. Almost as many Australians were casualties as well, and a hundred of their horses were killed. They could be thankful that Grant had decided to attack in the dark. The fighting ended about 5.30 a.m., except for two motor boats which escaped from the jetty – one was fired at, burst into flames, and sank.

Grant was in the process of extending his control over the surrounding area, particularly along the railway in the Yarmuk Valley, when he received orders to send the 12th Regiment north along the coast road towards Tiberias. There it linked up with an armoured car battery and the 8th Regiment, which had come across from Nazareth, to occupy Tiberias in the afternoon. Thus two vital links in Liman's hoped-for chain of defence was broken, the threat from Haifa was removed, and IV Army was defeated. The way was open for the cavalry ride northwards.[20]

---

[20] Hammond, *11th Light Horse*, pp. 129–36; Anglesey, *British Cavalry*, pp. 307–12; Falls, *Official History* Vol. II, p. 542.

CHAPTER 12

Damascus and Beirut

ALLENBY had first mentioned Damascus as a target during his conversation with Chauvel on 22 September, but both Damascus and Aleppo had already been suggested as suitable targets for his continuing campaign – indeed, an attack on Aleppo had been mooted months beforehand. He had slapped it down then, and he did so once more in September. A 'cavalry raid' to Aleppo was, he said, 'not feasible'. As he explained – and this should have been obvious in London – the distance from Nazareth to Aleppo was 300 miles and there were probably 25,000 Turkish troops in the Aleppo region, with more on the way. This latter point had already been made by Wilson two days before, when he claimed that Allenby's victories had already had its effect on Turkish operations in the Caucasus and in Persia (though the evidence for this is non-existent now, and it was probably only a guess on Wilson's part).[1]

Allenby was 'firmly of the opinion that the only sound policy is to advance by stages', and that the first stage was to 'advance to the line Damascus-Beirut'. The three cavalry divisions of the Desert Mounted Corps would head for Damascus, and an infantry division, supplied by sea at a succession of ports, would move along the coast to Beirut.[2] He did not wait for approval or comments from London, but that same day, 25 September, drew up the orders to his forces and wrote to Prince Faisal (copying in Lawrence) of his intention to march on Damascus: 'there is no objection to Your Highness entering Damascus as soon as you consider that you can do so with safety.'[3]

Allenby's plan was ready by the 25th, and on the following day he had a conference with his corps commanders.[4] By this time he did not need to set out in detail what was to be done, giving precise targets and so on. What had become clear in the various relatively minor actions at Haifa and the Jordan and Samakh in the previous few days was that the army was capable of operat-

---

[1] Hughes (ed.), *Correspondence*, pp. 158 and 160, Wilson to Allenby, 23 and 24 September 1918; p. 162, Allenby to Wilson 25 September 1918.

[2] Ibid., p. 162.

[3] Ibid., p. 150, Allenby to Prince Faisal, 20 September 1918; p. 151, Allenby to King Husain, 21 September 1918.

[4] Falls, *Official History* Vol. II, p. 563.

ing without detailed supervision. After the conference Chauvel sent out his orders for Damascus in a telegram in which he laid down only two targets and a few details about traffic priorities. The Australian Mounted Division, which had done less fighting than the others in recent weeks, would lead, followed by the 5th Cavalry Division, but together they would make the final advance in order to 'provide as imposing a force as possible on approaching Damascus'. The 4th Cavalry Division would use the Yarmuk route to Deraa to deal with the retiring Turkish IV Army, and would then head for the city.[5]

This required a shuffling of brigades. Even before the conference with the generals, infantry units had been moving north to take over from the cavalry. The 28th Brigade of the 7th Division was on the move from Tulkarm towards Haifa, and the 2nd Leicesters arrived there by lorry on the 25th.[6] The 3rd Division began to move north along the railway, and its 7th Brigade was at Jenin also by the 25th.[7] These movements allowed the cavalry to concentrate and accumulate supplies: the 5th Cavalry Division did so at Nazareth, and the Australian Mounted Division proceeded to collect itself at Tiberias. Parts of the 4th Cavalry Division were already at the Jisr el-Mejami bridge, and others were arriving.

The Arab Army had kept the railway in the Deraa region under threat since before the great battle began, and now the soldiers could begin moving north on the 26th, along with a large number of 'irregulars' who came into the rendezvous at Azraq. These were, of course, opportunistic groups who were joining the winning side, like the Beni Sakhr. Lawrence had by this time wholly adopted the Arab cause as his own, and he wanted the Arabs to achieve something notable which would justify their receiving rewards at the post-war peace conference. The capture of Damascus would do very well, and Allenby's message to him and to Faisal that day was a clear signal that he was leaving the city to them. Chauvel's orders to the Australians and the 5th Division in his telegraphed instructions reflected this – 'on arrival at Damascus a defensive position will be taken up on high ground commanding the town and dispositions made by leading division to secure all hostile approaches. Town will be left under its present civil administration, and no national flags will be flown.'[8]

The destruction of the Turkish VII and VIII Armies had opened up the land

---

5   Ibid., Appendix 27.
6   Wylly, *Leicestershire Regiment*, pp. 194–5.
7   Mackay, *7th Gurkhas*, pp. 77–8.
8   Falls, *Official History* Vol. II, Appendix 27.

west of the Jordan to the invasion of the Australian and the 5th Divisions, but much of IV Army still existed and was under command. The movement of the Ma'an force north effectively pinned down most of Chaytor's Force for the next few days, while a goodly part of the rest of IV Army was moving north along the Hejaz railway. The breaks in the line caused by Lawrence's men delayed the Army's progress, and it was threatened by the local Arabs, now pleased to join the winners and to see the backs of the Turks. The Army was, however, still numerous, had a clear goal, and most of it was clearly capable of standing off any Arab attacks.

Other Turkish units, including the surviving elements of the VII Army, were scattered about the east bank. They also headed for Damascus. If they reached the city before significant Allied forces, the latter would clearly be in difficulties. When the cavalry set off, some had only one day's fodder and two days' food, and 4th Cavalry Division was requisitioning supplies before reaching the city,[9] a process never calculated to gain friends. If the Turks could block access to the city for even a short time, the Allied cavalry would soon be too weak to challenge them. With Damascus and its resources at its call, the Turkish Army, even battered and reduced as it was, could clearly hold up the British and defy the Arabs with some hope of success.

The 4th Division had the main task of tackling IV Army, along with the Arabs, and by crossing the river at the Jisr el-Mejami the division could come to grips with the Turks close to the railway at Deraa. The Australian Mounted and 5th Cavalry Divisions, on the other hand, were west of the river, and in the north faced an even more awkward obstacle. First, there were the two lakes, the Sea and Lake Huleh, which were major obstacles in themselves. They channelled any movement from Palestine towards Damascus into the ten miles of the river valley between them. North of Lake Huleh was an area of marsh and many streams flowing from Mount Hermon; with no roads it was virtually impassable. South of Lake Huleh there were more marshes, and on that stretch of the river it was crossed by just one bridge, the Jisr Benat Yakub - the bridge of the daughters of Jacob. This had been one of Liman's key posts in his aim to hold the Jordan-Yarmuk line; the Turks had formed a camp on the east side, and blew up part of the bridge.

In fact, Liman von Sanders claimed in his memoirs that he intended only delaying actions, and that he did not aim to hold Damascus; this was his new notion following the defeats at Haifa and Samakh. He was also now thinking of

9   Barrow, *Fire of Life*, p. 208.

Aleppo as a backstop and sent his staff there, but for the present he was mainly concerned to collect up as many of his troops as possible, and push them on north so that they could recover and be sorted out and rearmed. The troops at the bridge were therefore now organized as the Tiberias Group, and their task was to delay any attack and make a fighting withdrawal so as to enable the retreating IV Army to reach safety.

Liman's new front was to be, as he said, from Rajak to Kuneitra to es-Sanamein.[10] Plotted on the map, this was an L-shaped line. Rajak – or Riyaq as the British called it – was in the Bekaa Valley, the long valley between the two great mountain ranges of Lebanon and Anti-Lebanon. Kuneitra and es-Sanamein were towns on the two main roads south of Damascus – and es-Sanamein was close to the Hejaz railway. So his aim was to hold as long as possible at the Jordan and Deraa, then at Kuneitra and es-Sanamein. This line has no obvious geographical significance, but in social and political terms it was significant. Kuneitra was the social and political centre of the Circassians of the Golan area, Ottoman loyalists. Es-Sanamein lies on the edge of the Jebel Druze, the region inhabited by Druzes, believers in a heretical Islamic sect. The Druze chiefs had been carefully courted by Liman before he headed for Damascus, and, like the Circassians but for different reasons, they were fearful of rule by the Sunni Arabs of Arabia. So Liman's line was flanked by two regions which were inhabited by active Ottoman loyalists, whose belligerency would be useful in providing recruits. They would deter the Arabs, and could make life difficult for the Allies generally. But by moving north and deciding not to fight for Damascus, Liman was tacitly abandoning these allies. He also arranged for the preparation of another defence line a few miles south of Damascus where a line of rocky basalt hills, the Jebel al-Mania, could be the base for the defence, along with the town of Kiswe.[11]

Liman's primary concern was to see that as many of his soldiers as possible reached Damascus. There they would be funnelled through the Barada Gorge, where the Barada River breaks through the Anti-Lebanon, an ideal defensive position. His fortress would thus be the Bekaa Valley, but he needed manpower to be its garrison. The only way the British could foil this intention was by destroying IV Army during its retreat, preferably by capturing Damascus in a speedy cavalry raid before IV Army could reach and pass the city. The 4th

---

[10] Liman von Sanders, *Five Years*, pp. 296–7.

[11] Ibid., p. 290; the Kiswe line was used by the Vichy French against the British and Free French in 1941 with some success.

Division probably could not do it, since it was following the IV Army – that is, it was behind it; therefore only the Australian and 5th Divisions could complete the task, by riding across from the south-west to cut IV Army's retreat along its preferred route. And that meant defeating the Tiberias Group at the bridge and then at the successive defence lines Liman had designated on the way.

At first, however, it was 4th Division which made the most progress. The Australian Division set off from Tiberias towards the Jisr Benat Yakub on 27 September, but by that time there had been considerable movement on the east bank. The Arab Army had moved two days before and by the 27th had cut the railway in two places and captured a train at Ghazale Station. Early on the 27th the next station up the line Izra, about twenty-five miles north of Deraa, was taken by an Arab detachment, and the main force reached Sheikh Sa'd, so controlling another route north.

The Arabs captured a disorganized group of Turks, Germans, and Austrians, and were warned by a reconnoitring aircraft that there were two more large groups of Turks heading north from Deraa. Lawrence concentrated on the smaller group, and reached it as it was fighting at the village of Tafas three or four miles north of Muzeirib. After the Turks marched on, it was found that the village had been sacked and some of its inhabitants murdered, women and children included. (How many died is never stated.) Lawrence makes much of this in his account, which he uses to justify the equally nasty behaviour of the Arabs. The Turkish column was chased and battered until most of the men were killed. Only a well-disciplined German unit resisted successfully.[12] The real explanation for the Turks' behaviour was surely that they were in mortal fear of the Arabs, whose cruelty equalled their own, and that in response to the defeat of the Turkish armies the local Arabs were rising in rebellion. The head man of Tafas, Talal, was one of Lawrence's officers, as Lawrence himself says; no doubt the Tafas villages were in arms – every Arab seemed to be armed – and the Turkish commander launched his lancers on the villagers in order to get through. None of the participants come out of this affair with any credit or honour. Lawrence's account is transparently tendentious and misleading.

The 4th Division began its move eastwards on the 26th, the day after the Arab Army and the day before the Australian Division left Tiberias. The aim was to reach Deraa, but the division also had to get into touch with Lawrence's Arab forces. This was tricky since they might mistake each other for the enemy

---

[12] Lawrence, *Seven Pillars*, pp. 505–9.

– indeed, the RAF bombed some of the Arabs as they were entering Deraa. The 2nd Lancers regiment was sent to explore the route, which turned out to be difficult. It took all day on the 26th to reach the village of el-Bariha, several miles short of Irbid, the day's target. The first resistance was encountered there and was quickly dealt with, but Irbid itself was reported to be held by 2000 Turks. The thought that they might quickly give in was rudely dispelled when the strength of the Turkish position was seen. By this time it was late in the afternoon, there was no obvious source of water except in Irbid, and the major in command of the 2nd Lancers decided that he would gallop through the town. So an attack was launched without conducting any preliminary reconnaissance. The result was a near disaster, and a clear defeat. Without serious machine-gun or artillery support, and with mistakes of geography to compound the errors, the 2nd Lancers suffered about fifty casualties. And in the night the Turks withdrew, unmolested.[13]

Not surprisingly the 2nd Lancers were now replaced as the leading regiment by the Dorset Yeomanry, who were again confronted by a Turkish rearguard at er-Remte, a few miles short of Deraa. As the Dorsets deployed to attack, the Turks withdrew. Then a mistake over a white flag in the village resulted in the Yeomen angrily and systematically scouring the whole village for any of the enemy – all of which successfully delayed the British advance. Meanwhile the Central India Horse, the third of the regiments in the 10th Brigade, sent three squadrons in pursuit of the Turks who were again retreating towards Deraa, riding them down and taking a couple of hundred prisoners.[14]

The Central India Horse now stopped, uncertain as to the situation in Deraa, which had in fact been taken by the Arabs earlier that day. The two Allied forces finally met the next morning, the 28th, in a series of encounters which exemplified the touchy relationship they would have from then on. The whole event is complicated by Lawrence's account, which is partly defensive, partly invented, partly guilty, partly aimed at pushing his own Arab agenda, and thoroughly unreliable.

Lawrence reached Deraa just before the Central India Horse, who could hear firing in the place, and, reasonably so after their recent experiences, had

[13] Whitworth, *2nd Lancers*, pp. 153–61; Anglesey, *British Cavalry*, pp. 317–21; Watson, *Central India Horse*, pp. 398–401; Falls, *Official History* Vol. II, p. 580; Barrow, *Fire of Life*, p. 208.

[14] TNA, WO 95/4510, War Diary of 4 Cav. Div., 27 September 1918; Watson, *Central India Horse* pp. 401–2; Thompson, *Dorset Yeomanry*, pp. 109–12; Anglesey, *British Cavalry*, pp. 321–2.

paused to make sure of their situation. He rode out on camelback to meet them. His account of the encounter is romantic nonsense; there are several other accounts of the meeting, mostly contradictory, though Lawrence's is generally accepted. It seems that he met a member of the Dorset Yeomanry in the person of the Lt de Montezuma, asked him what his regiment was, and then, in a typical Lawrentian display of one-upmanship, asked to be taken to 'Colonel Mason'.[15] (The division's war diary, reversing the game, merely says that 'touch was gained with the Sherifian forces'.)[16]

Lawrence was taken to meet General Barrow, commander of the 4th Division, and again Lawrence's account is constrained by his own agenda, to the extent that he claimed his camel so affronted the horses that 'the General Staff bucked along in the ditch', while his camel strode proud in the centre of the road. Lawrence's political aim was to establish Arab authority in the town of Deraa, with an Arab military government and police. This intention was largely wrecked by the behaviour of the Arabs, who had found a train full of wounded Turks. They were busy looting it, and, in the process, casually killing off the patients. Barrow's account claims that when he protested Lawrence explained that 'it was their way of war'; Barrow said that if Lawrence didn't stop the massacre, his own troops would clear the Arabs from the train. Lawrence replied, 'If you attempt to do that I shall take no responsibility as to what happens.' Barrow answered, 'That's all right; I will take the responsibility.' He immediately gave orders for his men to clear the station, which was done quickly. This episode demonstrates Lawrence's unreliability (he alludes to the whole episode of the train only obliquely – hardly surprising given the outcome), his uncertain command of the Arab irregulars, and the diametrically opposed policies of the British and Arabs.[17]

For 4th Division all this had been more arduous and time-consuming than expected. Some fodder was found at Deraa for the horses, but there was not a great amount of food for the men, and both men and animals needed rest. Barrow put the 10th Brigade, which had done the fighting in the previous days, to picquet and police Deraa – so much for Lawrence's plots and intentions –

[15] Lawrence, *Seven Pillars*, p. 509; Thompson, *Dorset Yeomanry*, p. 113.

[16] TNA WO 95/4510, War Diary of 4 Cav. Div., 27 September 1918.

[17] Barrow, *Fire of Life*, pp. 209–11; Barrow's account is a sustained display of anger at the misrepresentation of Lawrence and his followers. He repeatedly comments on their inventions and lies. Given Lawrence's alterations in his stories, his personal and political agenda, and the need always to cross-check his accounts against those of others, Barrow's memory is preferable.

and he sent the other two brigades to Muzeirib five miles away. Here there was a better water supply and improved human conditions. The division was only able to move forward again on the morning of the 29th. Most of IV Army had escaped their attack.

The Australian Mounted Division had set off northwards from Tiberias at dawn on the 27th; the 5th Cavalry Division, which had ridden in from Haifa during the previous two days, followed soon after. The Australians reached the river crossing at Jisr Benat Yaqub early that afternoon, and collected much information about the situation and the local geography from the inhabitants of the Jewish settlement village at Rosh Pina. The bridge was broken, and a defensive position mainly manned by German troops (the Tiberias Group) had been established on the east bank. Further, that force was well equipped with motor transport, which would allow it to retire quickly when seriously threatened.

The Australians searched for the ford which was known to exist nearby. The 3rd Brigade moved against the bridge itself to pin down the main enemy force, and the Notts Battery of the RFA efficiently tackled and silenced opposing guns. The 5th Brigade searched for the ford at el-Min, a few miles south of the bridge; the 10th Regiment (3rd Brigade) searched for a ford known to exist north of the bridge. The idea was to envelop the enemy post from both sides, but this did not take account of the condition of the land across the river. The southern crossing was found without much difficulty by the 4th and 14th Regiments, but the ground on the east side was almost impassable, and they could not get further than a mile or so from the ford. On the north the 10th Regiment was prevented by the enemy forces from using the ford they found until dark, and then they found getting forward almost as difficult.

By seven o'clock that evening the 10th were all across on the eastern bank of the Jordan, and pushing on towards the Damascus road, the remainder of the brigade following. B squadron (Major Hamlin) was sent to clear up the situation at the bridge, whilst the remainder of the Regiment, C squadron leading, moved over terribly steep and stony ground easterly to cut the road. A most trying time was experienced before the road was reached. Only a goat track here and there could be discovered in the darkness, and the horses had to be led, sometimes dragged, up over loose boulders until the level ground was gained.

B Squadron located a rearguard post near the road, charged it, and dismounted in the dark, using the enemy's fire to give them a target. The fight was hard, and even when the post had been taken, the Australians still had to find the road. It was not until midnight that they reached and blocked the road, about two miles east of the bridge. By then, the enemy – alerted by the crossing and by the noise of the fighting at the post – had withdrawn.[18]

The Corps Bridging Train came up and built a trestle bridge across the river; the Australians meanwhile pushed forward to Kuneitra, which was not seriously defended. The water supply there made it a good camping spot, and in the afternoon the 5th Division crossed by the new bridge, though the troops did not reach Kuneitra until midnight. The Australians noted that the local inhabitants were Circassians, and that a cavalry force – part of the Turkish 3rd Cavalry Division – was in the area, 'but when we attempted to engage them they scattered and fled into the mountains.' 'A sweet piece of work by Sergeant Fitzmaurice of A Squadron [of the 10th Regiment] resulted in the capture of eight Circassian horsemen who had sniped at the column.'[19]

The capture of Kuneitra, following the crossing at Jisr Benat Yakub meant that two of Liman's proposed lines of resistance had fallen in two days. The Australians were clearly heading for Damascus, and there was little in the way of forces capable of resisting them. Meanwhile the 4th Division, with the Arab Army on its eastern flank, was heading north along the railway for the same destination. The Australians were held up again at Sasa, twenty miles or so from Damascus, by another rearguard well posted behind a ridge. The fight was much the same as at the bridge, if drier. The rearguard fought until out-flanked – again by the 10th Regiment – and then withdrew in lorries; again the delay to the invaders had been minimal.[20] A regiment was left at Kuneitra to intimidate the local Circassians.

The Australians were now in an open undulating plain, littered with small groups of retreating Turks. Over to the east the remnants of IV Army were still retiring before the advancing 4th Cavalry Division, but were going fast enough to avoid being held up. Any stragglers were killed and stripped by the local Arabs; their bodies were seen by the advancing 4th Division.

The routes of the two parts of the Desert Mounted Corps were now con-verging. The Australian Division was stopped once again at Kaukab, Liman's

[18] Olden, *Westralian Cavalry*, pp. 270–2; Hammond, *11th Light Horse*, p. 137; Holloway, *Hooves, Wheels and Tracks*, pp. 200–1; Darley, *9th Light Horse*, pp. 150–2.

[19] Olden, *Westralian Cavalry*, pp. 272–4; Hammond, *11th Light Horse*, p. 137; Darley, *9th Light Horse*, p. 152.

[20] Olden, *Westralian Cavalry*, p. 275; Darley, *9th Light Horse*, pp. 153–5.

final line, about ten miles short of the city. The 5th Division, having now more or less caught up with the Australians, went across to intercept the Turks on the other road, north of Kiswe, the route along which IV Army was moving. The Turkish rearguard at Kaukab was outflanked while being pinned down in the same way as at Sasa and the bridge. On the Kiswe road, General Macandrew used one of his brigades to crash into the front half of a large Turkish column, forcing the rear half to turn back; the other two brigades then dealt with it.[21]

The successive, careful and generally well-organized retreats of the Turkish forces before the advance of the Australian Division made it clear that they were by no means finished, though they were evidently not expected to hold the several lines for very long. The aim was only to delay the British long enough for the fugitives to reach Damascus. The days of small mounted parties of British or Australian horsemen capturing masses of Turks were over. Two troops of the Gloucester Yeomanry were sent to capture a major German radio station just south of Damascus. It was being destroyed as they arrived. By a charge they drove the demolition party away, though not until the buildings were blown up.

> The enemy, taken by surprise, offered no resistance, and some 150 to 200 were captured and driven down the road. After going a short distance they refused to accompany the patrol. By this time many more had joined them. General fire was opened up in all directions and the patrol, who were outnumbered by about 12 to 1, were ordered to charge. Three Germans and 12 Turks were killed by the sword and many more wounded, while the Hotchkiss gun inflicted further loss on the enemy. One NCO and two horses were wounded from the patrol.

The Gloucesters' patrol was driven off, though their account tends to read like a victory. The action showed clearly enough that Germans and Turks were still defiant.[22]

The removal of the Turks from Kaukab opened the way to the city, but Damascus itself was not the most important target. It was now clear that the city was not going to be seriously defended, but was merely, in military terms,

---

[21] Falls, *Official History* Vol. II, pp. 571–5.

[22] Fox, *Gloucestershire Hussars*, pp. 280–2, partly quoting from Massey, *Allenby's Final Triumph*.

the funnel through which the retreating Turkish and German forces were moving. They were going directly for the main route north-west through the Barada Gorge, some by rail, others by road, to get into the Bekaa Valley. The gorge is narrow, with steep sides, and provides an admirable defensive situation – but only if the heights on either side are held. And this the Turks omitted to do.

The French cavalry regiment with the Australians had outflanked the Kaukab fight and had ridden up to a ridge on the west, the Qalawat al-Mezze, which led them towards the gorge. They were directed to cut the road through the gorge by seizing the heights and bombarding the road beneath. By 4.30 p.m. they were beginning to fire on the Turks in the valley below, and were joined by the 2nd New Zealand Machine-Gun Company, and armoured cars. Just like the RAF at the Anebta Defile, the task was basically simple: firing caused vehicles and motors to crash, thus blocking the route. Those unable to advance therefore had to go back to Damascus to save themselves. Later a squadron of the 8th Light Horse Regiment performed the same service further along the gorge. Several trains were also compelled to return to the city.[23]

There were still parts of the IV Army south of the city being attacked by elements of the Arab Army and pursued by the 4th Division. Those Turkish forces which had got through the city by that time were well scattered. Considerable numbers had passed through the gorge and were on their way towards Riyaq (where the airfield had been bombed on the 29th). Another group had ridden north-east out of the city in the direction of Homs, along a poor road east of the Anti-Lebanon. Large numbers were still in the city itself, where great clouds of smoke were arising from destroyed stores, and ammunition dumps were exploding.

The capture of Damascus has been a source of controversy since it occurred. Lawrence claimed, as did Faisal, that the Arab Army got there first; the Australians claimed to have been the first into the city, without claiming to have conquered it;[24] and there were various groups inside the city who were interested in seizing power. It is evident that there was much confusion in the city. At one point the citizens were entertained by a firefight between Turkish and German soldiers over transport to take them out. Most citizens were in fact

23 Olden, *Westralian Cavalry*, pp. 278–9; Holloway, *Hooves, Wheels and Tracks*, pp. 201–2; Falls, *Official History* Vol. II, pp. 572–4; Anglesey, *British Cavalry*, pp. 323–7.
24 E. Kedourie, 'The Capture of Damascus, 1 October 1918', in *Chatham House Version*, 33–51; Hughes, *Allenby and British Strategy*, ch. 6.

only too pleased to see both sets of occupiers leaving. They were by no means pleased, however, at the prospect of being occupied by someone else, British, Arab, or French.

The priority of the British forces was to capture as many of the Turkish soldiers as possible. On the morning of 1 October the Australians and Arabs both entered the city. Who got there first is of little account, for the two forces had differing priorities. The 3rd Australian Light Horse Brigade, headed by the 10th Regiment once more, aimed to intercept the Turkish force which was known to be escaping northwards along the Homs road; the men of the Arab Army, with Lawrence in precarious control - some of the Arabs had in fact got into the city the day before, signalling their presence by firing their rifles - were more interested in enjoying the fruits of the city, while their leaders aimed to establish their authority with a view to claiming the city at the peacetime negotiations.

The 10th Australian Light Horse had struggled to clear a way through the wreckage beside the Barada River, and rode into city because it was the only way to get to the Homs road. Colonel Olden called at the Town Hall, the Serail, looking for guides to lead his regiment to the Homs road. His regiment had already captured a trainload of Turkish troops at the station, and had been fired on briefly from the barracks. In the city:

> dense masses of people were seen to fill the streets and squares. It was a heterogeneous mob. There were Moslem Arabs of every class in their long *galabieh*s, milder-mannered Syrians – many in European dress – armed uniformed men – later proved to be the *gendarmerie* – wild-looking Druzes from the Hauran, with their distinctive headgear and painted cheeks – Turkish and Greek civilians, Jews, Armenians, and people of many other nationalities. A very large proportion carried fire-arms of some kind, and these they now proceeded to discharge in the air, at the same time uttering frenzied cries and chants.

In the Serail, Olden found that a city government of sorts existed, in the form of a governor, Said Abd al-Qadir, who had been appointed by Djemal Pasha a day earlier as he withdrew through the city. But the Emir Said could not control the Arabs who had come in earlier, and more were arriving with Lawrence. Further, it turned out that Said and his group were not the only claimants to local power, and in fact were the lesser group.[25] One cannot help feeling that

[25] Olden, *Westralian Cavalry*, pp. 281–93.

Djemal Pasha on his way through had deliberately selected the most awkward group to leave in command. For example, Said Abd el-Qadir was the grandson of a famous resistance leader against the French in Algeria. He cannot have looked with much favour on any European takeover, and nor would the French be likely to be able to bring themselves to work with him. So there were multiple authorities in the city – the city government, their rivals, the Arabs led by Faisal, and the Allied forces, of which the smallest contingent, the French, laid claim to the largest area.

It would clearly take some time for this to be sorted out. When the generals arrived they found that the Turkish withdrawal had produced an effective administrative breakdown: the medical staff in the hospitals were not working, the bazaar had closed down, the gendarmes had lost all authority. One of the major problems was that the Arab Army had lost much of its discipline, and it took a full show of strength by machine gunners, armoured cars, Indian Lancers, and Australians in slouch hats, contingents from every regiment in a march through the city on 2 October, to restore minimal order. The medical staff had to be compelled to go back to work. It was Deraa repeated on a much larger scale, and Damascus had much greater influence elsewhere in Syria. Lawrence and Faisal may have had their political agenda, but they did not have the power – hence the Arab insistence on their priority in reaching the city (as at Deraa), as a move in claiming their political 'rights'. The confusion in the city made it clear to everyone involved that Damascus was going to be a problem, but at least the lack of opposition to the Australians, or to the Arabs, made it clear that the city was no longer under Turkish rule.

During the Desert Mounted Corps' advance on Damascus the 7th Meerut Division had remained at Haifa. It began marching north along the coast road on 29 September, by which time the Australians were at Kaukab. 7th Division in fact could not move until it was replaced at Haifa by the first elements of 54th Division, which had been itself unable to move until the 28th, and which was only fully installed at Haifa on 4 October. The problem was bad roads, a shortage of transport, and perhaps a certain lethargy after recent exertions.

The 7th Division had also been delayed in starting off by the knowledge that there was a major obstacle before it at the Ladder of Tyre, Ras Nakura, which was impassable for its artillery. This was a pass along the cliffs at the Ras ('nose', therefore a cape), part of which consisted of stone-cut steps. The pioneers and the Royal Engineers very gingerly smoothed out the steps, which were ages old. There was a clear danger that using explosives would cause the whole pass to slide into the sea, but General Fane took the risk, which turned out to be worth it. (If the pass really had collapsed, his forces would either have had to find a new route inland, or be carried by sea, an ignominious prospect.)

The division, reinforced by the artillery which had demanded the engineering work at the pass, the XXI Corps Cavalry, and assorted pioneers, engineers, and other cavalry forces, marched in three sections, making a column ten miles long, by way of the Ladder, the city of Tyre itself, and Sidon. The first part of the column reached Beirut on 8 October. The size, length, and display of power of this column were impressive, deliberate, and wholly successful. There was no resistance. A march of about a hundred miles in eight days made a fine display. But the division's arrival brought the Allies into as complex a situation as at Damascus a week earlier.[26] Already a French warship had arrived in the harbour, and Sharifian intrigues to gain power there had taken place.

Almost as soon as Allenby had begun his latest campaign, the various Allied political authorities had begun to position themselves to take advantage of his victory. That victory had become clear by the end of the first day's fighting, though its eventual extent was only revealed after the capture of Damascus, when the Turkish Army had very largely been eliminated. The Arab Army campaigned alongside the 4th Division along the Hajj road and Lawrence pushed to make sure the Arabs had representative forces in Damascus as soon as, or sooner than, anyone else. Where Allenby's instructions to his Desert Mounted Corps had been that Allied flags were not to be flown in the city, somehow great numbers of Sharifian flags had appeared even as the Arabs arrived, and were flown as soon as the city was occupied.

In London, meanwhile, the Foreign Secretary, A.J. Balfour, had been reminded by the French ambassador of the earlier agreement that the French were to have a preponderant role in the government of post-war Syria. Allenby on 30 September laid out his administrative intentions, having been prompted by the War Office, which no doubt had been jogged by Balfour. The whole region was to be subject to a military administration, the Occupied Enemy Territory Administration (OETA), on the pattern of Palestine (where Allenby and just set up a separated system in the centre and south).[27] This made it possible to install an Arab government in Damascus and east of the Jordan, with Faisal and British 'liaison officers' respectively 'to safeguard the interests of the inhabitants'. Along the coast he intended to appoint French military officers. All this is more or less in line with a Sykes-Picot Agreement, but the main

[26] Wylly, *Leicestershire Regiment*, p. 195; Falls, *Official History* Vol. II, pp. 602–3.
[27] Hughes (ed.), *Correspondence*, p. 161, Allenby to War Office, 30 September 1918.

purpose was to preclude any final decisions until the peace conference. Yet on the next day, 1 October (and therefore a little late), the War Office 'authorized' Allenby 'to hoist the Arab flag in Damascus'.[28] He met Faisal in the city two days later and told him of France's promised role as 'protecting power' in coastal Syria, and that he would have inland Syria, but with a French liaison officer beside him. Faisal did not like this, though he cannot have been surprised.[29]

The rickety ineffective government installed so casually by Djemal Pasha as he left the city did not survive the arrival of the Arab Army. Lawrence claims to have driven out the Al-Jaziri regime, such as it was, surviving a knife attack in the process.[30] But he had to resist their further attempt to seize power by machine-gunning their supporters. As so often, Lawrence sanitized this event in his later account, but one of his associates, Colonel Stirling, reported that the streets were littered with the dead and wounded after Lawrence had finished. Like Napoleon, Lawrence was fully capable of ruthlessness; this was his equivalent of the 'whiff of grapeshot'.[31] Their rivals were Sherifian supporters. Lawrence installed Ali Ridha Pasha al-Rikabi, a former Turkish general, as governor in Damascus; he had done plenty to sabotage resistance to the conquest as commander of the Turkish garrison and had taken timely refuge with General Barrow as things fell apart in the city. He was a soldier of long experience, an Arab, and a Sherifian supporter whom Lawrence had contacted a year earlier. His familiarity with the city was particularly useful, and his Sherifian allegiance was reassuring.[32]

The group now in charge in Damascus sent one of their leaders, Shukri Pasha al-Ayyubi, technically Ali Ridha's superior, to Beirut. There, as General Fane and the 7th Division would later discover, a new local government had come into existence as the Turks withdrew.[33] Again the aim was to make a political point before the British arrived – they were known to be on their away. This local group smoothly replaced the Turkish authorities and included both Muslims and Christians, and flew the Sharifian flags. This was thus already a complex situation, and more or less as the 7th Division arrived French war-

28 Ibid., p. 167, War Office to Allenby, 1 October 1918.
29 Ibid., p. 176, Allenby to War Office, 6 October 1918.
30 Lawrence, *Seven Pillars*, pp. 517–21.
31 Ibid., p. 522; Stirling, *Safety Last*, p. 95.
32 Lawrence, *Seven Pillars*, pp. 516, 527; Barrow, *Fire of Life*, pp. 212–15.
33 Hughes (ed.), *Correspondence*, pp. 174–8, Allenby to War Office, 6 and 7 October 1918.

ships sailed into Beirut harbour. Allenby came and imposed a new situation, aligned with Sykes-Picot: the Sharifian flag came down, Shukri Pasha and the Damascenes were removed, and a French military governor was installed. This was Colonel de Piepape, who had been the commander of the French *Detachement*.[34] The gesture could not have been clearer.

---

[34] Ibid., pp. 179 and 181, Allenby to Wilson, 8 and 11 October 1918.

CHAPTER 13

Aleppo and Haritan

THE advance from the 'Auja-Auja line' had brought the British forces out of the region where major medical efforts had kept the toll of diseases within bounds The advance now took the soldiers into the regions were such efforts had not been made, or at least had not succeeded. Those troops who had been stationed for any length of time in the Jordan Valley had already been exposed to the local form of malaria, which was particularly virulent, but now just about all the troops were to be exposed to it.

This was not the only disease to attack them. The Spanish influenza epidemic had begun to affect several battalions in September, and from 6 October the pneumonic variety attacked the advancing British forces and spread with great speed. This was just at the time that the forces in Damascus began to move against the Turks in the Bekaa Valley. These had, as the British discovered, mainly retreated through the Barada Gorge, and others had gone northwards towards Homs. Liman's account claims that in both cases most of the troops involved got through, but that his 43rd Division, which had not been engaged and was mainly composed of Arabs and Arab officers, was unreliable, two complete companies having deserted.[1]

Colonel Olden's 10th Light Horse Regiment had got out of the city with the help of the guide provided by Abd el-Qadir at the Serail, though he was soon seen to be taking them by a roundabout route. Then they were guided by an English-speaking Greek from Jaffa, who was more helpful, and collected a British airman who had been a prisoner and who was now free; he joined in the fighting. Getting out of the city, they were informed from the air that the retreating force, which was stiffened by a considerable number of German machine gunners, was some miles ahead. The pursuit was thereafter regularly delayed by the enemy rearguard, until at Khan Ayash, seventeen miles from Damascus, the Australians found themselves facing twenty machine guns firing over level ground from 'a kind of medieval fortress', while most of the enemy force climbed the hill to the west, out of reach and out of range. Having

---

[1] Liman von Sanders, *Five Years*, pp. 305–6.

taken about 600 prisoners, and with horses and men both exhausted, a halt was called to the pursuit.[2]

This was a fighting retreat, not the rout which had been the case among some Turkish units further south. It was clear that the Turks, with their German supporters, were by no means finished. Nor was Liman too despondent. He had problems with acquiring information, and his account reflects the partial and at times inaccurate reports he was receiving. For example, he records that 'on October 1 ... the British had occupied Beirut', which did not occur until the 8th, but he added that the city 'declared its adhesion to the Arab government', which was correct. On the 1st he held a conference with Djemal Pasha (IV Army), Mustapha Kemal (VII Army), and Colonel von Oppen (Asien Korps). It was agreed that making a stand in the Bekaa Valley was not possible. Djemal would go to Homs to organize the fugitives there, while Kemal was to hold on at Riyaq and form the rearguard, collecting the men who had got through from Damascus or the coast. On the next day the effect of the fighting at the gorge showed through, and no more troops arrived from Damascus. Liman took the opportunity to retreat without further interference.[3]

The delay by the British forces in following up the capture of Damascus was partly due to the preoccupation of the commanders with establishing control in the confused city, and to the need to rest and refresh men and horses, but it was also due to the ravages of malaria. The incubation period of the disease was about fourteen days, so that the newly infected troops who were bitten in the low lands after the battle – in the Jordan Valley, the Plain of Esdraelon, Beisan (a notoriously malarial spot), the crossing of the Jordan near Lake Huleh – began to fall ill as they arrived at the city. The great numbers of prisoners which were collected into camps were also a source of infection – cholera briefly appeared, stimulating the medical staff to great efforts to suppress it.[4] The conditions discovered in the Damascus hospitals horrified everyone. General Chauvel ordered that the medical staffs should make the care of the sick and wounded prisoners in those hospitals their priority. This was, it turned out, as much a problem of organization and supply as one of medical care and personnel. The medical staff struggled for several days to put things right, not helped by a quarrel initiated by Lawrence over who had authority over the enemy prisoners. The seriously ill were kept in Damascus, the less seriously

2 Olden, *Westralian Cavalry*, pp. 286–7.
3 Liman von Sanders, *Five Years*, p. 306.
4 Downes, *Campaign*, 78, note 1.

ill evacuated south, and prisoners of war were moved out of the city to more healthy camps. By 5 October it was reckoned that 'the medical situation was for the moment under control'.[5] The net result was that substantial parts of the British forces had to be detached to guard the prisoners, and many more of them fell ill.[6]

It was not until that same 5 October that any serious further move forward was made. The numbers of Turks who had retreated by the Barada route implied that they were gathering in the Bekaa, while it was also clear that Homs was another point of concentration. Strategically it was necessary to drive the enemy from the Bekaa, for if they advanced by the road east of the Anti-Lebanon (along which the 10th Light Horse had pursued its quarry) the British would leave Damascus vulnerable to a counter-attack through the gorge. The 4th and 5th Cavalry Divisions were sent through the gorge therefore. The Australian Division remained in and about Damascus.

The advance, as Allenby had insisted when urged to 'raid' as far as Aleppo, was to be by careful stages. The Turks were known to be retreating. Air reconnaissance over unprecedented distances reported the concentration at Homs, but it also reported their disorganization. The airfield at Riyaq was bombed, but there were few other targets worth attacking.[7] Liman put Djemal in charge, and set up eating centres, as the best way of gathering the hungry troops. Then they could be sorted out into their units, and re-armed. Picquets on all the nearby roads also collected the strays. But recovery would clearly take time. He now decided that Aleppo should be his headquarters, and that the army should retire there when the forces at Homs were able to move.[8]

Allenby's decision to move north by stages was therefore not fraught with much risk for the British, but given time the Turks would certainly be able to produce an effective resistance. They were moving into territory in which supplies were more plentiful, and where they could be reinforced as needed from the forces in Anatolia. The only way for the British to keep them off balance and vulnerable was to chase them and keep attacking.

This, however, turned out to be difficult. It was on 6 October (just as the medical situation in Damascus with thought to be under control), as the 4th and 5th Divisions were occupying Riyaq and the southern half of the Bekaa,

5   Ibid., pp. 729–35.
6   Falls, *Official History* Vol. II, pp. 597–9.
7   Cutlack, *Australian Flying Corps*, pp. 168–9.
8   Liman von Sanders, *Five Years*, pp. 308–9.

that the influenza epidemic struck. On top of the malaria infection, which was particularly prevalent in the 4th Division after its stay in the Jordan Valley and at Beisan, this reduced the division to effective incapacity.[9] Both divisions were reduced seriously in numbers. Allenby nevertheless ordered them to move on, but 4th Division could only move a short distance into the northern part of the Bekaa; it was soon reduced to only 1200 men and Barrow protested that he considered that were it to be forced into further exertions it would cease to be viable as a military unit. Allenby had to accept that. Even before leaving Damascus, 10th Brigade was losing fifty men a day, and at Baalbek it was reduced to only 800 men.[10] The 12th Brigade had 180 men sick on 10 October, and 600 three days later.[11] In Damascus the French and English hospitals had 625 patients for 247 beds.[12] The great difficulty in a cavalry regiment when many men were sick was that those who were healthy had to attend to all the horses, which were, of course, still healthy. This was a very lengthy process, leaving no time for anything else, such as fighting.

With the Australians held in Damascus, and having to guard tens of thousands of prisoners, and 4th Division incapacitated, any further pursuit of the Turkish forces had to be by the remaining healthy (more or less) division, the 5th. Allenby ordered General Macandrew to go as far as Homs in the first instance; an equal force of the Arab Army travelled east of the Anti-Lebanon in parallel. The division reached Baalbek on the 7th, and sent a reconnaissance towards Beirut, while others inspected the railways. By this time the 7th Division had reached Beirut next day by the coast road, and being much healthier than the cavalry was able to move on along the coast as far as Tripoli.

There is a gap in the chain of mountains facing the Mediterranean just north of Tripoli, where the Nahr el-Kabur reaches the sea. This provides a route from Homs and the inland regions to the coast. Homs at the inland end of this valley and Tripoli at the seaward end were thus the natural targets for the next stage in the British advance. The coastal forces, in the form of the XXI Corps Cavalry and a Light Armoured Car Battery reached Tripoli on the 13th; the city had, of course, been abandoned by the Turks. The 5th Division meanwhile moved north along the Bekaa more or less in parallel with the 7th Division on the coast and the Arab Army to the east. Homs, also deserted by

---

9   Barrow, *Fire of Life*, pp. 215–16.
10   TNA, WO 95/4513, War Diary of 10 Brigade, 5–15 October 1918.
11   TNA, WO 95/4514, War Diary of 12 Brigade, 9–13 October 1918.
12   Downes, *Campaign*, p. 736.

the Turks by this time, was reached by the advanced guard on the 16th; the rest of the division came up soon after, and settled down to three days' rest.

The collapse of 4th Division necessitated the reinforcement of the weakened 5th, which was about 2500-strong, at Homs. Allenby ordered up a Light Car Patrol from the Egyptian Western Desert, and brought the armoured cars from XXI Corps across from Tripoli. But this was not really an imposing force to send 120 miles ahead of any support. It would face a revitalized Turkish army several times its numbers, about to fight in defence of its homeland. On 19 October Allenby ordered the divisions to advance on Aleppo, but then finally accepted that 4th Division was immobilized through sickness. Next morning the 5th Division had started out, but Allenby cancelled his instructions. General Macandrew was not pleased, and replied by telegram that 'Troops far in advance, and I propose advancing with armoured cars to Aleppo', and claimed that there was 'no opposition worth thinking of expected at Aleppo', though what intelligence this was based on is unclear, probably from air reconnaissance.[13]

By this time Mustapha Kemal had organized the Turkish troops in the Aleppo area into two divisions, the 1st and the 11th. Other forces were still not organized but were travelling north, and on 14 October another new division began to be organized; a fourth was moved into Alexandretta, where Allied ships had appeared in the Gulf, and a landing was feared.[14] (A landing at Alexandretta had been mooted more than once since 1914, and was being discussed again; it is perhaps just as well it was not considered necessary in 1918.)

Macandrew in his telegram reported that Hama was clear, and next morning he was given permission to go on. It is evident that the Turks were still retreating, and were not willing to attempt a stand in front of the 5th Division yet, though they had blown the bridge over the Orontes River at ar-Restan. Considering the map, it was obvious that they would not stand and fight in any serious way before Aleppo, but rearguard actions could be expected. Liman had also begun to move his headquarters into Cilicia, to Adana. Intelligence estimates put the number of Turks in or about Aleppo at 20,000, mainly rear area troops, and that the combat troops amongst them were demoralized – not an unlikely state, but not one it was safe to rely on.[15]

Macandrew, therefore, advanced with due caution, even if he was reckoned

---

13   Falls, *Official History* Vol. II, pp. 611–12, note.
14   Liman von Sanders, *Five Years*, pp. 313–14.
15   Preston, *Desert Mounted Corps*, p. 287.

to be, as Falls in the *Official History* II has it, a 'vigorous and headstrong commander'. He was given permission to move on to Hama, but was to halt there for a week. He had the assistance of aircraft, and a unit of RAF technicians who prepared temporary landing grounds for the reconnaissance planes. He was thus fully aware of the equally careful Turkish withdrawal in front of him. The order to halt at Hama was cancelled, and on 22 October the armoured cars made contact with the Turks, a lorried force which was caught up with north of Ma'aret en-Numan. The two forces clashed in a running fight, but the British cars drew too far ahead of the cavalry to risk a further advance once the Turks got away. A patrol located the Turks next day, entrenched before the city of Aleppo, and thought to be 3000-strong. Macandrew sent in a demand for surrender by letter. 'The commander of the Turkish garrison in Aleppo does not find it necessary to reply to your note', was the reply.[16]

This was a fully justified non-reply and the British cars then waited, several miles south of the city, for two days while the horsemen came up. From the east, having followed the railway, came 1500 Arabs commanded by Colonel Nuri es-Said (who had been one of the first into Damascus). From the south, along the road, came the 15th Brigade, now with only two regiments, the Mysore Lancers and the Jodhpore Lancers, Imperial Service regiments. By 25 October these forces were in position to attack from south of the city.

The 13th Brigade was some way to the south, and next day (the 26th) 'orders were received for the fittest brigade (as regards horses) to move on Aleppo';[17] the 14th Brigade was also sent north, though presumably not seen as being quite as fit. For the moment, however, any action at Aleppo depended on the two regiments of 15th Brigade.

It was more or less arranged that 15th Brigade would attack next day, the weary horses having had some rest. The Arabs, however, decided – whether spontaneously or by Nuri's decision is not known – to attack in the afternoon of the 26th. The city was a formidable proposition, especially for cavalry. Still walled, with gates especially designed for defence, it had a steep-sided Citadel in the centre, which, even if the main building was less than robust after four centuries of neglect, it would be extremely difficult to seize. The Arab force was perhaps 1500-strong, partly composed of men from the forces who had campaigned in the south, and partly opportunistic Bedouin collected on the

---

[16] TNA, WO 95/4515, War Diary of 5 Cav. Div., 23 October 1918; Falls, *Official History* Vol. II, p. 601.

[17] TNA, WO 95/4518, War Diary of 13 Brigade, 26 October 1918.

way. The first attack, from the south, failed; a second, from the east, broke into the city, and Arabs fought Turks in the streets. It seems that the Arabs reached the Citadel, even getting a few men inside, but were then driven out of the city altogether.[18] The 5th Division officers understood that there had been 'serious fighting, in which the Turks suffered heavy casualties', but this was clearly a report by the Arabs, whose lack of success renders such reports highly suspect.[19]

This failure of the attack should have reassured the Turkish commander, General Mustapha Kemal. The British armoured cars were no more suited to fighting in the streets and alleys of Aleppo than were the horsemen of 15th Brigade, all Lancers. The Arabs were unlikely to be able to make another attack after their defeat. So he should be able to hold the city, and he had other forces outside; the British and the Arabs might be caught between them. He had reinforcements on the way, and a considerable proportion of his troops were Germans. He did not have much in the way of cavalry, and no artillery to speak of, but well-placed infantry (behind city walls, for example) could hold off cavalry – and lancers were no good against walls.

Then he received a report that a column of British vehicles was approaching, and concluded that it was bringing infantry to balance the cavalry. In fact it was a supply column, bringing food and fodder for the men and the horses, and maintenance supplies for the cars. Kemal's force would not be able to combat a serious British infantry attack, which would be supported by plenty of machine guns and artillery from outside the city. So he brought out all his forces, and pulled back northwards for about five miles, placing his men behind a small ridge, with the road, the railway, and the river on his left. One of the main prizes in this area was the Muslimiye railway junction, just behind his position. This was where the railways to Mesopotamia, to Syria, and to Anatolia, joined. British aircraft had bombed this junction on the 23rd.[20]

The fighting in Aleppo had seen some of the inhabitants joining with the Arabs, and the Turks' withdrawal was harassed by some of the Arab horsemen. Liman von Sanders says that Bedouin were rising in revolt in the rear of the new Turkish position. So the Turks were under some pressure, and it was clearly more comfortable to be out of the city. The soldiers who were entrenched south of the city were withdrawn, the bridges were blown, and the

[18] Liman von Sanders, *Five Years*, p. 317.
[19] TNA WO 95/4515, War Diary of 5 Cav. Div., 25 October 1918.
[20] Cutlack, *Australian Flying Corps*, pp. 169–71.

railway bridge was blocked by a derailed vehicle, which meant the cavalry had to cross only one horse at a time.[21]

All this was done without the British in front of the city being aware. An air report suggested that the Turks were about 1000 strong, though it was clear that this was inaccurate. The 14th Brigade had caught up with the leaders on the 26th, and the Mysore Lancers and the Jodhpore Lancers rode round west of the city and north along the Alexandretta road until fired at by machine gunners. Again the report which reached the command staff was of only a small Turkish force, perhaps 200-strong. The brigade commander, Brigadier-General Harbord, believing that he faced a small, withdrawing enemy force, let the two lancer regiments attack, supported on the left by the machine-gun squadron. They were to be supported by the 12th Light Armoured Motor Battery, but when it advanced it came under fire, suffered several burst tires, and pulled back.

The Turks were located on and behind a rocky hill, and other troops were close to the Alexandretta road. The distance between these two positions was four miles, but it does not appear to have occurred to anyone on the British side that these were the flanks of a larger force. The rocky hill also was too far from the British machine guns for them to give support to the Lancers in their attack. The nearest place is Haritan, for which the action is named.

The Mysore Lancers were ordered to 'make a mounted attack on the enemy's left flank, with Jodhpore Lancers (less two squadrons) in support'. This brought the Lancers right across the front of the enemy position, fully in view of the Turks, whom they themselves could not see. Major W.J. Lambert made a personal reconnaissance, and found the Turkish left flank 'on a rocky knoll', and noted that 'columns of the enemy were seen retiring further back'. At 11.30 a.m. the Lancers charged the rocky hill in extended order, but faced artillery, machine-gun, and rifle fire, which was 'very heavy'; Mustapha Kemal was directing the firing personally. Major Lambert later claimed that 'The position, held by a party of 150 Turks, was carried, about fifty of the enemy being speared and twenty prisoners taken', though the war diary of the Mysore Lancers claimed that 'about 120 of the enemy threw down their arms, many being killed with the lance'. None of the numbers, except perhaps the prisoners, is any more than a guess. The Mysore Lancers pulled back, and even the bland *Official History* admits that they were 'shaken'. The Jodhpore Lancers moved forward, but before they could attack they came under fire also. The colonel

[21] TNA, WO 95/4519, War Diary of 14 Brigade, 26 October 1918.

was killed, then the captain of one of the squadrons, who was about to lead them in a charge, was also killed. At last an officer with a cool head, one of the Indians, ordered a retirement.[22]

At last also the British realized what they faced, and the number of the Turks, who were now moving forward intending to attack, was put at 3000. The attack did not actually take place, but the Turks began to entrench, and the two cavalry regiments could do no more. The British casualties are admitted to be eighty, whereas the maximum claimed for Turkish casualties is seventy (Lambert claimed a hundred), which is undoubtedly an overestimate.

This was a fairly stupid matter on the British side, and must count as a British defeat. The Turks withdrew during the night, but only to a new position a few miles to the north, where they were reinforced, and where they dug in – 'a very strong position', according to the 5th Division's war diary.[23] Added to the 1st and 11th Divisions, each of which built up to between 2000 and 3000 men, was the 43rd Division (the Arab formation which was considered unreliable), and there were four more divisions of much the same size within marching distance. The 3000 men whom the Lancers had faced at Haritan had grown to well over double that by the time of the Turks' withdrawal. Needless to say the withdrawal was regarded by Brigadier-General Harbord as a mark of his men's victory.

On the other hand, Harbord was no doubt much relieved to be joined by the 14th Cavalry Brigade during the night, and when Macandrew reached Aleppo next morning and understood the situation he – 'a vigorous and head-strong commander' – refused to make a new attack. In the next days both sides steadily built up their strength. The 13th Brigade arrived, putting 5th Division at its full strength, and the Australian Mounted Division began to march north, though it was only at Homs by 31 October.

The Turks had seen the reactions of the populations in the cities as the British forces successively reached them. Damascus, Baalbek, Beirut, Homs, Tripoli, Hama, had all seen popular demonstrations, flowers thrown, Sherifian flags on the buildings, speeches and banquets of welcome. At Aleppo some of the inhabitants had even joined the Arabs in the fight in the city – no other city had done this, but then Aleppo is different – and Macandrew met another joyous welcome on his arrival. These demonstrations, of course, were in celebration of the removal of Turkish rule, but not necessarily in anticipation of

---

[22] TNA, WO 95/4519, War Diary of Mysore Lancers, 26 October 1918.
[23] TNA WO 95/4515, War Diary of 5 Cav. Div., 28 October 1918

anything precise replacing it, though the production of Sherifian flags implied a wish to become part of the great Arab kingdom.

All this was as obvious to the Turks as to everyone else. Liman von Sanders records them all in his book. Mustapha Kemal and the Young Turks in the government were also fully aware of Arab sentiment. One of the motives for Kemal's withdrawal from Aleppo, and his successive withdrawals in the next days, was to cut the Turkish links with the Arab lands. The Young Turk movement was always a Turkish nationalist one, and the war had only emphasized that. Enver's final military moves had been to retake and extend Turkish rule into lost Turkish lands in the Caucasus and into north-west Persia. (And he died four years later attempting to raise a new Turkish Empire in Central Asia.)

Mustapha Kemal had, by the end of October, a force large enough to defeat any new British attack, given that the British had to use their forces to control the whole of Palestine and Syria, and could not gather a large enough force in the north for another couple of weeks at least. The Australian Mounted Division could not have reached Aleppo in less than another week, artillery was needed, the men and horses had to be rested and fed, supplies had to be brought up. Meanwhile Kemal's force could be doubled or tripled in numbers in that period, and his numerous machine guns could be supplemented by more, and he could acquire more artillery. At the end of October the prospect was of another great battle, one which the British must have looked to with some apprehension. Allenby had already noted that the Turkish railway running north from Riyaq in the Bekaa Valley was standard gauge and that his forces had captured very little rolling stock, so supplying his army in North Syria would require constant road convoys similar to the one which had deceived Kemal and Liman earlier. Meanwhile, at long last the railway tunnel through the Amanus Mountains had been completed, and Kemal would be able to receive supplies direct from Cilicia and Anatolia.

It was therefore with some relief on the part of the British command staff that they heard that the Turks, at a meeting with the British admiral in the Mediterranean, Admiral Calthorpe, had agreed to an armistice.

CHAPTER 14

The Occupied Territories

THE penetration of British forces into northern Syria brought them into a very different political society than they had found in Palestine. The political turmoil in Damascus, and the complex doings in Lebanon, showed this even in the first week of the British conquest, and the French were already establishing a presence. The political issue, however, was much wider than merely Syria and Palestine. The Ottoman Empire still existed and was still relatively well armed – the armistice did not require Turkish disarmament – while the king of the Arabs had strong ambitions for expansion and had a right to expect consideration from his allies. Then there was President Woodrow Wilson of the United States of America.

The framework for the control of the conquered territory, which stretched from the Sinai desert to beyond Aleppo, had been laid out the year before. It was known as the Occupied Enemy Territory Administration (OETA) until the status of the land was decided at the peace conference, and its deeds were then ratified. Syria-Palestine was thus left in suspense, a condition conducive to much intrigue and disturbance.

This suspense continued for a year, during which the war with Germany was won, refreshing elections in Britain confirmed Lloyd George's coalition government in power, and President Wilson sailed the Atlantic. The peace conference was convened early in 1919, but the Middle East, as it was to be called after the American fashion, was well down the agenda of everyone except the inhabitants, and only a few of those were consulted. During this time, the variety of ambitions entertained and the promises that had been made, principally by the British, emerged to enhance the confusion. Meanwhile Allenby's OETA established British power more or less nakedly in Palestine. Colonel Ronald Storrs – a bureaucrat from the British administration in Egypt (the 'Colonel' was a non-military rank) – was installed as Military Governor of Jerusalem, and military men governed elsewhere – General Sir Arthur Money was in charge of the Palestine OETA.

The whole region had suffered greatly during the war. Turkish requisitions had been notably thorough, and this in a region which had had little wealth even before the fighting. Operating the railways had required the destruction of much forested land, including cutting down fruit trees. The country had little industry, and what there was lost its European markets in 1914. Agriculturally it was largely a peasant society, though Zionist villages had developed some fruit exports – also these had lost their markets during the war. The British intelligence summary in the early days of the conquest after 19 September was blandly optimistic: 'The harvest has been good ... though the area under cultivation is less than normal [and] animals are short.'[1]

For its size, the whole region must be regarded as under-populated. The Ottoman census of 1914, probably only approximate, suggested a population of perhaps 2.5 million in the provinces of Halab, Suriye, Kudus, and the Transjordan lands. Of these, about 700,000 lived in Palestine, half of which was under British control before September 1918.[2] These numbers had fallen considerably during the war. A famine in the Lebanese area in 1915 is said to have killed 'tens of thousands', and may have reduced the population by a fifth.[3] other areas had no doubt suffered proportionately. When the British forces reached Lebanon they were shocked at the evidence of continuing famine, and more than one regiment adopted starving children for a time until they could be placed with a charity.[4]

To safeguard the health of his army, Allenby put much effort into improving public health, notably by suppressing malarial mosquitoes, and partly by encouraging the development of medical services, which were extended from the troops to the general population. The effect was highlighted by the widespread infection of the army when the battles of September brought the British troops into the Turkish areas where such public health measures had been less effective. These improvements were soon extended to all of Syria, though they took a long time to have full effect. One of the effects was the eventual decline in child deaths, and the subsequent expansion of the population, an expansion which has continued until the present day. (The population of the five countries of greater Syria was over 40 million in 2007).[5]

The oppressive conditions of Turkish rule during the war had included the execution of a number of men in Beirut and Damascus who were identified as enemies of the Ottoman state. These men were certainly anti-Turkish, but

[1] GHQ EEF, Intelligence Summary, 25 September 1918.
[2] Karput, *Ottoman Population*.
[3] Petran, *Struggle over Lebanon*, p. 28.
[4] For example, Blackwell and Axe, *Romford to Beirut*, p. 169, and Gibbons, *1/5th Essex*, p. 162.
[5] *The Economist, Pocket World in Figures*, 2010 edition.

then by 1916 so was the great majority of the Syrian population, and much of the fear engendered by this general opinion operated in the mind of Djemal Pasha (the Greater). The Syrians were, however, hardly politically organized. The secret societies had existed before the war, but were largely dismantled. Their ideas of nationalism and independence spread, but exactly what form the wished-for independence would take was not clear. The removal of Turkish rule was perhaps for many the main, and a sufficient, aim, but beyond that no clear plans could be made. Faisal, the son of the 'King of the Arabs', had contacted prominent Syrians before Husain began his rebellion, and was promoted by Lawrence as a future king of Syria. (Faisal also visited the city clandestinely during 1917, at considerable personal risk.) On the other hand, many Syrians had some European education, largely from France or under French influence, and a Syrian republic might be their preference.[6]

In the Lebanon area there were particular local ideas. The Mutasarrifiyya of 'The Mountain' was abolished by the Young Turks in 1915 as part of their modernization programme. The restoration of that autonomy was a widespread wish within the old province. Its extension, to take in the Bekaa Valley, which would expand the food supply for the coastal region, was also a local ambition. This ambition for both expansion and restoration conflicted to some degree with the general assumption among Syrians that 'Syria' meant the lands from Sinai to the Taurus Mountains. This might conflict with the rivalry which existed between Aleppo and Damascus, capitals of separate provinces, while Palestine might also wish for autonomy. None of these aims were, of course, irreconcilable, and a federal Arab monarchy for all Syria – 'Greater Syria' as it is now termed – was quite possible. That this did not happen was largely the result of the imperial ambitions of the European powers, but they were greatly assisted by divisions amongst the Syrians themselves.

In command of conquered Syria, Allenby, on instructions from London, had already taken measures which undermined the agreements made with Britain's allies during the war. It was clear that Britain was not going to relinquish the hold which Allenby had fastened on Palestine. The Balfour Declaration had also made that clear. These measures undermined the Sykes-Picot Agreement which had been made with the French, in which Palestine was supposed to come under an international administration (whatever that meant), and simultaneously indicated to King Husain and his sons that the kingdom of the Arabs would not include Palestine. Since the revelation of the Agreement

---

6   Petran, *Syria*, pp. 52–3; Longrigg, *Syria and Lebanon*, pp. 49–52.

in November 1917 by the Bolsheviks in Russia, it was clear that France would expect to be compensated for its sufferings by imposing itself on the coastal part of Syria at the very least.

Allenby, however, was not able to discern any clarity in the intentions of the London government, largely because that government did not itself know what it wanted in the Middle East. He therefore took as his text the Sykes-Picot Agreement. This had marked Palestine for international administration, Mesopotamia for Britain, coastal Syria (from Ras Nakura to the Gulf of Alexandretta) to France, while the interior was to be part of the Arab kingdom. By now, the notion of the international administration in Palestine had faded away, and Britain had made it clear that Haifa and Acre, with the very useful Bay of Haifa, would become British. He had indicated that Damascus was to be taken by Faisal and the Arab Army. The installation of Ali Ridha al-Rikabi as governor, to rule the city in Faisal's name, was done under the authority of Allenby as Commander-in-Chief.

Allenby's adherence to the surviving fragments of the Sykes-Picot Agreement, in default of any other plan, was sufficient to install Faisal and his people in authority in Damascus, but on the coast it meant the suppression of early movements to do the same. When the 7th Division reached Beirut on 8 October, a Sharifian government was in post and claimed to have authority in the old Lebanese province, though this was not something the locals were happy about. But this was the region which the agreement assigned to France. Allenby dismissed the Sharifians and put in Colonel P. de Piepape as his military governor in Beirut,[7] and other French officers were soon controlling other Lebanese coastal towns, such as Tyre and Sidon.

When Allenby's forces took Aleppo, therefore, the occupation system was all set up. There were three OETA areas: 'South' was Palestine, firmly under British control and administration; 'North' was the Lebanese and Syrian coast as far as Alexandretta, under a French administration; 'East' was the rest, roughly bounded by the coastal mountains – Lebanon-Jebel Ansariyeh-Amanus, and including the Bekaa Valley – which was the area under Arab administration. This was all set up explicitly on the authority of Allenby as Commander-in-Chief. The military governors in Jerusalem and Beirut, of Damascus and Aleppo, British, French or Arab, were appointed by and responsible to Allenby.

---

7   Hughes (ed.), *Correspondence*, pp. 175 and 177, Allenby to Wilson, 6 and 7 October 1918.

It was also explicitly temporary, which did not prevent the French and the Arabs operating as if they had full and permanent powers.

The Arabs claimed to rule Syria in nationalist terms, since all the people there were Arabs. The French, on the other hand, could use this Arab claim against Husain and Faisal, since many of the people – 'communities' – in Syria spoke Arabic, but were not Muslim – and the Sharif Husain was one of the most prominent Muslims in the world. As early as the beginning of November Allenby was complaining that Capt. Mercier, the French officer installed as the liaison with Faisal, was making promises to the Druzes in the Jebel Druze that the French would protect them against the Arabs.[8] The Druzes had been allies of Liman von Sanders until the conquest of Damascus, and many of them had made themselves notorious by their assiduous looting in the city until they were expelled. There were other 'communities' in Syria who feared Muslim Arab rule. In the north in the Jebel Ansariyeh were the Alawites, another heretical Muslim group; in Lebanon there were Christian (Maronites especially, but also Greek Catholics), Muslims (Shias, Druzes), and smaller groups; each of these contended with the others, which was one good reason for the Lebanon to be treated differently from the rest of Syria. But the several blocks of territories inhabited by these minorities also made Syria as a whole a difficult region to rule. In many ways it was tailor-made to be a federation.

The various agreements and treaties made during the war had entangled Britain and France, King Husain and Faisal, in a mix of obligations and promises, and others had an effect on affairs in Syria. The Balfour Declaration promised that Britain would regard Palestine as a 'National Home' for the Jews. This was an undertaking to which both the United States and France were parties, the latter by a similar mechanism - a letter from the French Foreign Minister to a French Zionist. It was, however, a device invented for short-term reasons, mainly to persuade Jews in the United States and Russia to support the Allies' war effort, but also to pre-empt a similar move which, it was understood, was being contemplated in Germany. What the promise meant was unclear, but some thought it would have indicated that one consequence would be to boost the Zionist cause, part of whose ideology was that the Jews should 'return' to Palestine. There were several Zionist settlements there already, established before the war, which tended to be regarded with suspicion by the Turks – a

---

[8] Ibid., p. 190, Allenby to War Office, 4 November 1918, quoting a report from Faisal of 2 November.

suspicion fully justified, since the Zionists tended to support the Allies, spied for them, and when the Allied armies arrived, helped them.[9]

The Allied alignment with the Zionists meant increased pressure from Zionists to settle in Palestine when they were able. A high-powered Zionist Commission arrived in March 1918 and made emotional gestures to publicize their requirements. It also brought cash to subsidize Jewish-Zionist activities and ambitions, helped local Zionists to gain and maintain control over the local Jewish communities, and pressed for such things as a Jewish mayor for Jerusalem. A copy of the Torah from Jaffa, which had been hidden at Petah-Tikveh from possible Turkish molestation, was ceremoniously recovered and carried to Jerusalem. So, even though the text of the Balfour Declaration was not fully known in Palestine - it was not published there until 1920 – it was quite obvious to the local Arabs, from the reception given by the OETA to the Commission, that Jewish and Zionist demands were at least being listened to.[10]

If the British government did not appreciate this consequence, the local Palestinian Arab population quickly did. A group of Syrians in Cairo proposed to send a telegram to the Foreign Office asserting that Palestine was part of Syria, though it was suppressed before being sent; Muslims in London pointed out that Jerusalem was regarded as a holy city in Islam; Arabs in the United States also protested.[11] The publication of the Sykes-Picot Agreement about the same time also brought the suspicions of King Husain to a higher point than ever. In all this the future conflict over Palestine was clearly foreshadowed.

President Wilson stirred the pot further in January 1918 with his Fourteen Points. Self-determination was one of the ideological foundations of the American political system, and he sought, in his evangelical way, to extend this 'self-evident' concept to others. As the 12th 'Point', he included the oppressed inhabitants of the Turkish Empire, even though the United States was not at war with Turkey. The news spread rapidly through those oppressed populations, and each group inevitably interpreted it in its own interests and in accordance with its own ambitions.

A group of seven Syrian Arabs in Cairo enquired directly of the British whether they endorsed the concept of independence and federation for the Arabs; they thought that the reply they received was unsatisfactory, particu-

9 Sheffy, *British Military Intelligence, passim.*
10 Shepherd, *Ploughing Sand*, pp. 39–40.
11 Tibawi, *Anglo-Arab Relations*, pp. 236, 265, 273; Monroe, *Britain's Moment*, pp. 44–5.

larly after the welcome extended to the Zionist Commission in Palestine.[12] Already in July 1918 there was a dispute between Jews and Arabs in Jerusalem after a clumsy Zionist attempt to buy land near the Wailing Wall from the Mufti of Jerusalem.[13] About that time D.G. Hogarth, an academic who had been working in the Arab Bureau in Cairo since 1914, toured Palestine in early 1918. His report to the Foreign Office made it clear that there was widespread dislike of the prospect of French authority and of Zionist aspirations.[14]

So within nine months of the Balfour Declaration, there was plenty of evidence that the British policy of promoting Zionist activities would be opposed by the inhabitants of Palestine. These had been referred to vaguely in the declaration as 'existing non-Jewish communities', and an equally vague promise was made that they would be protected. It was obvious that the Arabs of Palestine would be seen by the British rulers as second-class citizens when compared with the Jews. Balfour made this explicit as early as 1917: 'Zionism is more important than the "desires and prejudices" of the 700,000 Arabs who now inhabit it'.[15]

The conquest of northern Syria therefore only increased the potential for disputes among the Allies, and added general suspicion, even hostility, from the existing populations of the 'Occupied Enemy Territory'. The British were regarded with particular suspicion in Palestine, but in the northern areas it was the intentions of the French which were of especial concern. Faisal in Damascus had expressed his concern to Allenby as early as 8 October, which he repeated a week later,[16] and this is a regular theme in Allenby's correspondence during the next year. He could only reply that the situation was temporary, and only the peace conference would settle things finally.

The implementation of the armistice terms proved to be slow and difficult.[17] The German soldiers in Turkish territory were to be 'evacuated', which meant first gathering them together at Constantinople, then sending them on to Germany through the Black Sea ports, principally Odessa. The Ukraine descended into chaos, however, and the remainder, 10,000 men, were taken through the Mediterranean to the North Sea ports. This took some time, but it did leave

[12] Tibawi, *Anglo-Arab Relations*, pp. 275–7.
[13] Ibid., pp. 286–9; Gilbert, *Jerusalem*, pp. 69–70.
[14] TNA, FO 371/3381, pp. 107–11; Tibawi, *Anglo-Arab Relations*, p. 280.
[15] Quoted, without attribution, by Shepherd, *Ploughing Sand*, p. 14.
[16] Hughes (ed.), *Correspondence*, p. 179, Allenby to Wilson 8 October 1918, p. 183, Allenby to War Office, 17 October 1918.
[17] The terms are reprinted in Falls, *Official History* Vol. II, pp. 625–7.

the Turkish armies under sole Turkish command for the first time in several years, and many of the Turkish generals were not willing to accept the British interpretation of the armistice terms.

In truth the terms were carelessly worded. The assumption on the Allied side was that the Turks were as beaten and submissive as the Bulgars, but this was not so. The terms had been arranged by Admiral Sir Somerset Gough-Calthorpe, the British naval commander in the Mediterranean (sent to conduct the negotiations in order to supersede the French admiral in the Aegean). It was intended that British and naval priorities should predominate, and the terms show naval influence; those concerning the army are notably vague. In particular the clause dealing with the demobilization of the Turkish army could be easily evaded, and Turkish commanders took full advantage. The soldiers were to be demobilized immediately 'except for such troops as are required for surveillance of frontiers and for the maintenance of internal order' (clause 5). Just how many this referred to would be determined later, but in the immediate aftermath it meant that any Turkish general who wanted to do so could keep all his men under the pretence of guarding the frontiers (unspecified until the decisions of the peace conference) or maintaining 'internal order'.

The rationale of this clause is obvious. Most of Turkey was unconquered, and some of its frontiers, particularly that with Russia, were particularly disturbed. None of the Allies had any wish to become involved in defending Turkey against, say, Bolshevik Russia, nor did any of the Allies relish the prospect of becoming responsible for police duties in Anatolia. But to leave everything vague was merely asking for trouble.

There were also specific geographical clauses in the terms which were equally vague. For the Syrian theatre of war, these were that the Allies would occupy the 'Taurus tunnel system' (clause 10); Turkish forces were to withdraw 'except those necessary to maintain order', from Cilicia; the isolated forces in Arabia, Tripolitania and Cyrenaica were to surrender (clauses 16 and 17). There proved to be plenty of room for argument over territory for delay in these terms. The Turks appreciated as much as the Allies that the physical occupation of territory would be a crucial point in any of the peace negotiations. This had been one of the reasons for the risky British advance as far as Aleppo. In Mesopotamia the supine British army had finally pushed forward in the month before the armistice was agreed in order to seize more territory. This was why the French put their officers into Lebanese port-cities, and even landed a battalion at Alexandretta and two at Mersin in Cilicia, one of their targets. In the same way, Turkish commanders could use the provisions of the armistice to hold on to territory. At least two commanders, Nihad Pasha, who took over from Mustapha Kemal in the land north of Aleppo and Cilicia, and Ali Ihsan Pasha in Mesopotamia, shifted large numbers of their soldiers into the gendarmerie, while evacuating others. They thus continued in occupation – to maintain internal order – until Allenby, having tried persuasion, finally pushed his own forces northwards.

They had to cope with a variety of problems, in some cases simple brigandage, which had always troubled the region. As the Turkish forces withdrew, an unpoliced area opened up between them and the British. The Poona Horse, based at Jerablus on the Euphrates from January 1919, soon instituted regular patrols of the surrounding area, and their replacement, the 53rd Sikhs, were still troubled by raids in September.[18] In the south it became necessary to send patrols across the Jordan, where Bedouin raids had to be countered; the Deccan Horse became involved in a regular battle at one point.[19] The Arab government in this area was obviously ineffective.

The second type of problem was unrest in the cities. The Bombay Pioneers, the only infantry unit in the northern region, were used to control Hama after attacks on British soldiers who were acting as police.[20] There were threats of riots or massacres, and actual violence in several places, usually due to the detestation that Turks and Armenians felt for each other after the Armenian troubles during the war. This element pulled the British into several towns in the north. The Sherwood Rangers had to deal with a riot in Aleppo in February 1919, and then had to picquet the town.[21] Hodson's Horse moved into several places, dealt with bandits, and patrolled the villages. In February the regiment marched to Marash to prevent a threatened Armenian massacre.[22] In this way the British control gradually extended from Aleppo to the Taurus Mountains - indeed a detachment of the Duke of Lancaster's Own Yeomanry was sent in December 1918 into part of these mountains. The regimental history plaintively says 'there is no record of their doings, but they remained there until August 1919'.[23]

It was not therefore until 26 December that Nihad Pasha was compelled to withdraw his forces from Cilicia, and French troops could expand throughout

[18] Wylly, *Poona Horse*, pp. 164–5; Anon., *53rd Sikhs*, p. 253.
[19] Tennant, *Royal Deccan Horse*, pp. 171–3.
[20] Tugwell, *Bombay Pioneers*, p. 336.
[21] Tallants, *Sherwood Rangers*, p. 172.
[22] Cardew, *Hodson's Horse*, pp. 220–1.
[23] Brereton, *Chain Mail*, p. 81.

that region,[24] which then became a new OETA region. (But the French used two Armenian battalions, whose presence merely aggravated local anger. In the end Allenby insisted on their withdrawal to garrison, and their replacement by French metropolitan troops.)[25] Ali Ihsan Pasha, east of the Euphrates, was even more difficult to shift; he delayed until winter gripped the area. Part of it was occupied by the British 28th Indian Brigade (the already mentioned 53rd Sikhs at Jerablus) late in December, but the occupation of other areas was even more delayed. It took a visit by Allenby personally to Constantinople to get Ali Ihsan Pasha superseded in his command,[26] and he resisted attempts to reinforce the French forces.[27]

It had been just as difficult to remove the Turkish IX Army from Medina. General Fahr ed-Din Pasha was determined never to surrender, no matter what the armistice terms might say. There were also other Turkish forces further south in Asir and Yemen and Aden who, if united with the Medina army, could have caused much trouble. King Husain in Mecca and Ibn Saud in Riyadh were now almost at open war, and a Turkish intervention there could bring Allied disaster. A map in the daily intelligence summary of 30 October shows that the Turks still controlled 300 miles of the Hejaz Railway from Medina northwards, with '4010 Rifles, 49 M[achine] G[un]s, 64 guns'; this was not a negligible force.[28]

For the Allies, that is, the British, therefore, it was just as well that Fahr ed-Din's officers were much less committed to the need for continued resistance than he was. He held out for two months, but then he fell ill, and these officers carried through a *coup*, arrested him, and organized the surrender.[29] As it happened this simply left the local field open to Husain and Ibn Saud – both British allies – to fight it out. Eight thousand Turkish troops (from Medina and Yemen and Aden) went into captivity in Egypt, to join the tens of thousands already there.

[24] Falls, *Official History* Vol. II, p. 622.
[25] Hughes (ed.), *Correspondence*, p. 201, Allenby to Wilson, 4 February 1919.
[26] Falls, *Official History* Vol. II, p. 623; Hughes (ed.), *Correspondence*, p. 198, Allenby to Wingate, 15 January 1919.
[27] Hughes (ed.), *Correspondence*, p. 201, Allenby to Wilson, 4 February 1919.
[28] GHQ EEF, War Diary Intelligence Summary, 30 October 1918.
[29] Wasti, 'Defence of Medina,' in *Middle Eastern Studies*, 642–53 at 27.

CHAPTER 15

Problems with the Army

THERE was a widespread misapprehension in November 1918 that the war was over. The successive armistices with Bulgaria, the Ottoman Empire, Austria-Hungary, and Germany certainly brought the fighting to an end, and the insistence in all cases that the defeated armies be largely demobilized at once made it clear that the Allies had the victory, and that the fighting was unlikely to be resumed. But an armistice was only that – an end to fighting – not a peace. For the British soldiers who were stationed in northern Syria in 1919, the difference would be clear – that were still substantial numbers of Turkish soldiers in arms, either as soldiers or as gendarmes, or even as bandits in several parts of the region. There was even a complete Turkish army in Arabia which did not surrender until January 1919. There could be no confusion between an armistice and a peace here.

Yet in other, more tranquil, areas the confusion of an armistice with the restoration of peace was understandable, and for soldiers who were a long way from home and who had enlisted in, or been conscripted into, the army for the duration of the war, the time had clearly arrived for them to be returned to their homes, and this was expected with some impatience. This was not the view of their commanders, nor of the politicians who made the rules, and who understood all too clearly that it was going to take some time to organize a proper peace. In order to make the terms which would fasten the peace securely in place, it was necessary that a substantial, indeed an overwhelming, military force be retained. Yet the rapid reduction of enemy forces did convince the generals and politicians that the war was unlikely to be resumed. It followed that a substantial reduction of Allied armies was possible. This could be seen just as clearly by the rank-and-file as by the generals: the soldiers' expectations of repatriation and demobilization were soon transmuted into agitation.

The problem did not affect the regiments and battalions, both Indian and British, who were professional soldiers and who regularly underwent training and exercises even in peacetime. It was usually these units who were employed in the troubled areas in northern Syria and across the Jordan. It would not be sensible to risk 'hostilities-only' soldiers being killed in mere police duties.) It was perhaps the memories of such training which lay behind the methods used to keep the amateur soldiers busy. At first military training in the normal way went on, but this was fairly quickly replaced by sports and by education schemes. Football, swimming parties, competitions, hunting, all took place. The officers of the Indian cavalry regiments were particularly obsessed by attempting pig-sticking; packs of fox hounds were established, at least briefly, at Aleppo and at Tripoli; even point-to-point meetings were organized.[1] In Egypt particularly, an extensive system of education courses, with a wide variety of subjects, often of a practical nature, was set up.

All of these initiatives were more or less successful in retaining the interest of most of the soldiers. Many, of course, were quite happy to have little or nothing to do and to be given free food. But the main concern of all of them was always demobilization, a subject that was raised, for example, as a question after a lecture at Kantara as early as 27 November.[2] This was a decision for the British government, but one which could not be made until the results of the general election in December was known. In January a bureaucrat's demobilization scheme was announced, whereby those men with civilian jobs to go to were to be discharged first. This caused rumbles of discontent, when men who had been in the army for four years saw some with only a few months' service leaving before them.

It rapidly became clear that the soldiers were angry at both the delay in announcing anything and then at what had been announced. This was speedily transmitted by the commanders-in-chief in France, where most of the British army was stationed, to the politicians in London. The installation of Winston Churchill as War Minster after the election brought a politician's sensibility to the subject to replace the bureaucrat's practicality. He quickly discerned that the best way was to discharge the longest-serving men first. In a fortnight the bureaucrats' scheme was discarded and the new scheme was arranged.[3] There are repeated references in the memoirs to '1914 men' being discharged and repatriated.

But in Palestine there were other problems, and still others developed in Egypt (next chapter). The local Arabs, particularly the Bedouin, were addicted to petty thieving. This had been more or less tolerable in wartime, but became an increasing annoyance as the British soldiers settled into one camp for long

---

[1] These activities are mentioned in most accounts; a summary example is in Preston, *Desert Mounted Corps*, pp. 301–2.

[2] Pryor and Woods, *Great Uncle Fred's War*, p. 48.

[3] A clear account of the development of the new scheme is in Gilbert, *World in Turmoil*, Chapter 10.

periods. In addition there were many firearms in civilian hands, stolen or collected as loot from the battlefields. This was a combustible mixture to start with, but on top there was a generalized feeling of contempt amongst the soldiers for the local Arabs. This was particularly so among the Australian and New Zealand troops. One author indulges in a long diatribe of complaints about 'the thieving propensities of the Arab', going right back to Rafah in mid-1917, and citing the stripping of the dead at Rafah and Ayun Kara 'which took place close by Surafend, and there is not the slightest doubt that these villagers were responsible'.[4] ('Not the slightest doubt', of course, implies much uncertainty.)

These men made a virtue of their lack of military discipline when not fighting. They were chronically incapable of addressing offices as 'sir', and they rarely dressed in the way British soldiers – and above all Indian soldiers – did, preferring a more relaxed, even untidy, style. There are numerous anecdotes in which Australian officers are patronized by their British juniors – some of the stories might even be true – and which were really the result of antipodean carelessness in dress which made it difficult to discern rank. This was all regarded as a democratic virtue, a deliberate repudiation of the class-ridden British army, whose structure reflected the class-ridden British society. It extended to relaxed relations between officers and men, and a resulting unwillingness to obey orders which the men did not like.

The forces in Palestine were gradually withdrawn to Egypt, some of them, 54th Division, for example, going as early as mid-December. This was partly because it would be from Egyptian ports that they would be repatriated, and partly for good logistical reasons, since most supplies were unloaded in Egypt before being sent on into Palestine. Allenby was intending to locate his general headquarters at Haifa, and work was begun there in February 1919.[5] By the end of 1918 the headquarters of five of the infantry divisions had been moved to Egypt, and the troops were following.[6] The Desert Mounted Corps, now consisting of two cavalry divisions only (the 4th and the 5th) was to form the 'Army of Occupation' along with the 3rd and 7th Indian Divisions as the infantry component. The cavalry was mainly occupied in the north, the infantry in the cities and the south. The plan was for the 75th Division alone, reconstituted

4 Porter, *New Zealanders in Sinai and Palestine*, p. 266.
5 Hughes (ed.), *Correspondence*, p. 198, Allenby to Wingate, 15 January 1919; Pryor and Woods, *Great Uncle Fred's War*, p. 55.
6 Falls, *Official History* Vol. II, p. 623.

as a professional force, to remain in Egypt; the rest would be withdrawn and disbanded as their battalions were repatriated. The great majority of the forces left in Palestine would therefore be from the Indian army.

The Australian and New Zealand troops could only be withdrawn slowly, since shipping was difficult to come by. They were, like the British, to leave in order of enlistment, '1914 men' first. They were in camp near Richon-le-Zion, south of Jaffa, but in December the Anzac Division was pulled back and stationed in the desert near Rafah as a collective punishment for the conduct of a fairly small group of men at the camp at Surafend.

The 'Surafend Incident' is an extremely nasty affair whose reverberations continue in some form in New Zealand to this day. The background was the rising anger among the men at the petty thieving by local Arabs. On the night of 9/10 December one of these Arabs got into the tent where Trooper Lowry of the 1st Machine Gun Squadron of the New Zealand Brigade was sleeping. Lowry woke up and chased the intruder, who eventually turned and shot him; he died soon after.

This, for the New Zealanders, was the last straw. They had come to the conclusion, whether it was justified or not, that nothing would be done to apprehend and punish the murderer. They had long complained that they were compelled to pay if they caused damage to crops or palm trees owned by Arabs, but they suspected that damage was being invented – one example was sheep that had supposedly been stolen. At the same time they also complained – and this is endlessly repeated in the accounts of what happened – that British, Australians, and New Zealanders who were caught stealing were punished, but that Arabs got away with their crimes. This is because they could not be identified and were protected by other Arabs, particularly the headmen of their village. Surafend was claimed to be a hotbed of such thefts.

There was no doubt something in this, though it has the air of an oft-repeated complaint which became exaggerated and distorted over time and repetition, and which was based on little evidence and much prejudice. It was an odd way to justify oneself by complaining that New Zealanders who caused damage had to pay for it, or that those who stole were punished, while remonstrating that others did not pay or were not punished – thereby proclaiming their own carelessness and criminality. The obvious solution to the thieving was by being constantly vigilant, employing armed guards, and patrolling the perimeter at all times, but these measures seem to have been ignored once the general fighting ended. It was always difficult to get these 'democratic' soldiers to do the basic military chores. It would not have been difficult to deter trespassers if they had really wanted to – a fence around the camp would be easy to construct.

In the day that followed, the anger of the New Zealanders towards Lowry's death rose and was stoked by the involvement of some of the Australians who felt the same way. A set of footprints was identified as those of the murderer, and were thought to lead to Surafend village; it was noted that a number of men had departed from the village the next morning, and that one man was keeping a sharp lookout towards the squadron's camp. This was all taken as evidence of guilt – though it could well have been justified apprehension, or merely normal precautions. The military police reportedly found no evidence in the village, which may mean there was none to be found, or that it had been removed. The New Zealanders persuaded some Australians to join them, and on the night of the 10th, at about 5 p.m. they set out to raid the village. The generally accepted account is that they pushed the women and children out and then they beat up all the men, using pick helves as their weapons – they did not take guns in case they shot at each other in the dark, an excellent example of the deliberate nature of their raid. Reports of the violence vary from beatings, to a mass castration, to mass murder; and the numbers of casualties are as various as the accounts. It is clear that the perpetrators themselves did not know how many were either attacked or killed. (There is a distinct and unpleasant air of gloating in far too many accounts.) Having indulged their predilection for violence they then set fire to the village and to a Bedouin camp next to it.

It seems that it was this fire which finally alerted others to what was going on, but even after the fire was reported the officers in the guilty units were conspicuous by their absence, a fact which brought angry and scornful comments from Generals Chaytor and Allenby. They came to inspect the New Zealand units and Allenby reputedly called them 'murderers', which does imply that they had caused several deaths. The men replied at the least with resentful murmurs, and reportedly with a 'counting-out', a mass chant of 'One-two-three' up to 'ten', followed by a shout of 'out', as if at a boxing match. It seems unlikely that this happened, but some insist that it did, but only in accounts written out much later. It is probably another of the false memories with which the affair is liberally adorned.

No New Zealand account shows any sign that the consequences of such behaviour were appreciated.[7] The charge of being murderers is still resented,

---

7   Every book on New Zealand's participation in the war has an account of this 'incident' or 'affair' – it is never called what it really was, a murderous near-riot.

even though it is quite clear that a number of men were killed. Allenby's anger was partly at the failure of discipline which the whole affair, including the killing and burning, represented, but he was just as much concerned that the example might be contagious, that the political results would ripple out to affect relations with the Palestinian Arabs, the Hejazi Arabs, the French, and the Peace Conference. No New Zealander seems to have thought of this, then or since.

The irony is that the culprits were acting in just the way the British forces always did in circumstances of theft and guerrilla attacks. Several months later Hodson's Horse were moving south from Aleppo, having been relieved there by the French. Their camp was raided, and three of the thieves were killed by the guards. The rest fled back to the local village. There, 'a threat to blow up the house of the local sheikh resulted in the recovery of all the purloined property'. The difference was, of course, that the New Zealanders were a murderous mob, and the Hodson's Horse was under command and under control.[8] Note also the role of the guards; had the New Zealanders had a proper guard, Lowry would not have been killed.

There was a court of inquiry into the Surafend Incident. The record consists of a single typewritten sheet together with various statements concerning Lowry's death.[9] A second file concerned with the 'incident' considered issues of discipline. Again there was a series of witness statements designed on the one hand to determine the timing of events, and then to discover who did what. The witnesses were mainly officers, none of whom had taken part in the events until it was all over. They submitted their statements in written form, which were produced as a result of a 'circular letter'. (No doubt they had coordinated their stories.) They are mainly written with a view to indicating that the officers did not know what was going on, and only became involved when the fires in the village were reported.

The second set of statements, apparently this time the product of direct interviews and questioning, looked at the military police investigation.[10] Some men from the 2nd Light Horse Regiment reported that there were New Zealanders 'soliciting' Australians to join in the attack on the village – none of

Every account is also different, and the later ones are the wilder; among the better versions are Porter, *New Zealanders*, p. 266, Preston, *Desert Mounted Corps*, and Moore, *Mounted Riflemen*, pp. 169–71, though none can claim to be at all objective.

[8] Cardew, *Hodson's Horse*, p. 224.

[9] ANZ WA 1/3/6, XFE 1063.

[10] ANZ WA 2/1/90/60a.

these men took part, of course, nor were they able to identify either the New Zealanders who solicited nor the Australians who responded. In fact it seems that no names were ever found, yet it was glaringly obvious that it was Lowry's own unit, the 1st Machine Gun Squadron, which had taken the lead and whose members were the raiders. The involvement of Australians was clearly designed deliberately to widen responsibility.

The last item in the file is a letter from General Chaytor criticizing the opinion of Brigadier-General Meldrum who was, it seems, trying to smother the whole affair. Chaytor makes several points about the timing of the reactions of the officers, and ends by saying, correctly, that 'no officer took the elementary precaution of seeing what the men were about'. He pointed out that they must have been aware of trouble 'since the disturbers must have passed through, or close to, the New Zealand Mounted Brigade lines when moving from Khirbet Surafend to the Bedouin camp via Richon'. He finally points out that the officers commanding the Auckland and Wellington Regiments were informed about what was going on but took no action.

The inquiry was clearly aiming to go through the motions but was quite determined not to assign blame. This attitude clearly went as high as the brigade commander. In such circumstances Chaytor could do nothing other than put on record in his letter his disagreement and anger. In fact, of course, the murdering mob and the delinquent officers were all at fault. And the essential basis of the matter was that the officers were scared of their men, in part through too great a familiarity and in part through sheer lack of professionalism.

Since it was impossible to single out any individual or individuals as having taken part - the tight lips of guilt clearly operated – and since the discipline of the division was clearly very poor, Allenby finally removed the whole Anzac Division south into the desert near Rafah. This removed them from temptation. He was also reported to have refused to pass on recommendations for the decorations which were being handed out to all units at the end of the fighting. The New Zealanders took this badly, deliberately separating their 'work' as soldiers from their guilt as murderers, and claimed to be entitled to the medals being withheld. Allenby issued a special order of the day, early in January, in which he insisted that 'courtesy and consideration to the inhabitants of these countries were never more essential ... than they are now'.[11]

---

[11] Hughes (ed.), *Correspondence*, p. 196, Special order, January 1919.

It was so unlike Allenby to continue expressing anger at something – his outbursts were usually brief, if explosive – that it is clear that he was very worried indeed by the possible consequences. Now that the New Zealanders wanted something, of course, the 'harm being done to Imperial and Commonwealth relations' by his failure to recommend decorations was invoked, whereas the harm done by the murderers to relations with the Arabs and others, and to the dead men themselves, was never considered. In the end it was apparently the recently appointed historian of the Australian campaign, the (recently demobilized) journalist H.S. Gullett, who, speaking as a civilian, is said to have finally persuaded Allenby to pass the list of decorations and to issue a commendatory tribute to the work of the troops, though he managed to include a barbed comment that they were 'somewhat impatient of rigid and formal discipline'.[12]

The 'Surafend Incident' was not repeated, though the indiscipline and bad behaviour of the antipodean soldiers was neither new nor finished. What was in fact more ominous, though perhaps not appreciated as such at the time, was the reaction to what happened by the Jews at Richon and other pre-war Zionist settlements, whose people were being fired up by the antics of the Zionist Commission in the previous months. 'Many messages were received from Jewish settlers and senior officers of other formations that this disturbance would have a very good effect on the natives', is a claim made by a near-contemporary author.[13] While one may doubt, indeed disbelieve, the assertion's reference to the 'senior officers' – wholly unspecified and without any corroborative detail anywhere – the messages from 'Jewish settlers' is all too likely. It is further evidence of the malign effects of the Balfour Declaration on Jewish-Arab relations within only a year of its issuance. Already the Zionists were seeing Palestine as their own, and the Arabs as 'natives' to be subdued.

One of the other effects of the Declaration and the presence of the Zionist Commission in Palestine was to stimulate the two Jewish battalions which had been formed in the last year of the fighting and which had fought in the Jordan Valley as part of 'Chaytor's Force'. They were officially battalions of the London

---

[12] Starr and Greenway, *Forward*, pp. 156–7. Gullett had been the editor of a regular news sheet between March and December 1980 for the antipodean troops, called *Kia Ora Coo-ee*. It included bland comments on the fighting, soldiers' essays and poems, jokes (often at the expense of the British or officers) and cartoons. The collected version has been published as *The Kia Ora Coo-ee, The Magazine for the Anzacs in the Middle East, 1918*, in Australia in 1981. In style, language, and humour, it is extremely dated, even adolescent.

[13] Porter, *New Zealanders*, p. 268.

Regiment, the 38th and 39th, and there was a third, the 40th, in Egypt, but to themselves they were the 'Jewish Legion'. As the number of British forces in Palestine shrank by demobilization and by removal to Egypt, the Jewish Legion stood out, and was allowed to recruit from among Jews – Zionists very largely – in Palestine. It reached, so it is claimed, a strength of 5000 men by early 1919, and had become the main British garrison in Palestine. The British, however, could not but be suspicious, and when it was possible the Legion was reduced in numbers and swamped by the return of other British forces into Palestine. Their suspicions were fully justified, for the organizers of the Legion, above all the Russian journalist, V. Jabotinsky, made no secret of the hope that the Legion would be able to remain as the main garrison in Palestine – and quite possibly carry through a *coup d'état* to seize power in the area. Needless to say, given Jabotinsky's tunnel vision, he blamed the later troubles in Palestine on the reduction in numbers of his Legion, though in fact it was quite likely that the very presence of the Legion was one of the causes of the troubles.[14]

---

[14] Jabotinsky, *Jewish Legion*, pp. 144–7.

CHAPTER 16

Rebellion in Egypt

SINCE 1914 Egypt had been the main base in the eastern Mediterranean for the British forces. It was the base to which the defeated army from the Dardanelles had retreated to lick its wounds. Alexandria and Port Said were the essential naval bases to patrol the local seas. It was the base where forces from Australia and New Zealand and India landed. It was the base from which the Egyptian Expeditionary Force, first under Murray, then under Allenby, had come to campaign into and conquer Palestine and Syria. In December 1918 it became the base to which those forces were withdrawn to prepare for their repatriation.

It was also the source of essential military supplies: cotton, camels, grain, even water (through the pipeline), and above all, manpower. Much of the labouring work for the army – road-making, transport, landing goods from the sea, and so on – was done by the Egyptian Labour Corps, the Camel Transport Corps, the Donkey Transport Corps, and other groups. By 1918 135,000 men were employed, on six-month contracts, all through Palestine and as far north as Homs.[1] But from December these men were paid off and discharged, returning home to Egypt. None of them got rich, but all of them experienced a taste of life outside their villages, and all gained a greater understanding of the system under which they lived – and probably the majority came to dislike it intensely.

The men in the various labouring camps were all volunteers, at least technically, until early 1918, but then Allenby complained that he did not have enough,[2] and the High Commissioner, Sir Reginald Wingate, tried to get the Egyptian government to initiate conscription. This was refused, both by the Sultan Fuad and by the Prime Minister and his ministers. But Wingate then suggested – insisted, perhaps – that a *corvée* system be applied, whereby the head man in each village would provide a set number of men. This worked,

---

[1] *Advance*, pp. 107–10 and plate 52; almost 20,000 Egyptians were also sent to work in France, Mesopotamia, and Salonika.

[2] Hughes (ed.), *Correspondence*, p. 115, Allenby to Wingate, 1 May 1918.

but at the cost of increased resentment.[3] Allenby distanced himself from the operation, but later he casually referred to 'press gang methods' being used.[4] There was little difference between the *corvée* and conscription, though the former was much more open to abuse.

Compulsion also opened the way for punishment. Allenby lamented in May 1918 that flogging was illegal,[5] but, having recruited unwilling men by compulsion, physical punishment became necessary to deter desertion. On 8 December Private Fred Mills of the Royal Engineers described punishment in the Labour Corps camp at Kantara: some men were tied to posts so that they could only stand on tiptoe; others held heavy stones above their heads; others were seated on narrow boards in stocks.[6]

Within Egypt the political situation had been frozen since 1914 when by proclamation Britain replaced the old relationship with a British Protectorate. The Egyptian political class accepted this on the implied assurance that it was temporary and would be replaced by a negotiated system once the war was won. So when on 13 November the war was seen to have been won, the Egyptian politician Sa'ad Zaghlul presented a set of political proposals to Wingate. It was ignored, as was a second proposal made a little later. This was partly due to the preoccupation of government ministers in London with the new circumstances in so many regions throughout the world, but it was also the result of British ignorance of the particular Egyptian situation – ignorance not only among the ministers in Westminster, despite detailed reports by Wingate, but also among the British in Egypt, who had been fully preoccupied for the past four years with the war.[7]

Here again the effect of the words and policy of President Wilson was evident. The entry of the USA into the war was widely seen as ensuring victory for the Allies, which some translated into an apprehension that the USA would become the most powerful of the Allies, and that Wilson could impose his ideas on the rest. In fact, of course, Wilson was addressing the European populace when he proclaimed his Fourteen Points, and was rather surprised that Indians, Chinese, and Egyptians should take them up.[8] It was also a surprise

3   The system is described, ascerbically, by Marlowe, *Anglo-Egyptian Relations*, pp. 222–3; Elgood, *Egypt and the Army*, pp. 316–19.

4   Hughes (ed.), *Correspondence*, p. 215, Allenby to Wilson, 16 April 1919.

5   Ibid., p. 72, Allenby to Robertson, 4 December 1917.

6   Pryor and Woods, *Great Uncle Fred's War*, p. 49.

7   Marlowe, *Anglo–Egyptian Relations*, pp. 228–31.

8   Manela, *The Wilsonian Moment*, pp. 63–4.

to the British rulers in Egypt, who were insulated from everyday Egyptian concerns by operating through the largely obsequious Egyptian government, whose ministers were living in European settlements, and socializing only with other Europeans.

The Egyptian contribution to the Allied war effort, in manpower and in supplies, was thus considerable, and it was widely expected among Egyptians that this contribution would be recognized once the war was over by a substantial adjustment to the governing system. The Protectorate was disliked, and would have to go, though it had been an acceptable institution for the war emergency. British interference in the sultanate would have to end, and, above all, the numbers of British officials in the country would need to be reduced, making way for Egyptians to take their place. Many of the administrative tasks were in British hands, thereby preventing ambitious and able Egyptians from doing this work. And this was on top of the wide experience gained by the poorer Egyptians who had served in the Labour Corps – the six-monthly contracts had meant that large numbers had been recruited for relatively short periods.

There were also substantial grievances amongst the Egyptian rural population. The *corvée* system had taken many farmers and peasants from their homes for part of the war, but even those undisturbed by this had been badly affected by government compulsion in other areas. Repeated requisitions of grain and animals had been made, with compensation dictated by the government, compensation which often only partly reached the victims as it was channelled through various agents, each of whom took a cut. Even more seriously, the animals – mainly camels and donkeys – were not replaceable. These were used in the villages for many tasks – such as ploughing, reaping, transporting to market, operating irrigation schemes – and without their animals, this work could no longer be done, or at least not done so easily. So the *fellahin* (farmers and peasants) were not merely being deprived of the market price for their goods, by government purchase at government-set prices, but they were also deprived of part of their means of working. Rural discontent, which was not visible to the British, was thus widespread, and, though they do not seem to have realized it, it was the British who were blamed.[9]

When the Peace Conference was convened, Egyptians saw that Arabs from the desert were present at the conference, and that delegations came from Cyprus, Lebanon, and Syria, none of whose contributions to the victory

---

[9] Hughes (ed.), *Correspondence,* p. 215, Allenby to Wilson, 16 April 1919.

matched those by Egypt.[10] The only conclusion which the political class and the educated Egyptians could draw was that Britain intended to continue the Protectorate, which was in effect treating Egypt as a mere colony, one from which much wealth could be squeezed.

It was against this background, combining resentment, exploitation, and suspicion, that Sa'ad Zaghlul's campaign to get the British to discuss the future for Egypt was conducted. The Egyptian ministers, having been upstaged by Zaghlul's campaign, necessarily made a similar request for discussions and consultation. They hoped to debate Egypt's political future in London with the British government, so to pre-empt Sa'ad Zaghlul, but they were refused. The Egyptian ministers resigned. After some dithering, the High Commissioner was recalled to London 'for consultations', though it was a fortnight before Lord Curzon, acting Foreign Secretary while Balfour was in Paris, bothered to see him – an extraordinary insult to an imperial official who ranked with the governor of one of the dominions.[11]

Sa'ad Zaghlul made some threatening moves while Wingate was away, mainly aimed at gaining access to power himself, and he conducted a campaign to arouse support for his policy. Wingate's deputy as Acting High Commissioner, Sir Milne Cheetham, decided that Sa'ad Zaghlul and his colleagues – by now regarded as a political party later called the Wafd – should be removed. Cheetham persuaded Major-General Sir Harry Watson, who was commanding the British troops in Cairo, to deliver a warning to Zaghlul, reminding him that martial law was still in force, and telling him, in effect, to be silent since his continued campaign would be likely to cause disorder. Pressure of this sort was exactly what Zaghlul was aiming to create, so the warning had in fact had the reverse effect of that intended. On 8 March, Zaghlul and three of his colleagues were arrested and deported to Malta.[12]

There was now no Egyptian government, no High Commissioner, and the leading opponents of British rule had been removed. It is unlikely that Wingate would have acted against Zaghlul in this way, for he understood something of the pressures in the Egyptian countryside, and would have appreciated the provocation which the deportation of the four men would have aroused. But he was disregarded in London, even though he was heard over dinner by Lord

---

[10] Ibid., and noted by Wavell, *Allenby in Egypt*, p. 37.

[11] Marlowe, *Anglo-Egyptian Relations*, pp. 228–35; Kedourie, 'Sa'd Zaghlul and the British', in *Chatham House Version*, 93–9.

[12] Marlowe, *Anglo-Egyptian Relations*, p. 233.

Curzon and Lloyd George. And yet no sense of urgency was imported, and there is little sign that either man accepted Wingate's warnings. He was, to be sure, somewhat verbose and circumlocutory in speech, so maybe these tired men simply did not take in his message.

The day after the Wafd leaders were arrested, groups of students were demonstrating in the streets in Cairo, and the protests rapidly spread to nearby towns and into the rural Delta; by 15 March Upper Egypt was also in turmoil. The disturbances were large enough to be perceived as a full-scale rebellion. In London, at last, Egypt became the centre of attention. Lloyd George rapidly decided that Wingate was no longer a suitable High Commissioner. Allenby was chosen as a comfortingly martial successor, and a man who had some experience already of Egyptian conditions. He was in Paris at the time, and set off for Egypt at once, on 21 March.[13]

By that time General Bulfin from Palestine had taken command. The disturbances in Egypt had cut across the process of repatriating many of the soldiers of the former Expeditionary Force. Most of the British units had already left, and the Indian and Australian forces were on their way, some having already left, including two of the Australian Light Horse regiments. Some of the others were in the throes of embarking, having disposed of their horses and most of their kit, including their weapons. When the rebellion blew up, they were hastily recalled, re-armed, and sent to a new campaign. It was the same with the Indian regiments, at least one of which had already sent an advanced party to India to arrange for the main body's return.[14]

Nevertheless there were large numbers of troops still available in Egypt. Most were in the Suez Canal area in the great camps at Kantara or Moascar, others were at Rafah. There was, however, considerable reluctance to use these troops. Australians in particular were extremely unpopular in Cairo, having behaved in ways which outraged the inhabitants in the past. These inhabitants complained that Australian misbehaviour – which included murders, thefts, sacking houses, extreme drunkenness, beating up anyone they disliked, and mere boorishness – was never punished by the British authorities. (It is curious that this is the exactly the complaint made by Australians with regard to the Palestinian Arab thievery in Palestine; the British were clearly frightened of annoying anyone.) The British apprehension was that the use of Austral-

---

[13] Hughes (ed.), *Correspondence*, p. 203, Curzon to Allenby, 21 March 1919; Wavell, *Allenby in Egypt*, p. 92.

[14] The regimental histories generally skip over their time in Egypt in a paragraph or so; only those which provide useful information will be detailed in what follows.

ians as a means of controlling crowds in Cairo would be incendiary.[15] Russell Pasha, the British chief of Cairo's Egyptian police force, described exactly such a situation, in which a group of Australians armed with improvised weapons (hockey sticks) almost collided with a more or less peaceful demonstration he himself was leading. It is clear from his description that the Australians were a marauding mob looking for trouble – Russell deflected them by putting them in charge of a wild British soldier who was threatening to shoot someone, and promised them 'some useful street fighting' elsewhere.[16]

Russell decided that the Egyptian army could not be used to control the crowds, because they sympathized with the demonstrators.[17] He was able, however, to rely very largely on his police force, but decided very early on that the safest option was to let the marches take place, and even to guide them himself. The marchers' leaders were also concerned to prevent violence, and co-operated.

These demonstrations in Cairo were on a large scale, usually led by students of the al-Azhar mosque-cum-university, but with ready and vociferous support from the general population. Normally the marches were more or less peaceful, if noisy and raucous, but the appearance of British soldiers, or above all of Australians, could well provoke fighting. British soldiers were ordered to go armed if they went into the city, but this might simply result in the arms falling into Egyptian hands if the soldiers were ambushed. Going in groups was also recommended, but in that case the soldiers, emboldened by support, might turn on the Egyptians. But forbidding soldiers to go about the city would simply hand the political game to the opposition. And life in the city was not merely marches and demonstrations.

There was also the problem that the preoccupation of the police with the demonstrations left areas of the city unpoliced. As in all such situations advantage was taken by the criminals of the city. This in fact operated in part to British advantage since the middle classes of the city – who included many of the marchers – rapidly realized the usefulness of having the police return to their normal roles, but before that change in perception occurred there were ugly events. Minorities, notably Greeks and Armenians, became targets for looting. The Wellington Mounted Rifles had a squadron in Cairo which was

---

[15]   A reasonably balanced description of Australians in Egypt is in Brugger, *Australians and Egypt*.

[16]   Russell Pasha, *Egyptian Service*, p. 197.

[17]   Ibid., p. 193.

called out to deal with looting of Armenian shops in the Bulak quarter. On the first occasion they dispersed the mob by a cavalry charge which involved the horses jumping a barricade; on the second callout, to the Bab el-Luk quarter, they found that looting had become murder. In the regiment's history, it is said that 'drastic measures were immediately taken by the men', which appears to be a cloak for a reverse riot. Details are given of the killings by the mob, but then the discreet euphemism – 'drastic measures' – hides the soldiers' overt actions.[18]

While the city was thus disturbed by demonstrations and marches, riots and looting, the countryside was more actively in rebellion. This was a major surprise to the British, who fondly imagined that they had earned the gratitude of the *fellahin* for instituting a more peaceful and more just regime, but had not taken into account the effects of their actions during the war – the forced labour, the requisitions, and the inefficiencies. The general self-sufficiency of the villages was too easily thought of as isolation from the rest of the world. The villagers in fact understood full well what was going on, and news of outside events spread rapidly. For instance, the students of al-Azhar, many of whom the sons of fellahin, kept in touch with home.

In the countryside the army was principally employed in 'restoring order', as the British conceived their task, or in suppressing the revolution, as the Egyptians saw it. The situation was certainly revolutionary, Egyptians aiming above all to remove British rule and British presence. No leader emerged to co-ordinate events, since the Wafd leaders were exiled, and Sultan Fuad, who might have put himself at the head of the revolt, was under close British supervision. In the absence of a leader or of any overall organization, the extensive spread of the revolt is all the more impressive, and a good indication of how much British rule was detested.

The nationalists were generally unarmed, or at least had few weapons, but they understood well enough that British retaliation could best be blocked by interrupting their communications. It is noticeable that none of the canals, neither those used for irrigation nor those for supplying water into the cities, was damaged (unless by the British forces, who were given the ultimate sanction, in cases of the determined opposition, of cutting off water supplies). Railways, telephone and telegraph systems, however, were instant and easy targets. By late March Cairo was largely cut off from contact with the rest

---

[18] Wilkie, *Wellington Mounted Rifles*, p. 239.

of the country.[19] Two railway junctions, Zagazig and Tanta, were particularly persistent nationalist centres, the latter described by Russell as 'a political hotbed' centred on a local mosque.[20] Trains were ambushed. A particular case was at Deriut on 18 March, when a train was attacked by a series of mobs until eight British soldiers and officials on board had been killed.[21] After that there was much attention given to evacuating isolated groups of 'Europeans' to safety. Isolated soldiers were killed, though more often they were attacked in order to seize their weapons.

Not only were the Egyptians inflamed against the British and all manifestations of British control, but the soldiers who were used to suppress the risings were by no means always amenable to higher control. The interruption to the Australian and New Zealand evacuation left many of the troops angry. One British observer remarks that they 'have vowed to kill 200 Egyptians for every white casualty'. This was, of course, largely angry rhetoric, but there were rumours which could turn such mindless comments into reality. It was generally assumed that the Egyptians had 'filled their pockets' as a result of the war and should therefore be grateful to the British – who had also saved them from Turkish conquest.[22]

These rumours were generally that officers had been killed and that 'nurses' – it is always nurses – had also been killed. There is no doubt that some soldiers died, but very few if any seem to have been officers, and there is no record of any European women, still less nurses, being attacked or killed.[23] (But almost the only European women with whom the soldiers had been in contact during the war had been the nurses, hence the instinctive assumption that they were endangered.) The effect of such rumours was to make 'every man eager for revenge', which was a bad preparation for suppressing a rising which was originally caused by resentment at British exactions and casual violence.[24]

Cairo's demonstrations were largely contained by the local police, with occasional military help in suppressing riots and looting, so the military problem resolved itself and control over the Delta and Upper Egypt was regained.

---

[19] Russell Pasha, *Egyptian Service*, p. 195.

[20] Ibid.

[21] Details were researched by Allenby and reported. See Hughes (ed.), *Correspondence*, pp. 210 and 216, Allenby to Curzon, 4 and 19 April 1919.

[22] Goodlad, *Letters*, no 19/8, 21 March 1919; Bostock, *Great Ride*, p. 205.

[23] Hughes (ed.), *Correspondence*, p. 223, Allenby to Curzon, 2 May 1919.

[24] Bostock, *Great Ride*, p. 205; Livermore, *Damn Bad Soldier*, p. 152; Hammond, *11th Light Horse*, p. 141.

These circumstances were different. In the south (Upper Egypt) the priority of the Bedouin was looting rather than engaging in politics, so they were as much a menace to the nationalists as to the soldiers. The desert Bedouin, on the other hand, did not take part; as Allenby said, in his typically imperialistic patronising way, they were 'quiet'.[25]

A mixed British force, composed of men from several regiments who happened to be available - Manchesters, Connaught Rangers, 'Scotties' (H.L.I. and Seaforths), 'Yeomanry', Rifle Brigade, Royal Irish - was built up around a group of Somerset Light Infantry. They were sent off 'into the blue' and were not pleased to be doing so. 'I pity any Egyptian or Arab we come up against', wrote Captain Goodlad to his wife. And sure enough they had 'one little battle', when they were fired on from a village. The village was seized, the women and children moved out, the buildings set on fire. Goodlad estimated the casualties at fifty-seven 'Arabs' dead and more wounded. He counted eight of his own men wounded. The force then set off up river by boat, intending to 'find the leaders and shoot them'. But in the same letter he claims to be having a 'really wonderful trip'. The disjunction between his actions and his perceptions is quietly horrifying.[26]

In the Delta a greater political sophistication led some areas to declare themselves republics, either as a model for the rest of the country or as a message of local independence. (Often the word 'Soviet' was attached, either by the proclamation of republic-hood or by the British as a means of hostile propaganda.) Ironically it was in part due to this which eventually persuaded President Wilson on 20 April to publicly recognize the British Protectorate for the first time; so the greatest republic and the proponent of self-determination was persuaded to promote the British colonial rule and the suppression of a move for independence. Egyptians were, to say the least, disappointed.[27]

It was not, of course, possible for the Egyptians, essentially unarmed, to maintain the conditions of local anti-British independence for long without securing international support. Only two countries could provide that support – the USA and France – and neither was able nor willing to do so. However much they may have wished to see the reduction of the British Empire, both required British support in negotiating the details of the peace agreements. Neither was in a military position to intervene anyway, though in both coun-

---

[25] Hughes (ed.), *Correspondence*, p. 206, Allenby to Milner, 26 March 1919.

[26] Goodlad, *Letters*, nos 19/9 and 19/10, of 27 March and 7 April 1919.

[27] Manela, *Wilsonian Moment*, pp. 145–8.

tries there were voices condemning the British oppression of the nationalists. However, in neither case were these anti-British voices actually in any significant way pro-Egyptian. Neither government did anything to hurt the British position.[28]

So it was up to the British forces and the nationalists to fight it out. In the Delta and the Canal regions the cities were garrisoned. Hodson's Horse went to Alexandria and were used to control the demonstrations. They had an uncomfortable camp, but were able to continue their training programmes, which in themselves were no doubt intimidatory.[29] At Suez the 13th Frontier Force Rifles took over as garrison in April; the police in the town were able to control most events, with the regiment occasionally displaying its teeth in marches in the town.[30] Outram's Rifles had much the same experience at Serapeum, Port Tewfik and Damietta.[31] None of the histories of these Indian regiments displays the bloodthirstiness so often found in those of British and Australian forces.

In the central area of the Delta, Australian forces were moved out from Moascar to Zagazig, whence six light horse regiments spread over the eastern Delta, and to Damanhur on the railway towards Alexandria. Three regiments essentially guarded that particular railway. There was violence at once at several places. Forty Egyptians were killed at Minat al-Qamh on 16 March when a crowd said to be up to a 1000-strong threatened a patrol of fifteen men of the 10th Light Horse Regiment who were guarding the station.[32] This is exactly the sort of action which could only incite further trouble. When Bulfin arrived the next day he sent out messages that villages nearest to the sabotaged railway lines would be held responsible for the damage and those villages could be burned in reprisal.[33] Patrols went along the lines, and many breaks were repaired by conscripting locals to do the work. Simply locking up and guarding the linesmen's tools prevented much sabotage, though in some cases the repairs had to be done several times.

More aggressive methods were also used. Mobile patrols were sent out into areas where violence had been reported. The method was to surround a village at night and search the houses during the day. The inhabitants were

[28] Ibid., pp. 149–55.
[29] Cardew, *Hodson's Horse*, p. 225.
[30] Anon., *13th Frontier Force Rifles*, p. 184.
[31] Rawlinson, *Outram's Rifles*, p. 184.
[32] AWM 183/17,423, Report of Capt. Palmer.
[33] TNA, WO 95/4551, War Diary of 54 Div.

also searched, and anything of any suspicious nature was confiscated, as were all weapons, whether held legitimately or not. Interrogations followed, and offenders were tried at summary military courts. Punishments, inflicted at once, could include fines or flogging, or even jailing for six months.[34] The difference between terrorizing the population and restoring order seems minimal. Needless to say, some Egyptians accused the soldiers of unnecessary violence. Several courts of inquiry met to consider such cases but they generally founded it impossible, in the face of contradictory evidence and adamant denials by the soldiers, to discover the truth. There was, of course, little incentive to find against the soldiers, but it may be taken as certain that such violence took place. It was inherent in the situation.

Allenby arrived in Egypt on 25 March. He announced that his programme was first to 'restore order', then to investigate why the disturbances had taken place, and third to put in place restitution measures.[35] This was a standard British response, which completely denied the main causes of the rising – the demand for independence – for that, of course, was the one thing the British would not (they would have said 'could not') grant. Allenby was not helped by a pronouncement by Lord Curzon, a member of the War Cabinet in London, that he was gratified to note the loyalty of the Egyptian officials - which led immediately to a widespread strike by those very officials, enforced by intimidation and strike pickets. They would probably have stayed at work but for Curzon's provocative comments, and were finally induced to return by a proclamation that any who did not go back to work would be deemed to have resigned.[36]

Allenby was thus rather more subtle in his approach than his bluff military reputation suggested – but then his military planning had always included much subtlety and misdirection. Unlike many of the soldiers, from Bulfin downwards, who saw the revolt in military terms, Allenby quickly came to understand that it could only be aggravated by military suppression, even if this was probably the only way for the British to recover full control. The military methods therefore needed to be less harsh than the soldiers wished to impose.

General Wilson, in command of the eastern Delta at Zagazig, described one affair involving the railway which gives some indication of the hostility

---

[34] Brugger, *Australians and Egypt*, p. 119.
[35] Wavell, *Allenby in Egypt*, p. 43.
[36] Ibid., pp. 43–4.

of the Egyptians and the firepower available to the British forces. A train was sent out, unknown to Wilson, to repair the broken line at Mit Ghamr, about twenty miles north-west of Zagazig. Unarmed and unescorted, the train was trapped when, having stopped to repair a break, the line behind it was also taken up. A second train, escorted by twenty-six Australians, went out to the rescue. At Mit Ghamr the first train was found, but the town was under the control of a local 'Vigilance Committee', and local hostility was such that the escort retreated, linking up with a second party which had been sent out to help the first. This second escort had also interrupted a party taking up the line behind the second train. In dispersing them, the patrol claimed to have killed thirty. A third Australian party, on a trolley which mounted a machine gun, found yet another group tearing up the line, and opened fire, killing, it was claimed, another fifty. A third train now set out, this time escorted by over eighty Australians. It reached the other trains, having dropped off groups of soldiers at intervals to guard the line. The three trains and the trolley joined, fired at another group of men bent on destroying the line in their path (ten men died) and returned to Zagazig, collecting the detached parties on the way. 'We had no further trouble on this line', claims Wilson, though it is clear that Mit Ghamr was outside his control, and that the line remained broken. What stands out is the determination, in the face of substantial casualties (though the numbers claimed by the Australians are not to be relied on) of the insurgents.[37]

One of the extra problems was the presence in parts of Egypt of large numbers of Turkish prisoners of war. When the 7th Light Horse Regiment reached Salhia, on the boundary of the Delta and the desert, they had to help guard a camp with 12,000 prisoners. Parties of the prisoners were used to build small redoubts 'to prevent any efforts at breaking out on the part of the prisoners, or any combined attempts by the civil population for their release'.[38]

Wilson sent out patrols along all the railway lines out of Zagazig, and they found the same conditions: lines broken in many places, rails thrown into the nearest canal, wooden sleepers and telegraph poles removed to the nearest villages as loot. The lines were gradually repaired, once the destroyers were 'dispersed', usually by machine-gun fire. The Mit Ghamr line was out of action for several days, until an armoured construction train escorted by a hundred

---

[37] Wilson, *Egyptian Rebellion*, pp. 11–12.
[38] Richardson, *7th Light Horse*, p. 114.

men restored the line. Local villagers were driven into the canals to recover the rails and sleepers, and those who resisted were shot at.

Using such measures, by the end of March General Wilson was reasonably confident that he had reconquered the eastern Delta. He had light horse regiments at Mansourah, Zagazig, Salhia, Abu Kebir, and Mit Ghamr, and had been able to send two more to other areas. He extended his reach to Damietta on the coast, where there had reportedly been no foreign soldiers seen since Napoleon's day, and where despite his claim to have brought order, his troops faced much hostility. They were reinforced by men from the 13th Frontier Force Rifles from Port Tewfik.

This is more or less the pattern elsewhere. A battalion or regiment would be based at a town and would send out patrols to visit all the villages in its region. If resistance was encountered there might be fighting. Tanta in the middle of the Delta maintained an attitude of hostility for longer than most places, in the face of occupation by the Canterbury Mounted Rifles.[39] Other New Zealanders went out to Hosh Isa on the western side of the Delta and found that it had been bombed by the RAF the day before. Not surprisingly this 'acted as a deterrent to their martial spirit'.[40] The Kumaon Rifles patrolled the railway line north-west of Tanta, and came under repeated pressure from local Egyptians, ranging from attempts to bribe sentries to railway demolition and regular gatherings of hostile crowds which had to be dispersed with or without shooting. On 16 April a 'mob' attacked a ration limber, killing one soldier and wounding three more. A nearby patrol fired at the crowd, and the town was then surrounded and searched, during which time some men 'resisted and were shot'. Nine Egyptians died, ten were injured. The village was then subjected to another, even more rigorous, search. This was not the end, for incidents of stoning and shooting continued for several more days.[41] Occasional manifestations of violence and defiance still went on in other areas as well, but the threat of the nationalists achieving the expulsion of the British forces had ended.[42]

Wilson's account is somewhat self-laudatory, and this feeling was increased by the usual messages of congratulation from his seniors. But the methods used had been very rough, and had caused a large number of casualties

[39] ANZ WA 40/3, 18 Apr 1919 – 9 May 1919.
[40] Moore, *Mounted Riflemen*, pp. 173–4.
[41] Overton, *Kumaon Rifles*, pp. 20–1.
[42] Wilson, *Egyptian Rebellion* pp. 15–17.

amongst the Egyptians – one crowd was even machine-gunned from the air. In other regions the initial response by the British forces had often been even rougher. South of Cairo, at the village of Azizia, the 10th Light Horse Regiment under Colonel Olden began a search of the village well before dawn, without any preliminary warning. This was early in the campaign of repression, on 23 March, when all the British were extremely nervous, and many groups had lost contact with others. Olden ordered that houses could be burned if his men were resisted. Since the houses were made of flammable materials and were often built close together, when one was set on fire, the whole village was soon destroyed.[43]

In a second incident of the same sort, at Abu Akdar, a sentry from the 3rd Gurkha Rifles was reported missing. A search found his body in a canal. The murderers could not be found, so the Ghurkas and the Australians of the 2nd Light Horse Brigade burned the village. General Ryrie claimed that he had been ordered not to do this, and implied that he had ignored that order, though he was given permission to 'finish village' in the telegram, whatever that meant (leave it? destroy it?).[44] Definitive orders that villages were not to be burned went out on 27 March, probably as a result of Allenby's arrival two days earlier. It was unsettlingly reminiscent of the Surafend matter only three months before, and, if the implication of Ryrie's words are correct, it may be that commanders were very liable to ignore orders from higher up and to indulge themselves in their own ideas. This was the age-old problem of the failure of the Australians to appreciate the necessity of military discipline.

This time Allenby did not berate the guilty soldiers, but on the same day he sent out the order that villages were not to be burned, he sent a message of approval for the work done so far.[45] Allenby himself, of course, was under pressure from London to get Egypt under control as quickly as possible, but to do so in such a way that no adverse criticism could be made of the methods used. As usual such instructions were seen as contradictory by those who had to carry them out. The perpetrators were always able to justify their atrocities in their recollections.

Allenby was also in the process of removing part of the cause of the uprising. He could do nothing about the general wish for independence – though he did insist that the expression of nationalist sentiments should not be a cause for

---

43 TNA FO 371/3718; Brugger, *Australians and Egypt*, pp. 130–3.
44 Brugger, *Australians and Egypt*, pp. 134–5.
45 Ibid., p. 135.

punishment[46] – but he could reduce the temperature. By 31 March he recommended to the Foreign Office that Sa'ad Zaghlul and his colleagues, detained at Malta, be released. After the Office and the government got over the shock, the men were released on 7 April, though they were not to be allowed back into Egypt for the present. (Sa'ad Zaghlul went to Paris to try to influence the Peace Conference.) Allenby was of course criticized for this, usually later, and usually by people not facing the immediate problem, but he was supported by two men in Egypt whom he trusted, General Bulfin, and the political officer Gilbert Clayton.[47] The critics claimed that to release the men was a concession to the violence, and therefore an invitation to other groups to act in the same way. But once they were released, and after demonstrations of joy and celebration, the violence died away. This was partly a result of the military repression, but also because rural disturbances interfered with the agricultural work, and because the arrest of the four men had, for many Egyptians, been the issue they were campaigning against. Not all of them were working for full independence as an immediate aim, but for the end of the Protectorate (and probably for the ending of the martial law measures which the British had instituted).

The combination of concessions and repression gradually worked to bring the violence to an end. An Egyptian government was in place soon after the release of the four detainees, and Allenby and his forces could pull back into the background. By mid-May the Australians and New Zealanders were withdrawn to the camps along the Suez Canal, and by the end of May they had all left to return to their homes. The Indian regiments left as well, though later on – their disciplined approach was much preferred to that of the Australians' nastiness.

The insurrection had its effect in London. A commission headed by Lord Milner was set up to investigate and recommend new measures, though it did not arrive until December 1919. In many ways therefore the uprising had been successful. It had compelled the British to pay serious attention to the problems of Egypt, and Milner's Commission did recommend serious changes which removed much of the British oppressive presence, paving the way for a proper settlement in 1922.

---

[46] Ibid., p. 125, quoting 'A Note on Nationalism', of 7 April 1919 (AWN 183/12, 423).
[47] See Wavell, *Allenby in Egypt*, pp. 44–5, for a summary.

CHAPTER 17

France and Syria

THE British had never, despite French assumptions, suspicions, and accusations, had any wish or intention of keeping control of any of Syria beyond 'Dan', in the north of Palestine. On the other hand they did look with favour on the extension of Arab control into the inland parts of northern Syria. By contrast, the French wished to secure clear control and rule over as much of greater Syria as possible, and were quite prepared to accept the restrictions implied by the mandate system, on the assumption that such restrictions were largely theoretical and could be easily evaded (an assumption fully shared by the British). It had become clear long since that their original hope for the acquisition of Syria from the Sinai Desert to the Taurus Mountains as a French colony was out of the question.

It was obvious that the British would hold onto Palestine and during 1919 British troops were active east of the Jordan, protecting the crops of the settled inhabitants against raids by the Bedouin ('Arabs longing to plunder Palestine and to kill Jews who defile the Holy City of Jerusalem', in Allenby's elaboration in May 1919.)[1] So French ambitions became concentrated on Syria and Lebanon, Cilicia and al-Jazeira east to the borders of Mosul. (Mosul was in fact disputed between Britain, France, and the new Turkish Republic for several years; in the event might succeeded, and the area became part of the new British-controlled kingdom of Iraq.) This northern sector, whose northern boundary was indefinite, would have doubled the size of the territory France actually acquired.

There was plenty of niggling conflict between the British, who had military control over most of the area claimed by the French until near the end of 1919, and the French, whose administration and occupation developed only slowly. There was also, of course, the Arab presence, generally favoured by the British, leading to further French suspicions. French officers were military governors in the towns along the coast from Tyre to Alexandretta, but for some time they had few troops of their own to use - only 18,000 as late as November 1919, by which time the British still had at least three times that in the region. An early

---

[1]   Hughes (ed.), *Correspondence*, p. 219, Allenby to Wilson, 17 May 1919.

attempt to make use of locally recruited Armenians failed because they were disliked locally and were poorly disciplined; Allenby replaced them with British forces until soldiers from metropolitan France could take over.

This lack of French troops, as well as a wish not to be part of the French Empire, encouraged local resistance to French authority and ambitions. This was particularly the case in the Jebel Ansariyeh, where Alawi chiefs raided into the coastlands and blockaded French posts in the hills. It took several military expeditions to subdue the region.[2]

The whole of Lebanon and Syria was in dire need of good government – food, clothing, medical attention, were all desperately needed. No currency was available, since Turkish money could not be used; for a time Allenby sanctioned the use of Egyptian money – yet another cause for French suspicions. For a time no banks could operate. Agriculture was dislocated, and there was little in the way of transport which could be used to move produce to market. The railways were short of rolling stock after the destructions during the last part of the fighting; much had also been taken away to Anatolia, and what was left was largely monopolized by the military for its needs. The British forces did what they could, bringing in and distributing food and clothing, gathering up abandoned children and women and providing them with shelter, or directing them to charities, but the real solution for the country's problems in this area was the recovery of trade, local and international. Such industry as had existed in Syria was largely wrecked as well, partly by damage in the fighting, but mainly because it was impossible to sell goods in the absence of currency, or transport to the ports – and the ports themselves, notably Beirut, were usually blocked by sunken ships. Crucially, no civilian ships were available to export the goods.[3]

Only a settled government could make a start on solving these interconnected problems, and that was not available for some time. Not only did the French have few men in the country, either as soldiers or as administrators, they also wished to extend their control from the coastal zone which they had been allotted by Allenby, into the Arab lands beyond the Lebanese mountains, and north into the Turkish lands. Allenby's continued insistence that nothing could be regarded as settled until the decisions of the Peace Conference was seen by the French as needless quibbling, by the Arabs as reneging on the agreements made with King Husain, and by the French again as a faith-

2 Longrigg, *Syria and Lebanon*, p. 80, note 1.
3 Ibid., pp. 76–80.

less favouring of Arabs over French claims. In this respect the French were quite correct, for the British did tend to favour the Arabs. This was largely in reaction to the boorish French behaviour, but the fact that the Arabs had fought alongside the British against the Turks, at considerable personal risk, also brought British goodwill.

While the British held to the figleaf of 'waiting for the decisions of the Peace Conference', both the French and the Arabs manoeuvred to secure their positions in Syria in advance of those decisions; the British had, of course, already done this in Palestine. In the unconquered parts of the Ottoman Empire similar political manoeuvres were taking place, involving the French, the Italians, and the Greeks; here the British were not interested, but they supported the Greeks. On his entry into Damascus on 2 October 1918 Faisal had assumed the government, only to be told the next day by Allenby of the French interest, and that he was himself still no more than an officer of Allenby's forces.[4] This was the message to the French military governors also, but still they were intrigued to secure local support. The Druzes had been contacted during October.[5] The Maronites of Mount Lebanon, old clients of the French, welcomed the French military governors, who made French intentions and ambitions in the area quite clear. As Allenby said of Col. de Piepape, whom he installed as military governor at Beirut: 'his inclination has been to congratulate the inhabitants of Syria on coming under the jurisdiction of France'.[6]

On 8 November Britain and France issued a declaration that their programme was 'to secure complete and definitive emancipation of the peoples so long oppressed by the Turks, and the establishment of national governments and administrations deriving their authority from the initiative and free choice of the indigenous populations'.[7] They had spent a month negotiating the wording of this declaration, having begun soon after the capture of Damascus, when it had become clear that there were difficulties ahead, but the declaration scarcely helped. It was clear that the final decision was in effect in British and French hands, but the wording led to the assumption amongst the Arabs that their independence was guaranteed. Also, while the British assumed that the French had agreed to the establishment of a Syrian state, the French saw

---

4   Hughes (ed.), *Correspondence*, p. 176, Allenby to War Office, 6 October 1918.
5   Ibid., p. 190, Allenby to War Office, 4 November 1918.
6   Ibid., p. 184, Allenby to Wilson, 19 October 1918.
7   Hansard, *Parliamentary Debates*, Vol. 146, col. 36 (25 July 1921); Zeine, *Arab Nationalism*, pp. 47–8; Tanenbaum, 'France and the Arab Middle East', in *Transactions of the American Philosophical Society* 68, 1–50 at 24.

the 'indigenous populations' as being all the separate 'communities', as they had been under Turkish classification, including various types of Christians, the Druzes, the Alawites, and so on, as well as the majority Sunni Muslims, not 'Syrians' or 'Arabs'. The declaration made the situation worse.

The Peace Conference was convened in January 1919, but the problems of the Middle East were not its priority. The German treaty was negotiated (amongst the Allies) first. From the point of view of those at the conference this was a reasonable priority, since the engine of the war had been Germany; the other Central Powers had been peripheral to Germany's efforts. This may have worked with Austria and Hungary and Bulgaria, but it was not how the war was seen by the Turks and the Arabs. Discussions on the future of the Ottoman Empire proceeded only fitfully for months, and Syria was not seriously considered by the 'Big Four' until May. Finally in December 1919 the two main Allies, Britain and France, agreed that Syria would be in the French part, while Britain took the rest, and it was not until April 1920 that the mandates were officially allocated. In the meantime the French had had to accept a visit by Faisal to France, though with ill grace.[8] He was able to address the conference, with Lawrence translating his Arabic, and impress everyone with his personal dignity, but had no real effect politically. The French brought delegations of Lebanese to speak to the conference, and introduced a long-winded member of the Syrian Committee which had been a lobby group in France during the war.[9] All this made little difference in the end, for, with the USA unwilling to become seriously involved in the Middle East (or, as it turned out, anywhere else), the issues came down to negotiations between the two Prime Ministers, Lloyd George and Clemenceau; when the latter finally agreed that Britain should have Mosul, the issue was essentially settled.

The screen behind which the extension of French and British imperial power was to be hidden was the calling of the acquisitions 'mandates'. All territories taken from the defeated states, at least outside Europe, were to be assigned to the League of Nations, which would nominate one of the Allies to govern and develop them on its behalf. The rhetoric was that the colonies were to be prepared for independence, but this was not taken seriously by the assignees, though the British did reduce their responsibilities (and expenses) by setting up quasi-independent governments in Iraq and Trans-Jordan.

---

[8]   For the French treatment of Faisal, see MacMillan, *Peacemakers*, pp. 401–2.

[9]   Ibid., pp. 402–3.

But for the French the long delay in finally reaching an agreement on the division of the Middle East had substantially reduced their spoils. During 1919 the Turks in Anatolia began a political and military revival which eventually enabled them to face down and defeat their enemies, and deprive the French of a large part of the Middle Eastern territory to which French politicians felt they were entitled. The French did make a serious attempt to secure those areas, and even if the Turks were successful in part, in the south it was the French who gained control.

The Arab government of Faisal made serious attempts to gain a grip on Syria, but it had even greater difficulties in doing so than the French. Faisal's administration was at least generally accepted by the population, though some groups were inimical. He had few competent administrators who could organize a governing system, except for former Ottoman officials.[10] The cities generally remained under the mayors who had welcomed the British forces, but they could provide little more than the skeleton of a system. The British forces managed to maintain order over much of the region while they were there, but as 1919 wore on, pressures developed more or less simultaneously – pressure on the British from their soldiers requiring demobilization and from the Egyptian rebellion; pressures on the Arabs in Damascus from the French, and on the French in the north from the Turks.

In Syria the institutions of government were gradually established, including the usual ministries on the European pattern, and a number of useful initiatives were begun. The whole was crowned in July 1919 by the formation of the Syrian National Congress, partly elected in the Arab areas, and partly appointed by local headman and notables. This last group came from the French and British areas – the coast, Lebanon, Palestine – for 'Syria' was seen in Damascus as 'greater Syria', and was assumed to include those regions. When it produced a programme the Congress defined Syria in these large terms, and maintained that the government should be a democratic constitutional monarchy. A commission sent by President Wilson to ascertain the wishes of the inhabitants – the King-Crane Commission (the British and French refused to participate) – declared the Congress to be more or less representative of the country.[11] The commission, however, had no real standing internationally, nor was the Congress the responsible authority in Syria, for the government was appointed by Faisal on the authority of the Commander-in-Chief, General

[10] Longrigg, *Syria and Lebanon*, pp. 83–6.
[11] Ibid., pp. 89–90; Petran, *Syria*, pp. 58–9.

Allenby. Only Faisal had any significant contact with the European powers, originally through Lawrence and his British colleagues with the Arab army, and then at Paris in the Peace Conference.

Meanwhile the British presence in Syria was thinning out. The evacuation of the British divisions to Egypt and then to Britain went on through December 1918 and January 1919, leaving competent and sufficient garrisons in most places, but it was clear that the British wanted to withdraw from all but Palestine as soon as they could. The French, of course, wanted them to go so that they could send in their own forces to take their place; the Arabs in Syria, however, did not, since the British presence was to a large extent their guarantee against a French takeover. For the British the need to get out of Syria and concentrate their forces on their own requirements was emphasized by the Egyptian rising which began in March 1919. As it happened, of course, the remaining forces available in Egypt, including the New Zealanders and the Australians, sufficed to put down the rebellion, but after May these troops also left for home, and the need for the British to concentrate on the essential elements of their empire was greater than ever.

Allenby, fully occupied in Egypt, also had to supervise events in Palestine and Syria. He fully agreed with the report from the Palestine administrator that 'the Palestinians want their country for themselves and will resist [the Zionists] by every means in their power, including active hostilities'.[12] In Syria, soon after Faisal returned to Damascus from Paris in April, Allenby reported that 'his dislike and distrust of the French are extreme'.[13] Allenby also had trouble in his army. He wanted more troops, for 'I have not enough troops for a good margin of safety', and asked for a British infantry division. 'My troops are behaving well but are tired of war and very bitter against the Egyptians for having stopped their demobilization. The Indian troops show no signs of unrest, yet; but, if the Egyptian revolution takes a religious hue, my Moslems will be sorely tried'.[14] Soon afterwards some of the men at Kantara in the demobilization camp refused to let any of their people go off to help run the trains, regarding this as 'strike-breaking' – an interesting take on the Egyptian situation.[15] It all added up to what would now be termed 'imperial over-stretch'.

---

[12] Hughes (ed.), *Correspondence*, p. 220, Allenby to War Office, 2 May 1919.

[13] Ibid., p. 217, Allenby to Wilson, 21 April 1919.

[14] Ibid., p. 215, Allenby to Wilson, 18 April 1919.

[15] Ibid., p. 217, Allenby to Wilson, 21 April 1919.

(A little later Allenby pointed out also that he was responsible for '112,000 prisoners of war.')[16]

The Egyptian agitation died down slowly in May, and could be said to be over by June. Meanwhile Allenby visited Faisal in Damascus, and reported to London that it was still necessary to keep his garrisons in Syria to prevent both a French incursion and an Arab declaration of independence. Faisal asked for equipment for a Syrian army of 14,000 men plus 6000 gendarmes, which Allenby interpreted as a sign that Faisal wanted to build up his strength to face the French. The presence of the British garrisons was thus the main obstacle to these two fighting each other. The request for arms was accompanied by a request for British advisers for the government departments in Syria – a transparent request for British protection. Allenby could do no more than refer the matter to London, where the requests died.[17]

At the same time an argument developed in Europe over the boundaries of the proposed mandates. The British wanted Mosul, and had provisional French agreement, which was based on the assumption the Britain would agree to a French Syria. But it now developed that the British were suggesting a boundary between their territories a good deal further north than the French expected; in particular the British wanted to add the Palmyra oasis to their area, and parts of southern Lebanon and the approaches to Damascus as well. Wilson, the CIGS, was the originator of this, though Lloyd George accepted it. Wilson had also evidently contemplated asking for Damascus as well.

Wilson's reasons were purely imperial, in the interests of ease of communication and travel between Palestine and Mesopotamia. He told all this to Allenby, and identified Palmyra as the essential element, asking if Allenby considered the occupation of the oasis to be 'feasible'.[18] Allenby visited Palmyra and in his pragmatic way succeeded in pouring cold water all over Wilson's scheme, instancing distances, bad or non-existent roads, shortage of transport, and that 'a small force at Palmyra would be indefensible', and subject to attack by local Arab tribes. He noted that (which perhaps Wilson did not know) the RAF had already established an airfield there, which only required a stockpile of fuel to come into use (and 'the local Sheikh has agreed to guard it').

[16] Ibid., p. 221, Allenby to War Office, 4 May 1919.
[17] Ibid., p. 227, Allenby to War Office, 14 May 1919.
[18] Ibid., p. 232, Wilson to Allenby, 22 May 1919; p. 234, War Office to Allenby, 23 May 1919.

He then, in an extraordinary paragraph which undercuts most of the imperial arguments for the British presence in Palestine, argued that Palestine and Syria should not be separated, 'which is contrary to the wishes and interests of the great majority of the population'. He added that 'the old frontier of Egypt' – by which he meant the line separating Egypt from the Ottoman Empire until 1914, just south of Gaza – 'gives a better defence than any in northern Palestine'.[19]

No more was heard of this Palmyra proposal. Clemenceau had rejected the idea explosively, and Allenby's good sense blew away all Wilson's bright ideas. The episode did, however, delay any discussion of British withdrawal from Syria for some time. This decision was finally taken on 15 September, at another meeting between Clemenceau and Lloyd George. It was in the nature of a real estate bargain – the French agreed that Mosul should go to the British (it had been in the French part in the old Sykes-Picot Agreement) and that the British should have Palestine and should withdraw from Syria, leaving the French in control on the coast, and the Arabs in the interior, but with certain undefined French powers of supervision. The withdrawal should begin on 1 November.[20]

This decision was probably not directly connected to the meeting two days before at Sivas in Anatolia of the new Turkish Grand National Assembly, but the coincidence was nevertheless significant. At Sivas, after several months of agitation by General Mustapha Kemal who had re-awoken Turkish pride, the Assembly had achieved a national consensus. He was helped substantially in this by a landing by Greek forces at Smyrna in May, which infuriated all Turks. The basic programme enunciated by the Assembly at Sivas was that the Allies were not to be permitted to slice up Anatolia between them like a pie.[21] It was one thing for the Allies to debate the future of Palestine and Syria, which they occupied militarily and which they had conquered, but they had few troops in Anatolia; in order to enforce their greed it was clear, after the Sivas programme, that they would need to fight for it. This was a different situation from that in which the British had pushed their forces north beyond Aleppo in late 1918; then their aim was to maintain order and prevent riots and

---

[19] Ibid., p. 239, Allenby to War Office, 29 May 1919; Barr, *A Line in the Sand*, p. 78.

[20] TNA, FO 31/4237; Tanenbaum, 'France and the Middle East', in *Transactions of the American Philosophical Society*, 33–4; Longrigg, *Syria and Lebanon*, p. 94.

[21] Davison, 'Turkish Diplomacy', in Craig and Gilbert, *The Diplomats*, 172–209, and in Davison, *Essays*, pp. 206–42, at p. 219; the 'pie' analogy is that of Harold Nicholson, *Peacemaking 1919*, pp. 332–4 (diary of 13 May).

massacres. The troops were still there, of course, but the decisions of the two Prime Ministers two days after the Turkish Assembly's meeting meant that the French would now take over those British positions from November.

Faisal, summoned to London, was told of this new arrangement a couple of days later. Horrified, he went over to Paris and struggled with a succession of French ministers and officials and generals to reach an agreement which would stop a direct French takeover of his territory. The French had already sent extra troops into the coastal areas and into Cilicia, where there was a good deal of trouble from local Turkish hostility. They had also selected as their commander and High Commissioner, General Henri Gouraud. Faisal eventually secured some French assurances that Arab rule would continue in the Syrian interior, but had to promise autonomy for Lebanon, the Druzes, and agree that the Bekaa Valley would be a neutral zone (which would leave it open to French penetration; this was an area which the Lebanese wished to have attached to Lebanon). He also had to agree that Syrian diplomatic representation would be in French hands, and that if any assistance was required by his government it would be provided by the French[22] – Syria was to be a French protectorate in all but name.

In Damascus the Congress had been adjourned while Faisal was in Europe, and his brother Zaid held his place. Faisal did not return to Syria until January, by which time there had already been clashes between French and Arab troops in several places.[23] The British forces began to withdraw, as scheduled, on 1 November, and Gouraud arrived at Beirut on the 21st. He clearly intended to assert French authority as the British left, and French troops moved into the Bekaa Valley in violation of the agreement – Gouraud made no secret of his intention to do this, even stating as much to Allenby. This was too raw, however, and they were withdrawn from Baalbek, though not from other parts, on Clemenceau's instructions.[24] Even before Faisal had returned, the Arab government in Damascus had begun to take measures of defence – conscription was introduced, though it could only operate effectively in the towns; in the towns themselves Committees of Defence were organized.

The agreement with the French contained little or nothing which would be acceptable to the Syrians, and never really got started. Gouraud's troops in the

---

[22] Longrigg, *Syria and Lebanon*, pp. 94–5; Tanenbaum, 'France and the Middle East,' in *Transactions of the American Philosophical Society*, 34–6.

[23] Longrigg, *Syria and Lebanon*, p. 95.

[24] Ibid., pp. 95–6; Tanenbaum, 'France and the Arab Middle East,' in *Transactions of the American Philosophical Society* 68, 1–50 at 34–5.

Bekaa were one sign of this; Arab conscription was another. When the Syrian Congress heard the details they rejected it, even though Faisal pleaded with them to understand that the alternative was French aggression and probably conquest. This did not have much effect, no doubt in part due to the over-estimate of Syrian strength as against the French, but also because, as a compromise, the agreement was clearly insufficient to restrain French ambitions, and so it was worthless. But the rejection of Congress to the agreement was sufficient in persuading the British to cease subsidizing Faisal and his government and the French soon followed them.[25]

Meanwhile the French forces in the region were built up to 32,000 men by January 1920, and those which had taken over the towns in the north from the British garrisons were coming under pressure. They never had complete control of the area, given the fact they were subjected to harassment by local partisans and irregular forces. These may or may not have been sent into action by the Kemalist government in Anatolia, but it was clear they supported its programme. Marash was put under siege by Turkish forces in mid-January, and the town was abandoned by the French on 13 February. Urfa (Edessa) was under attack by then, subjected to a series of assaults which lasted for two months, and requiring regular attempts at relief and re-supply. On the borders of French control in Syria the same type of raids and attacks developed, also inspired by, if not actually sent by, the government in Damascus.[26] Certainly official attempts were made to prevent, or at least slow down, the dispatch of French supplies along the Aleppo railway. To Gouraud in the first months of 1920 it must have looked as if the whole region was sliding into banditry and chaos. Nor could he accept that any of his enemies – Turks, Syrians, Alawites, Cilicians – had any legitimacy.

This activity was dangerous for both the French and the Arabs. It was clear during 1920 that the French could not cope with both of their enemies, and were liable to lose in both conflicts unless they took remedial measures. Since the French were fighting both Turks and Syrians, the possibility of a Turk-Arab alliance clearly existed, all the more so since the majority of officials in the Syrian government were former Ottoman men.

The siege of Urfa continued throughout March, and that of Bozanti, at the Anatolian end of the Cilician Gates, also began in that month.[27] On 6 March

[25] Longrigg, *Syria and Lebanon*, p. 97; Juffaut, *Du Caire à Damas*, pp. 333–4.
[26] Longrigg, *Syria and Lebanon*, p. 96.
[27] Ibid., p. 97 (note).

the Syrian Congress was addressed by Faisal, who demanded that the members decide their future. It was a call to make a declaration of independence for their country, a repudiation of the compromise agreement with the French which was actually letting the French in, and a rejection of the mandate which was about to be awarded. The Congress responded two days later with an offer of the kingship for Faisal, an effective declaration of independence. Faisal accepted, and was given homage by a great crowd in Damascus on 8 March.[28]

Those Lebanese who evaded French supervision to attend this gathering were jailed when they returned. The Christians in Lebanon were annoyed to have been included willy-nilly in the new kingdom, and their resentment was encouraged by the French. On 22 March a rival assembly at Ba'abda, the former seat of the Turkish governor, issued its reply, declaring Lebanese independence of Syria. In other words there was a division of opinion in Lebanon, one favouring union with Syria, the other choosing the French mandate regime. In the Damascus decision in March, Lebanon was offered autonomy, within its pre-war boundaries, but by this time the Christians wanted an extension into the Bekaa. Gouraud dismissed the council which had produced these varying reactions, and appointed a new one comprising his own supporters. Later the extension eastwards was decreed by France, which secured the support of the opponents of the mandate.[29]

A month after the Syrian proclamation of independence, and almost as though it had not happened, the decision by the Allied Powers was rendered at a meeting at San Remo, when the mandates of the Middle East were offered to Britain (Palestine, Trans-Jordan, and Iraq) and France (Syria and Lebanon). This became the legal basis for French actions in these areas, whose boundaries were yet to be defined, at least in the north.[30]

Meanwhile the problem of fighting two enemies at once prevented General Gouraud from doing much in Syria. Urfa fell to the Turks in mid-April, by which time Aintab had come under attack as well. Bozanti fell in May, with the loss of its entire garrison, opening up the Cilician Gates, and so enabling Turkish forces to reinforce their people in Cilicia.[31] The French came to the conclusion that it was necessary to renounce their hopes of a northward extension of their power. They were the more ready to do this as it would also be 'one in

---

[28] Ibid., pp. 97–8.

[29] Akarli, *The Long Peace*, pp. 186–87.

[30] Longrigg, *Syria and Lebanon*, 99; the text of the mandate is in Appendix D, pp. 376–80.

[31] Ibid., p. 97.

the eye' for Britain, who was extremely supportive of the Greek advances into Anatolia, an adventure that the French did not like, largely *because* it was supported by Britain. Kemal, meanwhile, was cunningly playing off his enemies against each other, ignoring Britain for the moment, but reaching a settlement with the Bolshevik regime in Russia (under pressure itself). In Cilicia Aintab fell on 25 May. The French press had built up the town as 'the Verdun of the Cilician hills', so its loss seemed more important than it was in reality. It was the last place under French control, and the Turks twisted the knife by renaming the place Gaziantep – 'Christian-fighting Aintab'. Once the fighting for the city was over, however, a truce was agreed on the 30th.[32] This gave both sides some breathing space. The treaty of peace with the Ottoman Empire (the Treaty of Sevres) had been presented to the Sultan in mid-May, and had assigned large areas in southern Anatolia to Italy and France. The Sultan lamented but could not evade acceptance; the Kemalists protested, and repudiated it. The fall of Aintab on 25 May lead to the truce, but it also extinguished most of the French hopes for gaining control of the land which was assigned to them in the Sevres treaty. The Italians had already left.

The Turks were attacked once again by the Greeks in the west, and so the truce in the south perforce continued. Gouraud was now able to devote most of his attention to Syria, and had at last acquired a large enough army to launch his attack. In June he pushed troops forward into the Bekaa, and early in June he sent an ultimatum to King Faisal demanding recognition of the French mandate and presenting a series of complaints about Syrian actions. These were clearly designed as excuses for further French invasions. Desperate measures by Faisal and his government followed, in an attempt to delay or stop the French advance. They sent messages of submission and agreement, though this provoked riots in Damascus, and a barely organized force, many of whose members were untrained volunteers, held up the French military at the Maysalun Pass for six hours in the face of tanks and aircraft. But it was hopeless. The French occupied Damascus by the end of the month, and Faisal was driven from his kingdom on 30 July.[33]

---

[32] Jouffaut, *Du Caire à Damas*, pp. 340–1; Longrigg, *Syria and Lebanon*, p. 97; Davison, 'Turkish Diplomacy', in Craig and Gilbert, *The Diplomats*, 215.

[33] Longrigg, *Syria and Lebanon*, pp. 100–4; Jouffaut, *Du Caire à Damas*, pp. 342–3.

Conclusion

NONE of the lands considered in this book were really settled at the end of 1920. It took perhaps another five years for the whole region to become more or less peaceful – and then a huge rebellion in Syria shook the French regime to its foundations. By then Egypt had reached a certain equilibrium, thanks to concessions suggested in the special mission headed by Lord Milner, and High Commissioner Viscount Allenby's insistence that they be implemented. A long tour by Winston Churchill in 1921 promoted local concessions and produced a more or less settled Palestine, though continued British favour towards Zionism predictably produced a major Arab rebellion in the 1930s. This was followed, after Hitler's War, by Zionist terrorism which an exhausted British government decided was not worth fighting. The British pulled out in 1948, finally making use of the mandate by 'handing it back' to the United Nations as the League's successor. This of course was followed by several more wars, revolutions, *coups d'etat*, and conquests. By then the British-French argument over Syria had also been resolved by a new British conquest of the Vichy regime in 1941, followed by British insistence that Syria and Lebanon be recognized as independent states.

By 1948, therefore, all these states were independent, and by 1952 even Egypt had at last rid itself of British forces. But none of these states was left with a stable government regime. Instead they had over-powerful armies, traditions of military *coups d'etat* and profound (and usually justified) suspicions about the interests and purposes of their neighbours. Such characteristics could be traced back without dispute to their status as mandate-colonies of European powers – though we must include also their inheritance from Turkish rule, notably the Turkish-cum-Muslim insistence on subdividing populations into religious groups, and dealing with them separately. This division is clearly at the root of Lebanon's troubles, and partly at the root of those in Palestine.

I have been writing this book in the shadow of the events in Syria which began with the expression of disgust at the Syrian governmental system by the people of Deraa early in 2011. This disquiet I can understand. When I toured Syria almost thirty years ago scarcely a day went by when a secret policeman did not cross my path. They were quite obvious, making their classification as 'secret' a nonsense, and were dressed in a scruffy and untidy manner, in contrast to the generally tidy population around them. They were ubiquitous, popping up, for example, in the country when I stood waiting to catch a bus, lounging in the bar at Baron's Hotel in Aleppo, clearly sponging off the proprietor, shooing me away from the tell of Homs I wanted to see. The people generally ignored them, as one would a nasty smell. In no country of the world I have visited have these unpleasant men been so obvious.

But this regime was also an inheritance from the colonial past, with its informers, its crust of ignorant civil and military men, its soldiers imported from elsewhere so that they would have no sympathy with the people they were ruling (who were referred to as Gippos, Yids, Arabs, wogs, blacks – lower breeds generally). The present Syrian regime has deliberately used soldiers from one part of the country against the people of another, just as the British used Indians in Palestine, and the French Senegalese in Syria. The real tragedy, however, is not that these practices were so well learned by the independent regimes, but that none of these regimes did much to alter them. It is one thing to blame the British and French colonialist inheritance for current attitudes – and they must carry some of the blame – and quite another to ignore the fact that the various dictatorships have happily gone along with it, or that the discrimination meted out against various minorities has not been abandoned.

It is also easy to play the 'what-if' game, but it does seem that the best chance of a normal peaceful life and development for Syria lay in its establishment as a united constitutional monarchy under King Faisal from 1918 onwards. (And Syrians have repeatedly attempted to set up a democratic system – in 1920, 1925, 1936, 1945–1948, and now in 2011–2012, only to be thwarted by the French or by their own army.) But the constitutional system, monarchy on not, would have involved Britain and France abandoning their normal imperialistic attitudes, and breaking their promises to each other in favour of an untried ruler in a devastated country. Faisal never stood a chance of holding onto a Syrian kingdom, certainly not once Britain and France decided that their imperial interests demanded that they gain control of parts of his land for themselves.

Maps

MAP 1. The Battleground (Modern Boundaries)

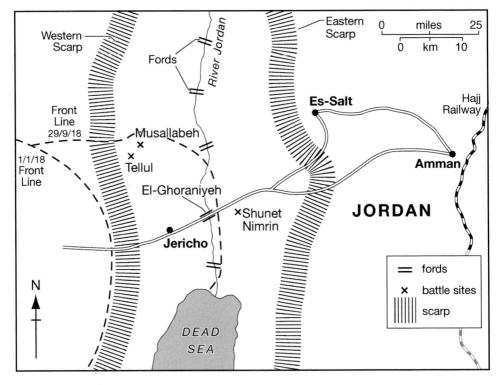

MAP 2. The Eastern Front

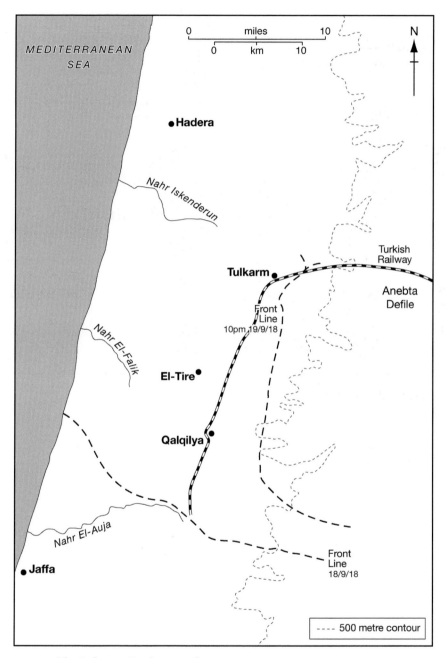

MAP 3. The Infantry Battleground

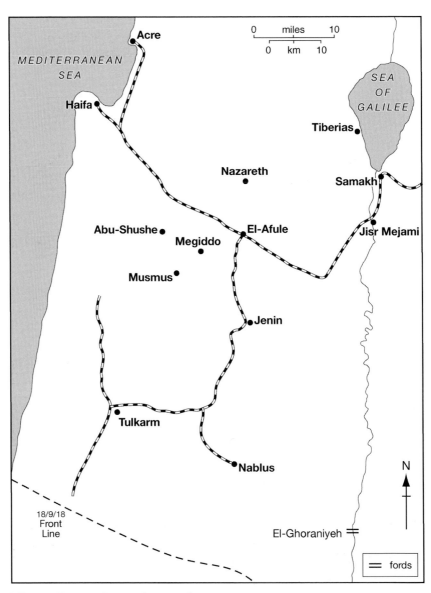

MAP 4. The Cavalry Battleground

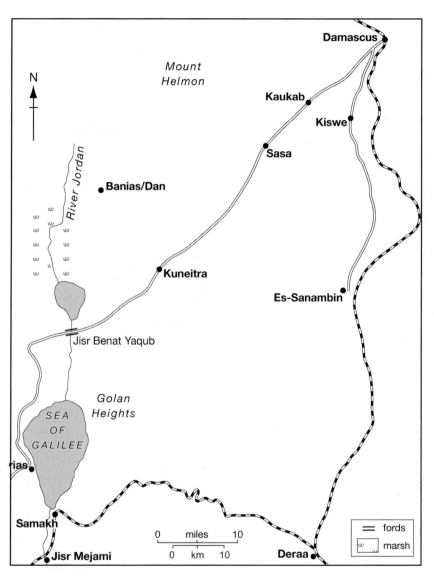

MAP 5. The March to Damascus

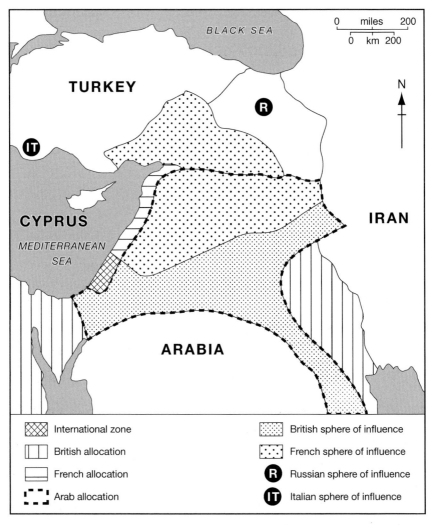

MAP 6. The Sykes-Picot Allocations

Bibliography

Abbreviations

ADM	Admiralty Documents
AIR	Royal Air Force Documents
ANZ	Archives New Zealand, Wellington
AWM	Australian War Museum, Canberra
AWM4	AWM4, Australian War Diaries
CAB	Cabinet Office Documents
FO	Foreign Office Documents
NZAM	New Zealand Army Museum, Waiori
TNA	The National Archives, Kew, London
WA	War Archives
WO	War Office Documents

Advance – A Brief Record of the Advance of the Egyptian Expeditionary Force, July 1917 to October 1918, London 1919.

Akarli, E.D., *The Long Peace: Ottoman Lebanon 1861–1920*, London 1993.

Andrew, Christopher M., and A.S. Kanya-Forster, *The Climax of French Imperial Expansion, 1914–1924*, Stanford CA, 1981.

Andrews, Ted, *Kiwi Trooper, The Story of Queen Alexandra's Own*, Wanganui NZ, 1967.

Annabel, N., *Official History of the New Zealand Engineers in the Great War, 1914–1918*, Wanganui NZ, 1927.

Anon., *Historical Records of the 20th (Duke of Cambridge's Own) Infantry, Brownlow's Punjabis)*, reprinted 2005.

Anon., *The Historical Records of the 53rd Sikhs F.F., 1847–1930*, Bournemouth 1931.

Anon., *Historical Record 110 Mahratta Light Infantry during the Great War 1914–1918*, Calcutta 1927, reprinted 2007.

Anon., *Regimental History of the 6th Royal Battalion 13th Frontier Force Rifles (Scinde), 1843–1923*, c. 1925, reprinted 2006.

Anderson, M.S., *The Eastern Question*, London 1966.

Anglesey, Marquess of, *A History of the British Cavalry*, Vol. 5, Barnsley 1994.

Aston, Sir George, *Secret Service*, London 1930.

Bailey, O.F., and H.M. Holler, *The Kensingtons, 13th London Regiment*, London 1936.

Badcock, G.E., *A History of the Transport Service of the Egyptian Expeditionary Force 1916–1980*, London 1925.

Barr, James, *Setting the Desert on Fire*, London 2006.

——. *A Line in the Sand, Britain, France and the Struggle that shaped the Middle East*, London 2011.

Barrow, Sir George de S., *The Fire of Life*, London 1948.

Bethan, Sir G., and H.V.R. Geary, *The Golden Galley, the Story of the 2nd Punjab Regiment*, Oxford 1956.

Black, G., *The 1/4th Battalion Wiltshire Regiment 1914–1919*, ed. G. Stanley, Frome 1933.

Blackwell, E., and E. C. Axe, *Romford to Beirut, via France, Egypt and Jericho: An Outline of the Record of B Battery, 271st Brigade RFA*, Clacton on Sea 1926.

Blackwell, S.M., and D.R. Douglas, *The Story of the 3rd Australian Light Horse Regiment*, 1952.

Bostock, Harry P., *The Great Ride, the Diary of a Light Horse Brigade Scout, World War I*, Perth 1982.

Brereton, J., *Chain Mail, The History of the Duke of Lancaster's Own Yeomanry*, Chippenham 1994.

Browne, G.H., *The History of the 2nd Light Horse Brigade AIF, August 1914– April 1919*, 1926.

Brugger, Suzanne, *Australians and Egypt, 1914–1919*, Melbourne 1980.

Cardew, F.G., *Hodson's Horse, 1857–1922*, Edinburgh 1928.

Chaldecott, O.A., *The 1st Battalion Duchess of Connaught's Own and the 10th Battalion the Baluchi Regiment*, (n.d.).

Cobham, Lord, *The Yeomanry Cavalry of Worcestershire, 1914–1922*, Stourbridge 1926.

Condon, W.G.H., *The Frontier Force Rifles*, Aldershot 1953.

Cutlack, E.M., *The Australian Flying Corps in the Eastern and Western Theatres of War, 1914 – 1918*, St Lucia, Queensland 1923.

Darley, T.H., *With the Ninth Light Horse in the Great War*, Adelaide, 1924.

Davidson, John, *Dinkum Oil of Light Horse and Camel Corps*, 1996.

Dawn, C. Ernest, *From Ottomanism to Arabism*, Chicago 1972.

Dinning, Hector, *Nile to Aleppo, with the Light Horse in the Middle East*, 1920, reprinted c. 2007.

Downes, R.M., *The Campaign in Syria and Palestine*, Part 2 of *The Australian Medical Services in the War of 1914–1918*, Sydney 1931.

Eames, F.W., *The Second Nineteenth*, London 1930.

Economist, The, Pocket World in Figures, 2010, 2010 Edition, London 2010.

Elgood, E., *Egypt and the Army*, Oxford 1924.

Elliott, Major W., and Captain A. Kinross, 'Maintaining Allenby's Armies – a Footnote to History', *RASC Quarterly*, 13, 1925, 114–28.

Erickson, E.J., *Ottoman Army Effectiveness in World War I, a Comparative Study*, London 2007.

Falls, Cyril, *Official History of the War, Syria and Palestine*, Vol. II, London 1929.

Fisher, J., *Curzon and British Imperialism in the Middle East 1916–1919*, London 1999.

Fox, Sir F., *The History of the Royal Gloucestershire Hussars Yeomanry, 1898–1922*, Southampton, 1923.

Fromkin, David, *The Peace to End All Peace, Creating the Modern Middle East, 1914 - 1922*, London 1989,

James L. Gelvin, *Divided Loyalties*, California 1998.

Geoghahan, S., *The Campaigns and History of the Royal Irish Regiment*, Vol. 2, Edinburgh 1937.

Gibbons, T., *With the 1/5th Essex in the East*, Colchester 1921.

Gilbert, Martin, *World in Turmoil, Winston S. Churchill 1917–1922*, London 1975.

——. *Jerusalem in the Twentieth Century*, London 1996.

Goodlad, S., *The Letters of Stanley Goodlad, Somerset Light Infantry, 1914–1919*, ed. Ann Noyes, Guildford 1999.

Goold-Walker, G., *The Honourable Artillery Company in the Great War*, London 1930.

Grainger, J.D., *The Battle for Palestine 1917*, Woodbridge, Suffolk 2006.

Gullett, H.S., *The Official History of Australia in the War of 1914–1918*, Vol. 7, *The Australian Imperial Force in Sinai and Palestine*, Sydney 1923.

Hammond, E.W., *History of the 11th Light Horse Regiment, Fourth Light Horse Brigade, Australian Imperial Forces, War 1914–1919*, Brisbane 1942.

Hansard, *Parliamentary Debates*, Vol. 146, col. 36 (25 July 1921).

Hatton, S.F., *The Yarn of a Yeoman*, London [1930].

Hill, A.J., *Chauvel of the Light Horse, a Biography of General Sir Harry Chauvel*, Melbourne 1978.

Holloway, D., *Hooves, Wheels and Tracks*, Melbourne 1990.

Holt, P.M., *Egypt and the Fertile Crescent 1516–1922*, London 1966.

Hopkirk, P., *Setting the East Ablaze*, Oxford 1984.

Hudson, Sir H., *History of the 19th King George's Own Lancers 1858–1921*, Aldershot 1937, reprinted 2007.

Hughes, Matthew, *Allenby and British Strategy in the Middle East 1917–1919*, London 1999.

Hughes, Matthew, ed., *Allenby in Palestine, the Middle East Correspondence of Field Marshal Viscount Allenby*, Army Records Society 2004.

Hurewitz, J.C., *The Middle East and North Africa in World Politics*, Vol. 2, 2nd ed., New Haven RI 1979.

Huxford, H.J., *History of the 8th Gurkha Rifles 1824–1919*, Aldershot 1951.

Inchbald, G., *The Imperial Camel Corps*, London 1970.

Jabotinsky, V., *The Story of the Jewish Legion*, New York 1945.

Johnston, Tom, *Orange, Green, and Khaki, the Story of the Irish Regiments in the Great War*, Dublin 1922.

Jones, H.A., *Official History of the War in the Air*, Vol. 6, London 1937.

Karput, Kemal H., *Ottoman Population 1830–1914, Demographic and Social Characteristics*, Madison WI, 1985.

Karsh, Efrem, and Inari Karsh, *Empires of the Sand, the Struggle for Mastery in the Middle East 1789–1923*, Cambridge MA 1999.

Kedourie, Elie, *Into the Anglo Arab Labyrinth*, London 1976.

——. 'The Capture of Damascus,' in *The Chatham House Version and other Middle Eastern Studies*, Hanover, MA, 1984, 33–51.

——. 'Sa'd Zaghlul and the British,' in *The Chatham House Version and other Middle Eastern Studies*, Hanover, MA, 1984, 93–99.

——. *Politics in the Middle East*, Oxford 1992.

Kemp, P.K., *The Queen's Own Royal Regiment in the First and Second World War*, Aldershot 1953.

Kennedy, J.J., 'With the 5th (Service) Battalion during the Great War,' *The Sprig of Shillelagh*, [1920].

Lacey, R., T*he Kingdom*, London 1981.

Lawford J.P., and H.P. Catto, *Solah Punjab, the History of the 16th Punjab Regiment*, Aldershot 1916.

Lawrence, T.E., *Seven Pillars of Wisdom*, 5th ed., London 1976.

Liman von Sanders, O., *Five Years in Turkey*, 1928, reprinted Nashville TN, 2000.

Lewis, N.N., *Nomads and Settlers in Syria and Jordan, 1800–1980*, Cambridge 1987.

Livermore, Bernard, *A Damn Bad Soldier*, Batley, Yorks, 1974,

Longrigg, Stephen H., *Syria and Lebanon under French Mandate*, Oxford 1958.

Mackay, J.N., *History of the 7th Duke of Edinburgh's Own Gurkha Rifles*, Edinburgh 1962.

MacMillan, M., *Peacemakers*, London 2001.

MacMunn, Sir G., and C. Falls, *Military Operations, Egypt and Palestine*, Vol. 1, *The Official History of the War*, London 1928.

Manela, Erez, *The Wilsonian Moment, Self-determination and the International Origins of Anti-colonial Nationalism*, New York 2009.

Marden, Sir Thomas O., *The History of the Welch Regiment*, Cardiff 1932.

Marlowe, John, *Anglo-Egyptian Relations 1800–1953*, London 1954.

Massey, W.T., *Allenby's Final Triumph*, London 1920.

Maunsell, E.B., *Prince of Wales's Own Scinde Horse*, Frome 1926, reprinted 2005.

Maurice, Sir F., *The 16th Foot, a History of the Bedfordshire and Hertfordshire Regiment*, London 1931.

Monroe, Elizabeth, *Britain's Moment in the Middle East, 1914–1956*, London 1963.

Moore, A. Briscoe, *The Mounted Riflemen in Syria and Palestine*, Auckland (n.d.).

Murphy, C.C.R., 'The Turkish Army in the Great War,' in *Soldiers of the Prophet*, London 1921 (originally in *RUSI Journal*), 175–96.

Newbolt, H., *Naval Operations*, Vol. 5, *History of the War at Sea*, London 1931.

Nichol, C.G., *The Story of Two Campaigns: Official History of the Auckland Mounted Rifles Regiment 1914–1919*, Auckland 1921.

Olden, A.N.C., *Westralian Cavalry in the War*, Melbourne, 1921,

Osborne, Rex, 'Operations of the Mounted Troops of the Egyptian Expeditionary Force', *Cavalry Journal* XIII, 1923.

Overton, J.F.A., *Historical Record of the Kumoan Rifles*, photocopy 1983.

Patterson, J.H., *With the Judaeans in the Palestine Campaign*, 1922.

Petran, Tabitha, *Syria, a Modern History*, London 1972.

——. *The Struggle over Lebanon*, New York 1987.

Petre, L. Loraine, *The 1st King George's Own Gurkha Rifles*, London 1925.

Porte, Remy, *Du Caire à Damas, Français et Anglais en Proche-Orient (1914–1918)*, Paris 2008.

Porter, C. Guy, *The New Zealanders in Sinai and Palestine*, Auckland, 1922.

Preston, R.M.P., *The Desert Mounted Corps: An Account of the Cavalry Operations in Palestine and Syria, 1917–1918*, London 1921.

Pryor, A., and J.K. Woods (eds), *Great Uncle Fred's War, an Illustrated Diary, 1917–1920*, Whitstable, Kent, 1985.

Ramsaur, E.E., *The Young Turks*, New York 1957.

Rawlinson, H.G., *Outram's Rifles, a History of the 4th Battalion 10th Rajputana Rifles*, London 1933, reprinted 2006.

Richardson, J.D., *The 7th Light Horse 1914–1919*, Sydney (n.d.).

Rolls, S.C., *Steel Chariots in the Desert*, London 1937.

Pasha, Sir Thomas Russell, *Egyptian Service 1902–1946*, London 1949.

Sainsbury, J.D., *The Hertfordshire Battery RFA*, Welwyn 1996,

Sheffy, Yigal, *British Military Intelligence in the Palestine Campaign 1914–1918*, London 1998.

Shepherd, Naomi, *Ploughing Sand, British Rule in Palestine 1917–1948*, London 1999.

Smith, N.C., *The Third Australian Light Horse Regiment 1914–1918*, Melbourne 1993.

Starr, Joan, and Christopher Greenway, *Forward, the History of the 2nd/14th Light Horse (Queensland Mounted Infantry)*, St Lucia, Queensland, 1989.

Stirling, W.F., *Safety Last*, London 1953.

Stonham, C., and B. Freeman, *Historical Records of the Middlesex Yeomanry, 1797–1927*, ed. J.S. Judd, Chelsea 1930.

Tallents, H., *The Sherwood Rangers Yeomanry in the Great War, 1914–1920*, London 1926.

Tanenbaum, J.K., 'France and the Arab Middle East, 1914–1920', *Transactions of the American Philosophical Society* 68, 1978, 1–50.

Tennant, E., *The Royal Deccan Horse in the Great War*, Aldershot 1939, reprinted 2008.

Thompson, C.W., *Records of the Dorset Yeomanry (Queen's Own), 1914–1919*, Sherborne, 1921.

Tibawi, A.L., *Anglo-Arab Relations and the Question of Palestine, 1914–1921*, London 1978.

Tugwell, H.B.P., *History of the Bombay Pioneers*, Bedford 1938.

Ward, C.W. Dudley, *History of the 53rd (Welsh) Division 1914–1918*, Cardiff 1927.

——. *Records of the Royal Welch Fusiliers*, Vol. IV, London 1929.

Wasti, S. Tanvir, 'The Defence of Medina, 1916–19', *Middle Eastern Studies* 27, 1991, 642–53.

Watson, W.A., *King George's Own Central India Horse*, Edinburgh 1930, reprinted 2005.

Wavell, A.P., *The Palestine Campaigns*, London 1931.

——. *Allenby in Egypt*, London 1943.

Whitworth, D.E., *A History of the 2nd Lancers (Gardner's Horse) from 1809 to 1922*, 1924, reprinted 2006.

Wilkie, A.H., *Official History of the Wellington Mounted Rifles, 1914 – 1919*, Auckland 1924.

Wilson, L.C., *Australian Imperial force in Egyptian Rebellion of 1919, Narrative*, typescript 1934.

Woodyatt, N.G., (ed.), *The Regimental History of the Queen Alexandra's Own Gurkha Rifles*, London 1929.

Wylly, H.C., *History of the Manchester Regiment*, Vol. 2, London 1927.

——. The *Poona Horse 1817–1932*, Vol. IV, 1933.

——. *History of the 1st and 2nd Battalions the Leicestershire Regiment in the Great War*, Aldershot 1979.

Zeine, Z.N., *The Emergence of Arab Nationalism*, Beirut 1966.

Index